The Lamp and the Cross

The Lamp and the Cross

A History of Averett College, 1859–2001

Jack Irby Hayes, Jr.

Mercer University Press
Macon, Georgia
25th Anniversary

ISBN 0-86554-854-4
MUP/H613

© 2004 Mercer University Press
1400 Coleman Avenue
Macon, Georgia 31207

First Edition.

Library of Congress Cataloging-in-Publication Data

Hayes, J. I.
The lamp and the cross : a history of Averett College, 1859-2001 /
Jack
Irby Hayes, Jr.– 1st ed.
p. cm.
Includes bibliographical references and index.
ISBN 0-86554-854-4 (hardcover : alk. paper)
1. Averett College—History. I. Title.
LD271.A83H384 2004
378.755'666—dc22
2004016731

Table of Contents

Illustrations

All illustrations and photographs are from the Averett University Archives.

Preface

The official seal of Averett College—an elliptical medallion with the words "Averett College, Danville, Virginia" surrounding a lamp and cross—was emblematic of the institution's history and mission. The lamp represented learning, while the cross stood for the Southern Baptist environment in which learning took place. Yet these two symbols were never static representations. Learning in 1859, when the college was founded, was designed to produce a "finished" young lady who could model high culture while attending to hearth and community. Refinement of this curriculum during the next four decades preceded dramatic change in the early twentieth century: job-related education, an elective system, and junior college status. Pre-professional programs came in the 1940s and 1950s. Coeducation and a baccalaureate program followed in 1969 with a career-oriented curriculum grounded firmly on the liberal arts. Next came new degrees (M.Ed. and M.B.A.) and new venues (Falls Church and South Boston, Virginia). The 1980s and 1990s brought an honors program, leadership studies, opportunities for study abroad, and non-traditional adult education that soon eclipsed the traditional program.

The symbolism of the cross evolved as well. The original Baptist setting entailed a personal new birth in Jesus Christ, coupled with mandatory church attendance and daily chapel. But at least as early as the 1930s, the college quietly espoused a measure of toleration and welcomed both Roman Catholic and Jewish students, although the faculty remained Protestant and the administration, Southern Baptist. Toleration expanded after Conwell Anderson became president in 1966; faculty began to be hired with little regard for denominational, or even religions, affiliation. When the college became a baccalaureate-level institution in 1969, adherence to simple Christian values replaced any remaining emphasis on attendance at church or chapel. The institution interpreted simple Christian values to be attitudes such as sacrificial

x

kindness in a lifestyle emphasizing social justice, responsible citizenship, concern for the worth of each individual, and moral judgment when confronting the ethical problems created by advancing technology and pluralistic society.

Just as the lamp and cross continued to be enduring motifs, the mission of the institution also reflected the purposes of education in the United States. Since colonial times, Americans have regarded education as essential to representative government. Our colonial forbears understood that without learning, voters and officeholders cannot effectively or wisely discharge their civic duties. By the 1820s Americans considered schooling essential to democracy, on the assumption that knowledgeable voters would not be swayed by demagoguery. In the emerging industrial age of the nineteenth century as financial necessity and opportunity continually challenged traditional female roles, Americans were forced to concede the urgency of educating women. Education has always been a key ingredient in equality of opportunity (at least for white males) because scholastic accomplishment places the poor youth on an equal footing with the prosperous one. America's colleges, in particular, have been expected to produce informed, liberty-loving, republican, egalitarian, and upwardly-mobile men and women who devote their energies to the betterment of self, family, church, community, state, and nation. The place of Averett College in this educational milieu is a secondary theme in this work.

I received generous assistance from many scholars and former employees of the college. Former presidents Conwell A. Anderson, Howard W. Lee, and Frank R. Campbell, former acting president Mary C. Fugate, and former professors Pauline Coll and Margaret Lanham graciously submitted to several hours of interviewing. David Gray kindly allowed me to quote extensively from his unpublished manuscript on Averett College, and James A. Davis from his on Curtis V. Bishop. Several hundred alumni returned questionnaires filled with memories and anecdotes of their Averett years. Nita Grant and Clara Fountain in the college library, Fred Anderson in the archives of the Virginia Baptist Historical Society, and Martha Beals at the Danville Public Library helped me uncover a wealth of primary source material. Clara Fountain's collection of photographs of the principals and presidents was invaluable. Dean of the College Malcom Huckabee and the faculty development committee granted me a sabbatical in 1982–83 for the purpose of preparing the history through 1983. Academic vice president Susan Dunton and another faculty development committee provided a second sabbatical in 2001–02 to carry it through June 30, 2001. Several scholars were kind enough to read, critique, and edit the manuscript: among these were George G. Shackelford of Virginia Polytechnic Institute, John Hammond Moore of the South Caroliniana Library, James O. Farmer of the University of South Carolina at Aiken, John Brinkley of Hampden-Sydney College, and Mary Fugate, Margaret Lanham, and Pauline Coll of Averett College. Secretaries Joyce Johnson, Mary Chamblin, Karen Nelson, Regna Worthington, and Gloria Robertson typed the manuscript. Bernadine Arnn Hayes, my wife, helped in all stages of manuscript preparation. The manuscript benefited from her suggestions for word usage, syntax, and appropriateness of information—as I benefited from her constant encouragement and sense of humor. To all these people I extend my heartfelt thanks and the assurance that all errors remaining in the manuscript are mine alone.

An Averett College Photograph Album

1. Nathan Penick, co-principal (1859–1861).   2. William A. Tyree, principal (1861–1863)

3. John C. Long, principal (1863).

4. Isaac B. Lake, co-principal (1863–1872)

5. Thomas Hume, co-principal (1867–1872).

6. John L. Johnson, co-principal (1872–1873).

7. Arnaud E. Preot, co-principal
(1870–1873).

8. Samuel W. Averett, co-principal
(1872–1887).

9. John T. Averett, co-principal
(1873–1887); president (1887–1892).

10. Patton Street building (original).

11. Patton Street building (post-1898).

12. Students and faculty on the steps of Patton Street building, ca. 1880.

13. Students in uniform, 1887.

14. RFC student in winter uniform, 1897.

15. *Echoes* (yearbook) staff, 1905.

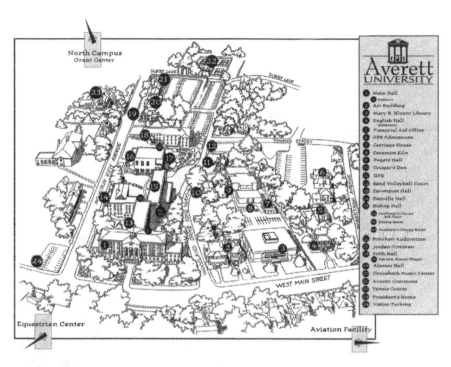

16. Aerial diagram of Main Campus, ca. 2001.

17. Main Hall, ca. 1910.

18. Basketball team, ca. 1916.

19. A party at the Lingernook, ca. 1930.

20. Music and Science Building (Danville Hall).

21. President's House (later North Hall and then Alumni Hall), built by President Cammack.

22. Charles F. James, president (1892–1902).   23. Robert E. Hatton, president (1902–1907)

24. John B. Brewer, president (1907–1914)   25. William W. Rivers, president (1914–1917)

26. Clayton E. Crosland, president (1917–1921).　27. James P. Craft, president (1921–1927

28. John W. Cammack, president (1927–1936).　29. Mary C. Fugate, ca. 1926.

30. Curtis V. Bishop, president (1936–1966); photograph ca. 1936

31. Curtis V. Bishop, ca. 1966.

32. Averett College in 1959.

33. Aerial view of Averett
College at the time of Curtis
Bishop's death in 1966.

34. The Daisy Chain, ca. 1947.

35. Scenes from May Day, ca. 1955.

36. Scene from Nativity Pageant, ca. 1955.

37. Participation in War Bond drive, ca. 1943

38. World War II veterans at Averett, exchanging uniforms for collegiate attire.

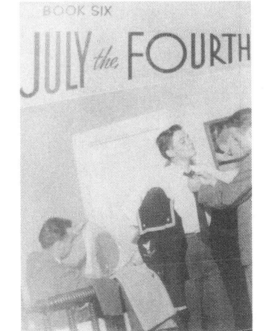

39. Dining family-style in the later Bishop years.

40. Dormitory life in the later Bishop years.

41. Mary C. Fugate, acting president (1966).

42. Conwell A. Anderson, president
(1966–1979), three scenes

43. Moving the Library Day, 1971.

44. Mary B. Blount Library.

45. Fine Arts Building (adjacent to Blount Library).

46. Averett students discuss issues on Vietnam Moratorium Day, 1969.

47. English Hall (Admissions building).

48. Averett-Stratford coordination, 1973–1974: boarding the bus at Stratford College

49. Howard W. Lee, president
(1980–1985).

50. Frith Hall, viewed from Jordan Common

51. The second President's House (Carrington donation).

52. Saturday's Warriors and Revelers, ca. 1984.

53. Frank R. Campbell, president (1985–2002).

54. President Campbell dons his rat hat for Rat Week, 1985.

55. The baseball team prepares for its first game on North Campus, 1998.

56. President Campbell and board chairman Dr. B. R. Ashby inaugurate Averett's football program, ca. 2000.

57. Grousbeck Music
Center.

58. Aerial view of the equestrian facility, 1999.

59. E. Stuart James Grant Convocation Center.

60. Averett Commons (apartment-style residence halls).

I. Pre-Genesis

1783–1859

1

An Antebellum Environment

In the seventy-six years between the founding of an independent United States of America in 1783 and the founding of Averett College in 1859, so great a change took place in national opinion concerning education that the two events seem to be separated by eons instead of by decades. In 1783 a precocious twelve-year-old named Lucinda Foote applied for admission to Yale University. Despite an acknowledgement by the school that she was "fully qualified" for admission as a freshman, Yale dismissed her application out of hand.[1] Women of Lucinda Foote's day were expected to be satisfied with hearth and home; higher education was men's domain. By 1859, however, times had changed. Protestant leaders sought denominational growth and societal change through new institutions such as women's colleges. Localities were beginning to found educational institutions for both sexes in order to answer demand and also to demonstrate their modern and progressive status. Finally, a period of reform, involving a cluster of movements, was sweeping over the United States, bringing educational opportunities for women.

The changing times began after the War of 1812 with the appearance of an antebellum era of reform, which included feminism and educational reform. The feminist movement made its national debut in 1848 at the first Women's Rights Convention in Seneca Falls, New York. The female delegates objected to laws and customs that treated them as legal minors, prevented their use and disposal of property, denied them the right to vote, allowed them to suffer physical abuse by spouses, and kept them uneducated. At Seneca Falls and at later annual conventions, they demanded nothing less than equality with men.

[1] Quoted in Frederick Rudolph, *The American College and University: A History* (Athens: University of Georgia Press, 1990 [1962]) 307.

Gradually, they were able to secure a measure of control of their property, gain admittance into professions such as nursing and elementary education, and win male acquiescence in their wish to be educated. Although Southern participation in feminist reform was almost nonexistent, some Southern women silently sympathized, especially with demands for expanded educational opportunities.[2]

More important to the establishment of female colleges than feminism was the educational reform movement. Antebellum reformers were convinced that education would usher in a secular paradise free of social problems. To that end, they were successful in persuading legislatures in state after state to create a system of public schools. In 1846, for example, an alliance of educational reformers, sincere civic boosters who argued that education was important to the growth of trade and commerce, and politicians who claimed education would contribute to democracy and republican government prodded the General Assembly of Virginia into creating a system of public primary schools for counties willing to levy taxes for its support. Reformers were also successful in establishing private and state-supported colleges. The usual pattern was for preparatory academies to add at least two years of collegiate work, thereby evolving into junior colleges and sometimes into senior colleges. So fashionable was higher education in antebellum America that approximately 700 colleges opened and closed by 1861. Another 250 colleges opened and remained open. Among those 250 survivors was Union Female College, the forerunner of Averett College.[3]

Although the antebellum reform movement made possible the chartering of a women's college in southside Virginia in 1859, a second ingredient—local boosterism—provided stronger impetus. By 1859 the citizens of Danville took pride in their community and looked for ways to enhance its reputation as a regional center of culture and progress. Tobacco and transportation had dictated the destiny of Danville, and the

---

[2] Alice Felt Tyler, *Freedom's Ferment* (New York: Harper and Row, 1944) 424–63. See also Barbara Miller Solomon, *In the Company of Educated Women: A History of Women and Higher Education in America* (New Haven CT: Yale University Press, 1985) 43–62.

[3] Rudolph, *American College*, 47; Tyler, *Freedom's Ferment*, 227–65: Win Kelley and Leslie Wilbur, *Teaching in the Community–Junior College* (New York: Appleton-Century-Crofts, 1970) 6–7; Cornelius J. Heatwole, *A History of Education in Virginia* (New York: Macmillan, 1916) 100–23; William Arthur Maddox, *The Free School Idea in Virginia before the Civil War* (New York: Arno Press, 1969) 126–69.

progress of the community from birth to maturity was impressive. Before the American Revolution, William Wynne of Brunswick County settled his family near the falls of the Dan River in present-day Pittsylvania County, where an Indian town once stood and where a north-south Indian trail crossed the river. Known as Wynne's Falls or Wynne's Ford and located almost within sight of the North Carolina border, the settlement became the center of a burgeoning tobacco culture. Inconvenienced by having to carry the leaves to Petersburg or Richmond for inspection, neighboring planters in 1793 successfully petitioned the legislature to designate an inspection station at the falls and a town on the south side of the ford. This town the legislature named Danville. In 1800 the United States government established the town's first post office. Soon, a successful flour mill operated at the falls of the river; in the next half century, the town added bridges across the Dan River, roads to Lynchburg and Rocky Mount, rail connections to Richmond, and steamboat connections to South Boston.[4]

Danville quickly blossomed as a commercial, transportation, and cultural center in the Virginia piedmont. Goods, people, and ideas routinely moved to and from mountain counties in the west, Pittsylvania and Campbell Counties to the north, the Dan and Roanoke River valleys of Virginia and North Carolina, and eastern markets in Richmond, Petersburg, and Norfolk. By the early 1800s, Danville had a private elementary school for boys. In 1817 schoolmaster Levi Holbrook set up a high school, which later became Danville Male Academy and, despite its name, admitted girls. In 1826 prosperous Danvillians with daughters to educate began to patronize the Female Institute of schoolmistress Ann Benedict, who faced competition five years later from the Danville Female Academy under Episcopal rector George W. Dame. In the 1820s Danvillians established a newspaper, a chapter of Masons at Roman Eagle Lodge, and the town's first church, First Presbyterian. Between 1830 and 1860, the town's population increased from 500 to 3,500. One bank grew to five, one newspaper to two, one church to four, three schools to five, and one tobacco factory to ten. One of the tobacco

---

[4] Jane Gray Hagan, *The Story of Danville* (New York: Stratford House, 1950) 1–5; Edward Pollock, *1885 Sketch Book of Danville, Virginia* (Danville VA: Womack Press, 1976 [1885]) 17–19; Maud Carter Clement, *The History of Pittsylvania County, Virginia* (Baltimore MD: Regional Publishing Company, 1973 [1929]) 231; Beatrice W. Hairston, *A Brief History of Danville, Virginia* (Richmond, VA: Dietz Press, 1955) 14.

factories was the second largest in Virginia. By 1861 Danville boasted an insurance company, a police force, a circuit court, a telegraph line, and a railroad, none of which the town had in 1830.[5]

Danvillians enjoyed a social life appropriate to a growing community in antebellum America. Washington's birthday was an occasion for balls at the Eagle Tavern. Barbecues and dances highlighted the Fourth of July. In the summertime, local society could repair to any one of six medicinal springs near Danville. Although accommodations at these miniature spas were comfortable, most Danvillians made daytime visits by buggy, driving home before moonlight could imperil Victorian propriety. The highlight of autumn was a week of races over the Danville Race Course.[6]

With good reason, Danvillians in the 1850s were self-confident and brimming with civic pride in their boomtown. Like other Americans they were thrilled to be living in an age of change and progress. They applauded the rise of industry and steam transportation, improved communications by telegraph and daily newspaper, labor-saving comforts such as the sewing machine, and, of course, education. Every town wanted whatever was modern—a factory, a railroad, a canal, a newspaper, a telegraph line, and a string of elementary and secondary schools. By 1856 Danville had these modern features. But one of the few things this young community lacked to be thoroughly up-to-date was a college. Naturally, Danvillians craved a college that would build Danville's reputation as an important urban center in the southern piedmont. A college meant modernity, prestige, progress, cultural primacy, an instrument for molding that illusive "better world."[7] With support from citizens in neighboring counties, a college could easily become a reality in Danville.

---

[5] Hairston, *Danville*, 127–28; Hagan, *Story of Danville*, 66–84, 104.

[6] Hairston, *Danville*, 26, 96, 129; Pollock, *Sketch Book*, 26–40.

[7] Rudolph, *American College*, 48.

2

The Flowering of the
Roanoke Baptist Association

While educational reformers and civic boosters were helpful in founding
Averett College, a third ingredient— the growth of the Baptist faith in
southside Virginia—was crucial. In the eighteenth century, Baptist
missionaries and families brought three distinct varieties of their
denomination to the Old Dominion. General Baptists, who proclaimed
universal atonement, settled in the southeastern Tidewater. Regular
Baptists, preaching limited atonement, inhabited northern Virginia. In
southside Virginia were Separate Baptists, former Congregationalists
who came from New England by way of North Carolina during the Great
Awakening. They renounced infant baptism and insisted upon baptism
by immersion following a vital profession of faith.[1]

Baptists in Danville and Pittsylvania trace their ancestry to Separate
Baptists. In 1755 the Reverend Shubal Stearns carried his tiny flock of
Separate Baptists from Connecticut to Guilford County, North Carolina,
where the Stearns colony quickly grew from sixteen to almost 600
people. Fired with missionary zeal, Stearns's converts crossed over into
southside Virginia. James Craig, an Anglican minister, noted that
"wherever the Baptists appear, the people flock over to them."[2] As a
consequence, in 1760 the converts in Virginia established the Dan River
Baptist Church in the Pittsylvania section of Halifax County. The
church's seventy-four members included sixty-three whites and eleven

---

[1] Reuben E. Alley, *A History of Baptists in Virginia* (Richmond: Virginia Baptist
General Board, 1974) 35; Charles F. Leek, *The History of Pittsylvania Baptist
Association* (Danville VA: Pittsylvania Baptist Association, 1963) 1–2.

[2] Leek, *Pittsylvania Baptists*, 2–3.

blacks.[3]

The majority of these members owed their conversion to Samuel Harris, one of the best-known Baptists in colonial and Revolutionary Virginia. Born in 1724 in Hanover County, Harris settled in present-day Pittsylvania County and became a colonial planter with ten slaves and 4,000 acres of land. A friend of George Washington, he served as justice of the peace, member of the House of Burgesses for Halifax County, vestryman of Antrim Parish, colonel of militia, and commandant of Fort Mayo on the Indian frontier near present-day Martinsville.[4] One day in May 1758, Colonel Harris was riding in Halifax County from Peytonsburg to Booker's Ferry when he noticed a crowd gathering at a private dwelling along the road. Learning that William and Joseph Murphy—celebrated evangelists from the Separate Baptist community in North Carolina—were about to preach, Harris dismounted, tied his horse, and slipped into the back of the meeting room. Baptists like to say God and Harris met that day for the first time. Harris returned home to convert family and friends, who banded together in August 1760 to form the Dan River Baptist Church.[5]

Although not ordained until 1769, Harris preached the gospel from 1758 until his death in 1799. With Pittsylvania as his base, Harris ranged from northern Virginia to North Carolina, organizing or helping to organize more churches—twenty-six—than any Virginia Baptist in history. The established Anglican Church unwittingly aided his efforts by allowing, and perhaps encouraging, mob violence against Harris's gatherings. On one occasion at Orange, Anglican ruffians knocked him from the platform and dragged him away by his legs and hair until friends were able to free him.[6] No doubt such Anglican hostility attracted liberty-loving Virginians to the Baptist faith. Apparently Anglican opposition was motivated by the effectiveness of Harris as an orator. One of his Baptist contemporaries, Robert B. Semple, noted that his forte "consisted chiefly in addressing the heart"; even the noted evangelist George Whitefield, Semple added, "did not surpass Harris in this respect."[7] Another commentator even doubted "if Patrick Henry could

---

[3] Ibid; Alley, *Baptists in Virginia*, 37.
[4] Leek, *Pittsylvania Baptists*, 36–37.
[5] Ibid., 38–39.
[6] Ibid., 40–41.
[7] Quoted in ibid., 46.

control a vast assemblage by a power superior to that of Samuel Harris."[8]

Harris also used his oratorical talents in the American Revolution. By then moderator of the General Association of Separate Baptists in Virginia, he spoke out for independence as forcefully as he preached the gospel. Harris also operated a wagon train carrying military supplies between Petersburg and the Continental Army depot at Peytonsburg.[9] With other Pittsylvania Baptists, he joined the fight for religious freedom in the Old Dominion in the late Revolutionary period. They rallied behind James Madison's Memorial and Remonstrance against religious tyranny in 1785. They even complained to the legislature that Episcopalians had every right to "prefer Episcopacy to any form of government," but for Episcopalians to insist upon an established Episcopacy, they said, "threatens Religious Liberty in its Consequences."[10] In addition, Pittsylvania Baptists lent vocal support to Thomas Jefferson's Bill for Establishing Religious Freedom, which passed the legislature in 1786 and made Virginia the envy of all friends of religious liberty. The bill's passage also paved the way for dramatic growth of the Baptist faith.

The late 1780s were banner times for Pittsylvania Baptists. In 1788 twenty-one churches formed the Roanoke Baptist Association under the leadership of Samuel Harris. The association took its name from the river system, which included the Dan as a tributary, in the area where the churches were located. Their "Plan upon Which We Associate" specified "one faith, one Lord, one baptism," congregational supremacy, and religious freedom.[11] The following year, 1789, when George Washington was chosen to be the first president of the United States, Harris wrote to him concerning federal guarantees for religious liberty. Harris also traveled to New York to attend Washington's inauguration.[12]

Prior to 1800, Pittsylvania Baptists were concerned primarily with securing religious freedom and founding Baptists churches. These goals met, they turned their attention to the Sunday School movement, foreign missions, and education. The Sunday School movement began in the 1780s in England when volunteer teachers began providing religious

---

[8] Ibid.
[9] Ibid. 37.
[10] Quoted in ibid, 8.
[11] Ibid., 23.
[12] Ibid. 19–24, 47.

instruction and basic training in reading and writing to children, many of whom worked six days a week and did not have the benefit of schooling. The movement spread to Virginia in the early nineteenth century, entering the Commonwealth through Baptist churches. Pittsylvania Baptists strongly supported the movement. They purchased over fifteen hundred books, enlisted hundreds of teachers, and planned a Sunday School convention in 1854 for publicity and recruitment.[13]

The nineteenth century was without question the Protestant century in foreign mission work, an effort in which Pittsylvania Baptists took a prominent part. The Roanoke Baptist Association founded its missionary society in 1816 and began to make generous annual contributions to the national Baptist Board of Foreign Missions, established two years earlier. The commitment of Danville Baptists to foreign missions was shown as early as 1834, when missionary Luther Rice was chosen to preach at the organization of the city's First Baptist Church. Nevertheless, the movement slowed in the 1830s when anti-missionary sentiment sprang up within the Roanoke Baptist Association. Several churches joined a national Anti-Missionary Movement, opposing the missionary bureaucracy with its centralizing tendencies. So bitter did battles in the association become that twelve pro-missionary churches withdrew in 1839 to form the Dan River Baptist Association. Seven anti-missionary churches followed suit in 1841 to form the Staunton River Anti-Missionary Baptist Association. Yet by the mid-1840s the Roanoke Baptist Association had recovered from the rupture. The association continued its generous annual contributions to the mission board and even employed its first missionary.[14]

Although committed to Sunday schools and missionaries, Baptists took longer to develop enthusiasm for higher education. In 1807 Presbyterian clergyman John Rice wrote, "It is a maxim firmly established amongst the Baptists...that human learning is of no use."[15] There is some evidence to the contrary. Rhode Island Baptists, for example, recognizing that ignorant clergymen could lead ignorant laymen astray, founded Brown University to foil "that old deluder, Satan." On the other hand, Baptists emphasized religious experience

---

[13] Alley, *Baptists in Virginia*, 141, 147; Leek, *Pittsylvania Baptists,* 102–3.
[14] Alley, *Baptists in Virginia,* 151–205; Leek, *Pittsylvania Baptists*, 86–87.
[15] Quoted in Leek, *Pittsylvania Baptists*, 59; Alley, *Baptists in Virginia*, 144.

rather than religious knowledge, the heart and not the head. Neither the well-educated clergyman nor the lettered layman who had not walked the Damascus Road had a place in God's kingdom, they insisted. Reuben Alley, historian of Virginia Baptists, wrote, "Evangelical Protestants, including Baptists, generally showed little or no interest in the education of ministers, believing that men in the pulpits needed only the spirit of God to qualify as preachers. Worldly wisdom, they argued, led ministers into sins of vanity and conceit."[16]

A change in Baptist attitudes did come eventually. In 1810 the member churches in the Roanoke Baptist Association responded favorably to a request for a statewide "plan for the education of young preachers."[17] The request bore fruit in 1832 with the founding of Virginia Baptist Seminary, which in 1840 became Richmond College (later the University of Richmond). Pittsylvania Baptists supported both the local Ringgold Academy and the Baptist ancestor of Hollins College, founded in 1853. In a report to the Roanoke Baptist Association the previous year, Elder Drury Blair contended that "in an enlightened community like ours...all should be educated."[18] Without fully accepting the desirability of universal education, the association praised Sunday schools as "a powerful means of grace" and bemoaned the acute shortage locally of educated laymen to serve as Sunday school teachers.[19]

Such popular and official pronouncements in the mid-1850s helped to assure the creation of a Baptist women's college in Danville. An important function would be to train future Sunday school teachers. A secondary goal would be training of future missionaries or wives of missionaries. It is worth noting that in 1850 Virginia Baptists ordained their first unmarried female missionary, Harriet A. Baker of Powhatan County, for service in China. Probably, the organization of a Baptist women's college in Danville was also viewed as an expression of support for the missionary side of the missionary–versus–anti-missionary

---

[16] Alley, *Baptists in Virginia,* 186; see also Rudolph, *American College,* 6.

[17] Quoted in Leek, *Pittsylvania Baptists,* 60.

[18] Minutes of the Roanoke Baptist Association, 23 August 1852, 9, Virginia Baptist Historical Society, University of Richmond. See also Alley, *Baptists in Virginia,* 189, 224; Garnet Ryland, *The Baptists of Virginia: 1699–1926* (Richmond: Virginia Baptist Board of Missions and Education, 1955) 288ff.

[19] Minutes of the Roanoke Baptist Association, 23 August 1852, 17.

squabble.[20]

Perhaps an equally important motive was belief that a Baptist women's college in Danville could combat prevalent antislavery arguments. Abolitionists said slavery violated not only fundamental American ideals embodied in the Declaration of Independence, but also the spirit of New Testament Christianity. With Harriet Beecher Stowe and the antislavery Grimké sisters of South Carolina as models, many Christian women were morally indignant about slavery. To an overwhelming majority of southern and Virginia Baptists, an obvious countermeasure was collegiate instruction that Mosaic law, the Hamitic curse, and the Pauline epistles justified slavery; that slavery made possible the glory and grandeur of Greece and Rome; that ethnology seemed to prove blacks were fitted to serve and whites to rule; and that blacks were better off slave than free.[21]

Another source of support for the school was the movement to educate partisans in the war against alcohol. Baptists provided both leadership and membership for the temperance movement in the Old Dominion. In the early 1820s, Abner W. Clopton, a Baptist minister in Charlotte Courthouse, helped organize a group that soon became the Virginia Temperance Society, with Clopton as secretary. He had support in the Roanoke Baptist Association, which labeled the use of spirits "highly injurious," "ruinous to domestic happiness," and promotive of "gross disorder in the churches." The association concluded, "In view of these things, we should, as patriots and philanthropists, but especially as Christians...use our influence to exterminate this scourge from among us."[22]

Not fully conscious among local Baptists was a motivation inherent in social mobility. Frederick Rudolph, the Mark Hopkins Professor of History at Williams College and noted educational historian, has written,

> For the Methodists and Baptists, founding colleges became
> a part of that apparently endless American process of coming to
> terms with an essentially middle-class society. As churches of
> the meek and disinherited, the Methodist and Baptist persuasions

---

[20] Ryland, *Baptists of Virginia*, 276; Hagan, *Story of Danville*, 91–93.

[21] In 1845, Baptists in the United States split into two camps over the slavery issue. See Alley, *Baptists in Virginia,* 215–19.

[22] Minutes of the Roanoke Baptist Association, 25 August 1851, 11.

had at first been able to get along without educated clergymen and educated laymen. But opportunity in the United States being what it was, no church could establish itself as a permanent refuge for the permanently meek and disinherited. American life did not work that way, and Baptists and Methodists discovered that they were at the very least candidates for rank in the middle reaches of society. With that discovery went the necessity of erecting colleges, institutions which not only catered to some of the requirements of middle-class life, but which also helped to lend an aura of respectability to Methodists and Baptists as they worked their way from poverty to plenty.[23]

Finally, local Baptists longed to have a school offering an education with a proper denominational flavor. Danville Female Academy operated under an Episcopalian, George W. Dame, who used his position as schoolmaster to swell the rolls of Epiphany Church. Danville Male Academy became Danville Military Institute, hardly a fitting place for a young lady. Methodists controlled the recently established Danville Female College, the forerunner of Stratford College. Worst of all from a Baptist perspective, for thirty-five years before the Civil War, schoolmistress Ann Benedict laced the curriculum of her Female Institute with heavy doses of Presbyterian Calvinism.[24] Baptist girls in Danville simply had no place to go for a proper education.

---

[23] Rudolph, *American College*, 57.

[24] George W. Dame, "Facts Concerning the Early History of Danville," typescript, Danville vertical file, Danville Public Library, Danville VA, 24.

II. GENESIS

1859–1892

3

An Infant Survives Troubled Times, 1859–1871

With incentives provided by the reform movement, local boosterism, and a dynamic Baptist faith, schoolmaster William Isaac Berryman founded the Danville Female Institute in September 1854. Located in his house across Patton Street from First Baptist Church in an area known as "Baptist Hill," this preparatory school enjoyed the support and patronage of both the local church and the Roanoke Baptist Association.[1] Berryman was new to Danville but not to the profession of education. After operating a private academy in King and Queen County for several years, he relocated to Danville in the early 1850s to teach at the Danville Male Academy. Immediately joining First Baptist Church, he quickly rose to positions of responsibility, including church treasurer, which brought him into contact with Peter William Ferrell, who served with him on the church's finance committee. Ferrell would later serve as an original trustee of the Baptist Female Seminary (the forerunner of Averett College) and, no doubt, encouraged Berryman to open the Danville Female Institute.[2]

By 1856 the school was well enough established for Berryman to place the following advertisement in the official organ of Virginia Baptists, the *Religious Herald:*

---

[1] David W. Gray, "A History of Averett College" (master's thesis, University of Richmond, 1960) 1–2, 17, 138.

[2] Clara G. Fountain, "The Presidents of Averett College," Averett University Archives, 1.

DANVILLE FEMALE INSTITUTE.

The exercises of the third annual session of this school will be resumed on the 1st September next, under the superintendence of the subscriber. Every department has been filled with competent instructors. The ten months' session will be divided into two sessions of five months each, without vacation. Pupils will be charged from the time of entrance and no deduction will be made for absence or subsequent withdrawal, except in cases of protracted illness.

Terms for Session of Five Months

Primary Department	$10.00
English Grammar, Geography, Arithmetic, etc.	12.50
Natural and Intellectual Philosophy, Botany, Chemistry, Rhetoric, Logic, Mathematics	15.00

Extras:

Latin, Greek, and French, each	$ 7.50
Music on Piano and Guitar	20.00 to 25.00
Use of Instrument	2.50
Painting in Oil	12.50
Painting in Water Color	10.00
Drawing and Embroidery, each	5.00
Contingent expenses, each pupil	.50

The principal is prepared to accommodate twenty boarders. The charge for board, every necessary included, is ten dollars per month. In order to insure a systematic progress in their studies, it is highly important that the pupil be present at the opening of the session. For further information address the subscriber at Danville.

Wm. I. Berryman.[3]

The curriculum at Berryman's school was thoroughly American. He retained both the language of the educated clergy (Latin) and the language of the gentleman/scholar (Greek) to enable young ladies to study theology, the Classics, and literature of the Renaissance. So

---

[3] *Religious Herald* 25 (4 September 1856): 139.

equipped, each would be a Christian gentlewoman who could do battle against the forces of heathenism and barbarism. Berryman also included French for a touch of High Culture. But what Americanized the curriculum was the incorporation of useful knowledge (mathematics, geography, and natural sciences) and the capacity to appreciate the mother tongue and use it effectively. At the same time, Danvillians, who were no more than three generations removed from the frontier, wanted their daughters to exhibit the trappings of civilization. Nothing did this quite as well as proficiency at the piano, easel, and embroidery hoop. What is uncertain, however, is the level of instruction at Berryman's school. At best guess, the Danville Female Institute combined elementary and secondary training with high hopes of eventually becoming a college.[4]

Despite a solid academic program, problems of management connected with the boarding department caused the Danville Female Institute eventually to suspend all operations.[5] This unfortunate beginning did not daunt the Dan River Baptist Association, which resolved in July 1857 "that the subject of female education demands a more serious consideration on the part of every Baptist within the limits of our Association, and that we recommend the establishment of a female school of high grade in our midst."[6] The association put words into action by appointing a seven-man committee to devise ways and means of founding another school. The next year witnessed the demise of the Danville Female Institute, but also considerable investigation of alternatives by the committee.

In autumn 1858, its labors bore fruit when Nathan Penick announced the beginning of a new school, the Baptist Female Seminary, which would use some of the facilities of the defunct Danville Female Institute.[7] Born in 1831, Penick was a native of nearby Halifax County, where he married Jane Elizabeth Averett, daughter of former

---

[4] Rudolph, *American College*, 40–44, 114–17, 222, 310.

[5] Berryman seems to have left the profession of educator shortly after the closure of the Danville Female Institute. He served for several years as town sergeant and Danville agent for the Richmond and Danville Railroad before his death in 1882 at seventy years of age. Fountain, "Presidents," 1.

[6] Minutes of Dan River Baptist Association, 6, 29–31 July 1857, Virginia Baptist Historical Society, University of Richmond.

[7] Gray, "History of Averett College," 5.

Congressman Thomas Hamlett Averett and sister of three future teacher/president/trustees of Penick's school. In the early winter of 1859, Penick placed the following advertisement in the *Religious Herald:*

BAPTIST FEMALE SEMINARY, DANVILLE, VA.
	Mr. N. Penick. Principal and Teacher of Latin and higher branches of English, Mrs. J. E. Penick, teacher of Music, French. and Elementary English.
	The first session of this school will commence on the First of February and close on the 30th of June, 1859.
	Board can be obtained in pleasant families at $10 per month.

Tuition in Elementary English	$12.50
Tuition in Higher English	15.00
Latin and French (each)	5.00
Music on Piano	20.00
Use of Instrument	2.50
Incidental Expense	1.50

The school is furnished with such *Chemical and Philosophical Apparatus,* as may be necessary in the study of the two sciences—also, Globes, maps and every other convenience and necessity that will in any wise tend to make the progress of pupils easy and rapid.
	Pupils will be charged from the time of entering the school to close of session and no deduction made except in cases of protracted sickness. Persons in the county wishing to patronize the school can address,
	N. Penick
	Danville, VA.[8]

Within a month, plans were afoot to add a collegiate curriculum to the seminary, a common occurrence in antebellum preparatory schools. The new name of the school would be Union Female College, reflecting the united efforts of the Roanoke, Dan River, and Concord Baptist Associations.[9] On 10 May 1859, the *Religious Herald* publicized the new

---

[8] *Religious Herald* 32 (24 February 1859): 31.
[9] Kelley and Wilbur, *Junior College Teaching,* 6–7; Gray, "History of Averett

college with the following notice:

UNION FEMALE COLLEGE, DANVILLE, VA.

This is an institution, which has lately been brought into being by the most pressing demands for a Female College in this part of Virginia. A large extent of country, composing the Roanoke, Dan River, Concord and parts of other Associations has never had a Baptist Female School of high order. We have been forced to send to expensive city institutions to obtain a thorough female education. Responsible and earnest minded men, in all this region, feeling this want, have gone to work to remedy it. A large and beautifully located edifice has already been purchased, and possession will soon be obtained. In the meantime, the exercises of the school have been commenced under the guidance of two able and experienced teachers, and the prospects of success are more than flattering.... The college is now, beyond the shadow of a doubt *a certainty*.... We want—*we will have*—a College that will meet the wants of those interested in a school on the line of the Richmond and Danville Rail Road—especially to the wants of the three Associations above named, under whose fostering care we earnestly desire to see it grow up....

J. W. McCown, Secretary[10]

The next two years were crucial ones for the struggling institution. In September 1859, Nathan Penick's brother-in-law, Halifax schoolmaster Joseph J. Averett, joined Penick at the college. The two men and their wives constituted the faculty of four. In December 1859 the General Assembly of Virginia incorporated Union Female College. In 1860 its sixteen trustees raised enough money through stock subscriptions to erect a building at Ridge and Patton Streets adjacent to the former Berryman residence on college land atop "Baptist Hill." A later college catalogue boasted of the edifice:

The College Building, erected at an expense of about

College," 6–7.

[10] *Religious Herald* 32 (10 May 1859): 39.

$25,000.00, is located in one of the most elevated, quiet, beautiful and refined portions of the town. It was constructed for the purpose for which it is now used. It is tastefully planned, has all the conveniences of the most approved school architecture, and affords accommodations for a large number of young ladies, besides a large chapel and a sufficient number of recitation rooms. The chambers are large, well ventilated and warmed by means of fire-places.[11]

The initial student body of forty in 1859 swelled to eighty-three in 1860–1861.[12]

The Civil War brought change and uncertainty to the college, which apparently remained in operation throughout the conflict.[13] When hostilities became imminent, Nathan Penick and Joseph Averett resigned from the college to become Confederate officers. Penick joined the artillery, Averett the infantry. A succession of clergymen-principals directed the affairs of the college until the war's end: William A. Tyree (1861–1863), John C. Long (1863), and Isaac Beverly Lake (1863–1872). In 1863 the trustees adopted a management plan that would be followed for half a century. Under this arrangement the trustees rented the land and the buildings to the principal in return for 10 percent of his receipts. The principal was responsible only to himself for recruiting students and faculty, providing quarters and meals, and setting curriculum and salaries. In 1864, after three years of embarrassment because of "Union" in the college name, the state legislature approved a change of name, and until 1904 the college was called Roanoke Female College, or RFC.[14]

The war years must have been a time of excitement mixed with concern. In 1861 the students undoubtedly joined the throng watching two companies of the 18th Virginia Infantry Regiment, a local troop of

---

[11] *Catalogue of Roanoke Female College, 1873–1874* (Danville VA: Waddill & Brothers [et. al.], 1874 [to the present]; hereinafter cited as *[Years Given] Catalogue)*, 10.

[12] Gray, "History of Averett College," 8–9.

[13] A lack of primary source material about the college during the Civil War prevents a description of the size of the student body, the length of the school term, and the nature of the curriculum. Since the trustees retained a principal throughout the war, students probably took classes at the college from September to June, 1861–1865.

[14] *The Danville Appeal*, 28 November 1863, 3; Gray, "History of Averett College," 9–10, 79, 142–45.

cavalry, and a battery of artillery march off to war. They also saw trains come and go with fallen warriors and with war materials for the supply depot in Danville.[15]

Prison camps located in town must have made the most lasting impression on young minds. Because Danville was far enough from the battlefronts to make Union cavalry raids unlikely, the Confederate government began transferring Union prisoners from Richmond to Danville in November 1863. Approximately 650 prisoners were housed in each of several three-story tobacco warehouses. Four of these structures were located at Union and Spring Streets, a fifth at High and Floyd Streets, and a sixth at Lynn and Loyal Streets. Excessive heat and cold, inadequate sanitation, poor hygiene, scanty provisions, and debilitating parasites, coupled with devastating epidemics, made these makeshift prisons true "houses of horror." Their stench and that of hospitals set up to treat ailing prisoners pervaded the atmosphere for hundreds of yards, certainly reaching the college only three blocks away. Only approximately 3,000 of the 7,000 prisoners survived the eighteen months during which Danville was a prison site.[16]

In early April 1865, Danville briefly captured the nation's attention after Confederate forces evacuated Petersburg and Richmond. General Robert E. Lee tried to maneuver his dwindling army to a position west and south of General Ulysses S. Grant's troops, in hopes of joining General Joseph E. Johnston's small army near the Virginia–North Carolina dividing line. Lee and Johnston's routes of retreat pointed toward Danville. Accordingly, President Jefferson Davis and what was left of the Confederate government arrived in Danville at 3:00 P.M. on 3 April 1865, having fled Richmond via the Richmond and Danville Railroad. In anticipation that Danville would become the new capital of the Confederacy, a ten-man arrangements committee tried to spruce up the town. Two of the ten, the Reverend Charles C. Chaplin and tobacconist Peter W. Ferrell, were president and secretary, respectively, of the trustees of Roanoke Female College.[17]

---

[15] Pollock, *Sketch Book*, 44–46.

[16] James I. Robertson, Jr., "Houses of Horror: Danville's Civil War Prisons," *Virginia Magazine of History and Biography* 69 (July 1961): 329–33; Pollock, *Sketch Book*, 46–50, 345.

[17] John H. Brubaker III, *The Last Capital* (Danville: Danville Museum of Fine Arts and History, 1979) 3, 5; Pollock, *Sketch Book,* 50ff., 158, 173; Benjamin Simpson, *Men*

The next six days were an anxious time indeed. Roanoke Female College sat in the middle of several blocks containing Confederate government offices, cabinet members' lodgings, and the William T. Sutherlin mansion, which accommodated the Davises. No doubt the college students caught glimpses of government officials who scurried back and forth to meetings. No doubt, also, they took advantage of every opportunity to see the Confederate president. Apparently he appreciated their attention. Author Myrta L. Avary, probably quoting Mrs. William T. Sutherlin, wrote:

> Another thing that cheered [Davis] in Danville was the enthusiasm of the schoolgirls of the Southern [Roanoke?] Female College; when these young ladies, in their best homespun gowns, went out on dress parade and beheld Mr. Davis riding by in Major Sutherlin's carriage, they drew themselves up in line, waved handkerchiefs and cheered to their hearts' content; he gave them his best bow and smile—that dignified, grave bow and smile his people knew so well. I have always been thankful for that bright bit in Mr. Davis' life during those supremely trying hours....[18]

One of the original trustees of Roanoke Female College played an important role in the last days of Confederate Danville: Captain William P. Graves, whom President Davis ordered on April 7 to locate and report on Lee's army. Originally from Caswell County, North Carolina, and a volunteer in the Mexican War, Graves had been a successful Danville merchant in the 1850s. Following the John Brown Raid at Harper's Ferry in 1859, he was elected to command the newly organized Danville Infantry Blues. In 1861 this outfit became Company A, 18th Virginia Infantry Regiment, C.S.A. He surrendered his command in 1862 to serve

---

Places and Things, ed. Duval Porter (n.p.: Dance Brothers & Co., 1891) 358; *1888–1889 Catalogue*, 19.

[18] Myrta L. Avary, *Dixie after the War* (New York: Doubleday, Page, 1906) 52. On 4 April 1865, a North Carolina soldier wrote from Danville: "The President is here and looks well and cheerful. Hotels are crowded, the Baptist Female College and other large buildings are turned into hospitals." One wonders if the RFC students, like Melanie Wilkes in *Gone with the Wind,* did not put aside thoughts of personal comfort and safety in order to nurse the wounded soldiers ([Raleigh] *Daily Confederate,* 11 April 1865).

on General George E. Pickett's staff. Captain Graves was later a mounted scout and in this capacity set out on President Davis's mission. Furnished with a special train, he moved through Halifax and Charlotte Counties to Pamplin, where he learned of Lee's surrender at Appomattox. Upon receiving the news from Graves on April 10, President Davis and the remainder of his government fled at once to Greensboro, leaving Danville to chaos, confusion, and Yankees.[19]

History does not record whether the collegians remained on "Baptist Hill" to witness the explosion of the arsenal the next day. Nor does anyone know how many of the girls remained under the watch and ward of Principal Lake, who presumably guarded them (and college property) from the disorder and looting of the next two weeks. Making matters worse were thousands of paroled Confederates passing through Danville on their way to homes farther south. Fortunately, Virginia Governor William Smith arrived in Danville just as Davis was leaving and countermanded the latter's order to ship southward all available Confederate supplies, thus giving the tattered, hungry, and often shoeless veterans provisions enough for a start toward home. But no sooner had paroled Confederates left when Yankee "bummers" (irregulars), free of responsible army controls, began looting. Danville's Confederate military commander, Colonel Robert E. Withers, was able to maintain some control by arresting and detaining eighty of them until April 27, when Union Major General Horatio G. Wright and the Sixth Corps restored Danville to the Union and assured law and order.[20]

At war's end, Nathan Penick decided not to return to Danville and settled instead in Culpeper, Virginia, where he operated the Culpeper Female Institute. Despite his absence, the postwar period found Roanoke Female College firmly established and ready to expand. This story of success is a tribute to the high caliber of those operating the institution. The Reverend William A. Tyree (1824–1884) was the college's first principal of the war years. A brother-in-law of Nathan Penick through marriage to Penick's sister, Susan, Tyree earned baccalaureate and master's degrees from Columbian College (now George Washington

---

[19] Pollock, *Sketch Book*, 56–58, 119–20, 173; Brubaker, *Last Capital*, 48–52.

[20] Pollock, *Sketch Book*, 62–64; Robert Enoch Withers, "Excerpts from Autobiography of an Octogenarian," typescript, 10–15, Danville vertical file, Danville Public Library, Danville VA; "Reconstruction Days in Danville," typescript, Piedmont Genealogical Society Collection, Danville Public Library, Danville, VA.

University) in Washington, DC, before becoming a pastor and college administrator. Tyree remained at the Danville college from 1861 to 1863, when he returned to Halifax County and the pastorate.

The next principal was the Reverend John C. Long (1833–1894), a brother of Confederate General Armistead Long. In 1856 he earned an undergraduate degree from Richmond College and went on to be pastor of several Baptist churches in Goochland County. Long was a natural choice to finish Tyree's unexpired term in 1863. Tyree baptized Long at the Baptist Church of Farmville and doubtless recommended the young pastor. In addition, during his days as a student at Richmond College, Long had befriended Charles C. Chaplin and J. W. McCown, both of whom acted as trustees of Union Female College in Danville in 1860. Long also served a year in higher education as a teacher at Florida State Seminary in 1857–1858. Nevertheless, he served as principal of the college in Danville for only five months before assuming the pastorate of the Baptist church in Charlottesville, his birthplace. He devoted the last nineteen years of his life to service as professor of ecclesiastical history at the Crozer Theological Seminary in Pennsylvania.[21]

Isaac Beverly Lake (1837–1922), principal or co-principal from 1863 to 1872, provided continuity between the war and post-war periods. He held the A.M., Th.G., and D.D. (honorary) degrees and taught at Chesapeake College in Hampton before coming to head Roanoke Female College. Several notables assisted Lake as co-principal. Hannon W. Reinhart served for the school year of 1866–1867. The fact that he not only was educated at the prestigious University of Virginia, but also had served as a captain of cavalry in the C.S.A., was certainly appealing to local planters with daughters to educate. The Reverend Thomas Hume, Jr., (1836–1912) assisted Lake as co-principal between 1867 and 1872. Hume, a graduate of Richmond College and the University of Virginia, taught Latin and English at Chesapeake College before the Civil War, served as chaplain of the 3rd Virginia Infantry Regiment of the C.S.A., and filled a pulpit ministry before coming to Roanoke Female College. More pertinent to his receiving the co-principalship, Hume's father baptized Principal I. B. Lake and doubtless recommended the son to him.

---

[21] Gray, "History of Averett College," 143–48; George Braxton Taylor, *Virginia Baptist Ministers,* series 4 (Lynchburg, VA: J. P. Bell, 1913), 202–20; ibid., series 5, 337–44; ibid., series 6, 113–15; Fountain, "Presidents," 1–6.

In addition, Lake and Hume both taught at Chesapeake College. Also, while at Richmond College, Hume befriended Peter W. Ferrell, a trustee of Roanoke Female College. After leaving Danville in 1872, Hume was a teacher-clergyman in eastern Virginia until 1885, when he began a twenty-two-year tenure as professor of English language and literature at the University of North Carolina.[22]

Roanoke Female College flourished under the guidance of Lake and Hume. Ninety-one students were enrolled in 1868, and the principals apologized for being unable to accommodate all applicants. Not unlike students in liberal arts colleges in the early twenty-first century, students at RFC translated and memorized Latin prose, read and critically examined English literature, practiced correct pronunciation of French words and phrases, polished their English grammar, learned practical but refined diction and enunciation, grappled with higher mathematics, explored the natural sciences, debated philosophical concepts, and studied the highlights of Western civilization. Instruction, the principals advertised, was "given by means of text-books and lectures." Because of RFC's dual function as college and finishing school, the students also immersed themselves in the Ornamental Department's music program, which, the principals promised, "develops and refines the taste, strengthens the mental powers, and ministers the highest enjoyment." Immersion in the music program involved daily practice, "regular rehearsals in the presence of the entire school, the Faculty, and a few invited guests," and periodic public performances. Testing in all other disciplines involved daily oral recitation, despite a claim by the principals that students were "encouraged to think for themselves—to investigate truth, and not simply to memorize." Comprehensive written examinations came at the end of January and again in June. The school term began September 10 and ended the last week of June, with Commencement held on the last Wednesday (the final musical concert) and Thursday (the graduation exercises).[23]

Four times in the nine-month term parents received progress reports

---

[22] See also *The Baptist Encyclopedia: A Dictionary*, ed. William Cathcart (Philadelphia PA: Everts, 1881) 968; *North Carolina Troops, 1861–1865: A Roster*, comp. Louis H. Manarin, 13 vols. (Raleigh: North Carolina Department of Archives and History, 1968 [1966–present.) 2:198.

[23] *Catalogue of the Roanoke of the Female College, Danville, Virginia, 1867–1868* (Lynchburg VA: Schaffler and Bryant, 1868) 8-15.

"showing the merits and demerits of the pupil as exhibited in her general deportment, attention to studies, and standing in her several classes." A week or so later, each student could expect to receive from home a letter containing the necessary "admonitions and encouragements." No doubt students had plenty of time to ponder these parental threats in required morning and evening chapel services and at required church services and Sunday school each sabbath. They likely also shared such letters from home with fellow boarders who ate family-style with the seven professors at a common mess.[24]

The student body in 1868 was heavily local. The forty-nine Danvillians who made up 54 percent of the student body probably would have commuted to RFC. More than 71 percent of the student body hailed from either Danville or nearby counties of Pittsylvania and Halifax in Virginia and Caswell in North Carolina. Almost 76 percent were from southside Virginia, the region shaped by a triangle extending from Lynchburg and Danville along the border of North Carolina to the southern portion of Hampton Roads. Only one student—Bettie Crump from Jefferson, Texas—was not from either Virginia or the North Carolina counties of Caswell and Rockingham. Her Christian name, however, was the second most popular at RFC. Among the student body ten students were named Mary, seven Bettie, six Ella, five Nannie, and four Mollie. Reflecting the fashion of the times, 40 percent of the Christian names consisted of two syllables and ending in "ie." Besides Bettie, Nannie, and Mollie, there were Pattie, Mattie, Sallie, Fannie, Eadie, Josie, Lizzie, Cattie, Maggie, Willie, Minnie, Nellie, Ginnie, Lettie, and Annie.[25]

Because Principal Hume accepted the pastorate of Danville's First Baptist Church in 1870 and could function for his last two years only as a part-time co-principal, the Board of Trustees brought in a third co-principal to assist Lake and Hume: Arnaud Eduard Preot (1818–1873). Co-principal Preot added international flavor to the Danville school. Born in Lille, France, and educated in Paris, Preot immigrated to America in 1837 and settled in New Orleans. After stints of teaching music and modern languages (he spoke five) in New York and Pennsylvania, he moved to Virginia, where he taught at Leavenworth

---

[24] Ibid., 16-17
[25] Ibid., 5-7.

Academy in Petersburg and Female Collegiate Institute in Buckingham before accepting a position at Farmville Female College (later Longwood College) in 1860. He served as president of the Farmville school from 1862 to 1869, leaving then to teach for a year at Danville Female College (later Stratford College), which closed temporarily in 1870. The unemployed Preot was fortunate indeed to land the co-principalship at Roanoke Female College, where he taught modern languages and music (organ, piano, and guitar). His wife and former pupil, Elizabeth Anne Hammatt of Chesterfield County, also taught French and music.[26]

Unfortunately, Preot was more notable in death than in life. He was in the habit of taking a little beer as a tonic for his poor health. In 1873, just before commencement, a keg of Preot's beer exploded in his face. One of his co-principals wrote of the incident:

> He went to bed and never got up. Dr. John William Jones and Dr. C. H. Toy, then Professor in the Southern Baptist Theological Seminary, were with us to deliver the sermon and literary address of the commencement exercises; but the death of Professor Preot on the night before…substituted a funeral for the exercises that had been expected. It became a time of mourning instead of one of general rejoicing.[27]

Assisting Preot as co-principal for the school year of 1872–1873 was the Reverend John L. Johnson, whose appointment continued a trend begun at the Danville school by Hannon W. Reinhart, a trend that would continue for the rest of the nineteenth century. In postwar Virginia former general officers of the Confederacy often served as senators and governors, former field-grade officers often served in lesser offices at the state level, and former company-grade officers were usually relegated to positions of local prominence such as college presidencies. So it was with Johnson, a one-time captain in the Confederate Army. Holding degrees from the University of Virginia, he was also a Baptist parson and former instructor at Hollins Institute. With Preot providing cosmopolitan and international airs and Johnson offering a combination of sound

---

[26] Rosemary Sprague, *Longwood College: A History* (Farmville, VA: Longwood College, 1989) 10–32.

[27] John Lipscomb Johnson, *Autobiographical Notes* (privately printed, 1958), 203.

academic credentials, Confederate service, and religious guidance, Roanoke Female College must have been attractive to parents and daughters alike. Unfortunately for the school, Johnson left in 1873 to become chairman of the Department of English at Mississippi State University, where he would remain for twenty years.[28]

The infant years of Roanoke Female College came during a troubled time, one that many similar colleges did not survive. RFC endured primarily because its founders and principals were respected, cautious, and pious men, many of them pastors or former Confederate officers, whose academic background was the best preparation available at the time and whose qualities of leadership and scholarship would later earn for them positions at the best schools in the South.

---

[28] Fountain, "Presidents," 6.

4

The Averett Years
1872–1892

Most important of the early principals at Roanoke Female College were the Averett brothers, Samuel Wootton and John Taylor, sons of Martha Wootton Averett and former congressman Thomas H. Averett (1800–1855) of Sedge Hill plantation in Halifax County. Samuel Wootton Averett, born 1 March 1838, was the sixth son and ninth child. Older brother John was born 24 December 1827, the third son and fourth child. Their father was a drummer boy in the War of 1812, attended Jefferson Medical College in Philadelphia, and practiced medicine in Halifax County, an area he represented as a Democrat in both the Senate of Virginia and the US House of Representatives. Two other children, Joseph James Averett and Jane Averett Penick, also taught briefly at Roanoke Female College before the Civil War.[1]

Considering the father's demise in June 1855 and the necessity of sharing a good, but not extremely large, estate with his widowed mother and so many brothers and sisters, Samuel Wootton Averett was fortunate to be appointed a midshipman at the US Naval Academy in Annapolis. He graduated third in the class of 1859. His first assignment was the screw sloop USS *Wyoming*, which put in to San Francisco in May 1861. When the twenty-three-year-old Averett learned the Civil War had broken out, he resigned from the US Navy and made his way to New Orleans to accept a Confederate lieutenancy and command of the CSS *Watson*, a towboat engaged in mounting the defenses. Soon he

---

[1] News clippings, Collected Papers and Scrapbooks of J. T. Averett, Danville Public Library, Danville, VA, hereinafter cited as Averett Papers; Gray, "History of Averett College," 141–42; Averett Family Tree, Averett University Archives, Danville.

commanded a floating battery at Island No. 10, the Confederate stronghold on the upper Mississippi River. The Federal capture of this position in April 1862 made him a prisoner until his exchange four months later. Averett joined the CSS *Florida* in October 1863. One of the most powerful Confederate vessels afloat, the *Florida* terrorized the Atlantic sea lanes before its capture at Bahia, Brazil, in October 1864, though Averett was not on hand for that event. Six months earlier, he had been detailed to carry dispatches from Bermuda to Richmond. While at home on leave, he was incapacitated by both a near-fatal bout with typhoid fever and a partial loss of vision in one eye as a result of an incorrect prescription to treat his deteriorating eyesight. His convalescence lasted until after the war. Afterward Averett secured a job as a teacher at the Culpeper Female Academy under his brother-in-law and RFC's founder, Nathan Penick. In Culpeper, Averett met and married Janie Russell Miller.[2]

In 1872 Averett came to Roanoke Female College, where his older brother, John Taylor Averett, had served as a trustee since 1859. The following year co-principal Preot died, co-principal Johnson resigned, and John Taylor Averett joined younger brother Samuel in a co-principalship that lasted until 1887 when the younger Averett left to become president of Judson College in Alabama. At RFC, "Captain Sam" taught French, physics, chemistry, and mathematics, while "Captain Jack" taught English, history, and Latin and also handled the school's finances.[3]

Even more than his younger brother, John Taylor Averett ensured the success of RFC. In 1848 he was graduated with honors from Emory and Henry College and subsequently married Louisa Frances Penick, sister of RFC founder Nathan Penick. After failing health prevented him from studying law, he became headmaster of the flourishing Ringgold Military Academy in neighboring Pittsylvania County. In 1859 he was one of the founding trustees of Roanoke Female College.[4] When the Civil War broke out, Averett was commissioned a lieutenant in Company D of the 38th Virginia Infantry Regiment under Colonel E. C. Edmunds, who fell at Gettysburg in 1863, and Colonel George K. Griggs, who went

---

[2] News clippings, Averett Papers; Gray, "History of Averett College," 149–51.
[3] Gray, "History of Averett College," 151.
[4] News clippings, Averett Papers; Gray, "History of Averett College," 153.

on to serve as a fellow college trustee and was pallbearer at Averett's funeral in 1898. Because of Averett's administrative ability, Colonel Edmunds arranged his appointment as captain and regimental quartermaster. Averett participated in the major campaigns of the Army of Northern Virginia and surrendered with Lee at Appomattox.[5]

In 1865 Captain Averett returned to his peacetime profession. He was to become not only a noted educator but also a participant in Danville's governing structure. From 1867 to 1872 he operated his own Danville Male Academy at the corner of Loyal and Jefferson Streets; in 1872 he became principal of Danville's first public school system. When he joined his brother as co-principal of Roanoke Female College in 1873, he also continued to serve as a college trustee.[6] He became a leader among Confederate veterans, educators, Baptists, and Masons. As editor of the *Tobacco Journal*, a local trade organ, he became the most important spokesman for Danville's leading industry.

Because of his attributes and position, John Taylor Averett was destined as well for political leadership, which came in the early 1880s when Virginians were preoccupied with race relations, readjustment of the state's debt, and the power of General William Mahone.[7] After the end of military occupation and reestablishment of native rule in Virginia in 1870, William Mahone became the most visible and potent force in Virginia politics. He had been the principal Confederate hero at the siege of Petersburg and was president of the Atlantic, Mississippi, and Ohio Railroad, which then stretched from Norfolk through Petersburg to Lynchburg. Initially he belonged to the Conservatives, a coalition of prewar Democrats and Whigs, who were opposed by Republicans. In 1879 he launched the Readjuster movement to address the problem of Virginia's prewar debt, which with interest amounted to about $45 million. The older generation of Conservatives, known as Funders, wished to pay the entire amount, claiming that Virginia's "honor" was at stake. The Readjusters wanted to scale down the debt to a "reasonable" figure, claiming the money was owed mostly to Yankee investors who made repayment impossible by devastating the Old Dominion from 1861

---

[5] News clippings, Averett Papers; Gray, "History of Averett College," 153–54.

[6] Dame, "Early History," 20; news clippings, Averett Papers.

[7] Pollock, *Sketch Book*, 108, 158; news clippings, Averett Papers; George W. Dame, *Historical Sketch of Roman Eagle Lodge, No. 122, A. F. and A. M.* (Richmond, VA: I. N. Jones, 1895) 99.

to 1865. This issue split the Conservative coalition. In the statewide elections of 1879, the Readjusters captured both houses of the legislature, which then elected Mahone to the US Senate over Funder candidate and former Danvillian, Colonel Robert E. Withers. Three years later the Readjusters scaled down the state debt. In 1881 Mahone joined the Republican Party in order to receive support for Readjuster policies and candidates from the Washington establishment. Mahone's political enemies, including John T. Averett, united to form the new Democratic party.[8]

Encouraged by an overhaul of Danville's election machinery by the Readjuster legislature, Mahoneites captured control of city government in May 1882. They elected seven of twelve city councilmen and all three justices of the peace. In turn, the city council appointed Mahoneites as policemen and as health officer, clerk of the market, and weigh master of the public scales. The majority of Mahoneites were African Americans who supported the Readjuster principle in order to prevent transfer of funds from public education to debt retirement. Racism undoubtedly swayed Danville Democrats such as John T. Averett to denounce the election and subsequent appointments, but Mahone's cynicism and corruption lent credence to their self-serving allegations.[9]

Danville Democrats responded first with the pen. They printed and distributed statewide the *Danville Circular*, which detailed the alleged abuses they suffered from local government and appealed for deliverance. "We cry out to you in our affliction," the document pleaded to white Virginians, "to help us throttle this viper of negroism [*sic*] that is stinging us to madness and death."[10] The circular defined deliverance as a vote against Mahoneites in the statewide elections of 1883. One of the authors was tobacconist William P. Graves, a scout for Jefferson Davis in 1865 and president of the trustees of Roanoke Female College in 1883. His close friend, John T. Averett, was a keen supporter of this appeal.[11]

According to Readjusters, the Democratic sword was mightier than

---

[8] Virginius Dabney, *Virginia: The New Dominion* (Garden City, NY: Doubleday, 1971) 376–77, 383–86.
[9] Pollock, *Sketch Book*, 85–89; Dabney, *Virginia*, 391; "Reconstruction Days" typescript.
[10] Quoted in Pollock, *Sketch Book*, 89–90.
[11] Pollock, *Sketch Book*, 85–90.

the Democratic pen. As the November elections in 1883 approached, emotions in Danville ran at fever pitch. On Saturday, November 3, three days before the election, white Democrats and black Mahoneites tangled with fisticuffs and gunfire on Main Street. Four blacks were killed, and two whites and three blacks were wounded. Republican newspapers across the nation dubbed the confrontation the "Danville Riot" and the "Danville Massacre." By contrast, Democratic newspapers in Virginia reported the affair as proof that Mahoneism inevitably led to black domination and attendant corruption and violence. In the end, these accounts frightened white Mahoneites in Virginia into voting Democratic, thus ending Mahone's political supremacy.[12]

Locally, Democrats also triumphed, despite the fact that black voters were a majority in Danville. For two days after the riot, armed white Democrats under William P. Graves patrolled the streets of Danville. No doubt, John Taylor Averett was among them. Their presence intimidated potential black voters and caused a low turnout, enabling Democratic candidates William P. Graves to win election as mayor and John T. Averett as city councilman.[13] The election of Graves and Averett convinced men of prominence in surrounding counties that Danville was a safe place for the education of their daughters.

Nevertheless, with the exception of the Danville Riot, postwar Danville was a city without explosive social and economic turmoil, a situation which helped the city and its Baptist college to grow and prosper. The city was Victorian in morals, manners, and appearance while New South in geographic and industrial orientation. In place of the mythical planter-aristocrat was the industrial baron as the heroic leader. Danville adopted the tenets of the New South with gusto: society should be organized to favor urban, not rural, and industrial, not agricultural, ways. "Beat the Yankee at his own game" became the motto. If Northern railroads consolidated, Southern ones must do likewise. If the North turned a blind eye to exploitation of mill hands, the South should, too. If a Northern capitalist was not keen to invest in the South, the new model

---

[12] Ibid., 92–98; "Story of the Danville Riot," typescript, 1–8, Danville Genealogical Society Collection, Danville Public Library, Danville VA; "Early Days in Danville," typescript, 21–25, Piedmont Genealogical Society Collection, Danville Public Library, Danville VA; Dabney, *Virginia*, 391–93.

[13] R. A. Schoolfield, "Reminiscenses of R. A. Schoolfield," typescript, 2, Danville vertical file, Danville Public Library, Danville VA; Pollock, *Sketch Book*, 115–20.

Southerner was willing to sell him material resources and tax immunity at bargain prices.

Danville founded an aggressive Chamber of Commerce in 1882 and soon got results. Local entrepreneurs established Dan River Mills. They invested in railroads to Lynchburg, Greensboro, Stuart, and Norfolk. They built scores of tobacco factories and warehouses. New jobs in transportation and industry tripled the city's population between 1850 and 1890. Over four hundred buildings were erected in Danville between 1876 and 1881 and another four hundred between 1881 and 1887. In the years 1875 to 1887, the value of real estate increased from $1.5 million to $5.2 million, and the value of personal property from $589,000 to $3 million. Facilities and public services kept pace. In the 1870s the city constructed a gas plant and courthouse, established a fire department, and laid water and gas lines. The 1880s brought streetcar service, streetlights, a hospital, and telephones. By 1890, students at Roanoke Female College had a thoroughly modern city at their disposal.[14]

This flourishing New South city gave rise to an elegant society. New York had its Fifth Avenue and Cleveland its Euclid Avenue; Danville's "Millionaires' Row" was the stretch of Main Street between Ridge and South Main where the nabobs of textiles and tobacco settled down to gracious living. Their mansions provided a profusion of turrets, gables, brackets, lattices, balusters, finials, cupolas, columns, embossed terra cotta, multicolored slate roofs, roof crestings, modillions, verandas, and cast iron fences set in granite. Architecture ranged from Classical Revival, Italianate, and Romanesque to Second Empire, Gothic, Queen Anne, and French Chateau. The interiors were eclectic, with mantels of Italian marble, parquet floors, plastered ceiling moldings, lincrusta wainscoting, gas chandeliers of brass and prisms, ornate ceiling medallions, and elaborately carved European furniture. Even well-to-do country girls at Roanoke Female College considered themselves fortunate to receive an invitation to dine with family friends in such a setting. It was a treat for all students to view the mansions from a passing streetcar.

The same postwar period that brought prosperity to Danville also

---

[14] Chesapeake and Ohio Railroad, *Historical, Industrial, and Statistical Review* (New York: Historical Publishing Company, 1887) 156; Hairston, *Danville*, 130–31; Hagan, *Story of Danville*, 145.

brought prosperity to its Baptist college. Enrollment increased from an average of seventy-nine students in the 1870s to 106 students in the 1880s. The 1873–1874 catalogue paints an inviting picture. There were three areas, or departments, of study: preparatory, collegiate, and ornamental. Preparatory departments were commonplace in higher education throughout America because of the uneven quality of elementary and secondary training. These departments guided students of various ages and levels of knowledge to graduation with the modern equivalent of a high school diploma before funneling them into the collegiate curriculum. The preparatory department at Roanoke Female College gave elementary and secondary training in history, geography, spelling, reading, writing, composition, arithmetic, and grammar. The collegiate department provided courses in ancient and modern languages, English language, English literature, mathematics, history, geography, moral philosophy, and natural sciences—in short, a liberal arts and sciences education. The ornamental course of study, which included music and painting and stressed both performance and appreciation, highlighted the college's supplemental role as a finishing school.[15] The catalogue touted this role with these words: "Need we say to our patrons that a knowledge of Music and Painting—the sister arts—are in our day conceded to be necessary to the completeness of a young lady's education.[16]

The collegiate curriculum was rigid and rigorous. Latin students read Julius Caesar (first class), Sallust and Virgil (second class), and Cicero, Tacitus, and Horace (third class). Greek classes struggled with Xenophon, Herodotus, Homer, and the dramatists. Students in English studied the notables: Chaucer, Shakespeare, Spenser, Bunyan, Milton, and Tennyson. Those in mathematics advanced through calculus. The natural sciences combined principles of chemistry, physics, and geology; and there were even courses devoted to the history of Virginia, the United States, England, the ancient world, and the modern world. Finally, girls in the collegiate program were expected to master moral philosophy. The curriculum was intended "to develop the mind, train the habits of thought and inquiry, and lead to the acquirement of useful

---

[15] *1873–1874 Catalogue*, 11–17; Gray, "History of Averett College," 46. Enrollment figures are not available for all years during this period.

[16] *1873–1874 Catalogue*, 17; see also Rudolph, *American College*, 281–82.

knowledge, and to the love of what is the beautiful and the good."[17]

The college awarded four degrees for students who mastered portions of the collegiate curriculum. The degree of "Proficient" went to students who completed a certain number of courses outside of a prescribed avenue of study. "Graduate in a School" was awarded for mastery of one of seven collegiate schools—Ancient Languages and Literature, Modern Language and Literature, English Language and Literature, Mathematics, Natural Sciences, Moral Philosophy, or History and Geography. "English Graduate" was given to students mastering the intermediate level in mathematics, attaining proficiency in Latin or French, and completing study in the following schools: English Language and Literature, Moral Philosophy, History and Geography, and Natural Sciences. Finally, "Full Graduate" was awarded to those earning "Graduate in a School" from seven collegiate schools and completing "a satisfactory essay upon some literary subject."[18]

Although these requirements suggest students did nothing but study, not all of the matriculates were awarded comprehensive degrees. Yet the regimen, to be sure, left little time for mischief. Sunday school, church, and devotionals twice a day were compulsory. Girls were limited in visiting and receiving visitors. They could not make "boisterous noise," play games of chance, read popular "dime" novels, talk from the windows, or answer the doorbell. Each morning before dawn, a maid came to each dormitory room to build a fire in the fireplace and bring water for bathing. The girls arose, bathed, and dressed at sunrise, ate breakfast an hour later, had devotionals and classes until 1:30 P.M., ate lunch, took classes until 4:30 P.M., enjoyed a "constitutional"—a brisk walk certain to induce "high thinking"—ate supper at nightfall, studied in a study hall until 9:00 P.M., and turned out lights at 10:00 P.M.[19] The Averett brothers were certain these rules would "induce a correct, lady-like and Christian deportment."[20]

For this educational environment, parents paid the following fees:

---

[17] *1878–1879 Catalogue*, 19; see also *1873–1874 Catalogue*, 12–16.

[18] *1873–1874 Catalogue*, 18.

[19] *1873–1874 Catalogue*, 19–20; *1874–1875 Catalogue*, 25–26; Frances Hallam Hurt, "Centennial of Averett College," *The Commonwealth: The Magazine of Virginia* 26 (December 1959): 8, 4–12.

[20] *1873–1874 Catalogue*, 19.

For tuition in Advanced English Branches	$50.00
For tuition in Primary English Branches	40.00
For tuition in Ancient and Modern Languages, each	20.00
For tuition in Music	50.00
For tuition in Oil Painting	50.00
For tuition in Drawing	25.00
For Use of Piano for practicing	10.00
For Incidental Expenses	10.00
For Board	150.00[21]

Most of the instructional fees went to pay the seven instructors. Three of them taught collegiate courses; three, ornamental courses; and one, preparatory courses. The remainder of the money covered instructional supplies, the tithe to the trustees, and profit to the principals. The boarding fees paid for all meals, with girls and professors eating family-style at common tables.[22]

Changes came gradually and without fanfare during the tenure of the Averett brothers. Ornamental courses such as organ, guitar, violin, waxwork, embroidery, and lace work were added, dropped, and added again as specialists came and went. Students were allowed occasional gentlemen callers, but only with proper letters of introduction to the principals and the "approbation" of the latter.[23] Even so, the 1888–1889 catalogue advised, "We deem it best to forbid...[written] correspondence with young gentlemen."[24] Students could leave campus one day a week, but only with permission and in the company of a chaperon. On the other hand, the Averetts strongly encouraged each student to send home once a week "a letter neatly penned and (in every sense) properly worded."[25] Parents, of course, were expected to respond just as often with "words of cheer and sound advice."[26]

More notable was the introduction in the 1880s of calisthenics, which reflected the new national emphasis in collegiate education on physical fitness. Beginning in the 1860s, colleges throughout America

[21] Ibid., 21.
[22] Ibid.
[23] *1874–1875 Catalogue*, 25.
[24] *1888–1889 Catalogue*, 32.
[25] Ibid.
[26] Ibid; see also *1878–1879 Catalogue*, 28; *1874–1875 Catalogue*, 21.

established departments of physical education and constructed gymnasiums to develop the body in ways not considered to be either vulgar or heathen. In keeping with the trend, by 1883 Roanoke Female College added a Physical Department in order "to secure the 'most complete education of the whole muscular system.'"[27] The advantages of calisthenics were legion, as the Averetts pointed out in 1883:

> Its beautiful games, graceful attitudes, and striking tableaux possess a peculiar fascination for girls. The exercises are arranged to music, and when performed by a class are found to possess a charm superior to that of dancing and other social amusements. This system of exercises will correct drooping or distorted shoulders, malposition of the head, and many other common defects.[28]

Roanoke Female College also was gaining an air of sophistication. By 1883 two literary societies, the Longfellow and the Tennyson, were active. On Friday evenings, members indulged in songs, plays, tableaux, poetry recitals, and original essays. By 1885 the college presented two concerts each year at the Danville Opera House. The first came in early March and the last in late May. These concerts were highly acclaimed. Freund's *Music and Drama* noted that "the greatest musical event of the [1885] season [in Danville] was the final concert of the Roanoke Female College.... The musical department of this institution still ranks above all others in this section and equals any in the South."[29]

Partly responsible for the luster of the music department was a young music teacher named Frederick (Fritz) Delius, soon to become one of England's foremost composers. Born of a German father and reared in Bradford, England, Delius left England in 1884 to manage a family citrus plantation, Solano Grove, in Florida. A largely self-taught musician, young Delius preferred teaching and performing on the violin in nearby Jacksonville to citrus farming on his St. Johns River estate. In 1885 Delius left Florida for Roanoke Female College, where he taught piano, violin, music theory, and composition for a year before moving on to

---

[27] *1883–1884 Catalogue*, 26; see also Rudolph, *America College*, 153.

[28] *1883–1884 Catalogue*, 33.

[29] Quoted in *1885–1886 Catalogue*, 39; see also *1883–1884 Catalogue*, 37.

study at Leipzig and to win fame as a composer.[30]

During his year in Danville, Delius became a close friend of fellow RFC music professor and Leipzig graduate Robert Phifer, to whom Delius would send an autographed copy of *Appalachia* in 1910. In later years, Phifer's wife remembered Delius as "the nice Englishman with such charming manners."[31] She recalled:

> There was rarely a day he did not come to our home on Jefferson Street, taking meals with us, telling jokes, amusing my children, and always scribbling music which he would sit down at the piano and play. He loved to extemporize and would take a simple tune and convert it into soaring passages like a tapestry of music which charmed us all.[32]

Danville was as generous to the young Englishman as he was to its citizens. Delius loved to take walks, which frequently led him past several of the city's thirty tobacco factories, where as many as three hundred black workers would be singing the lines of a work song called by a hand who served as song leader. These tunes became the basis of *Appalachia*, one of Delius's most famous symphonic works. Delius also loved to perform, and ample opportunities were afforded by small gatherings at the Phifer house, the city's two musical associations (the Beethoven and the Gottschalk), Fischer's Jewelry and Musical House, which billed itself as "the largest music store in the South," and college concerts. One such concert on 5 March 1886, featured Delius with a violin concerto by Mendelssohn.[33]

In June 1886, Delius left Roanoke Female College for Europe. His timing was propitious, because the college soon experienced a decline in enrollment. Apparently Dame Rumor was partly to blame; in the catalog the Averett brothers took pains to point out that only four deaths from malaria in as many Augusts made Danville the envy of American cities. The Averetts also began marketing the college more aggressively, hoping

---

[30] William Randel, "Frederick Delius in America," *Virginia Magazine of History and Biography* 71 (1971): 349–59.

[31] Gerald Tetley, "Delius in Danville," *Virginia Cavalcade* 9 (Summer 1959): 17.

[32] Ibid.

[33] Randel, "Frederick Delius in America," 360 (see also 349–61); news clippings, Delius file, Mary B. Blount Library, Averett College, Danville VA.

to entice country girls for whom RFC would be the epitome of high living. These advertised inducements included a healthy, attractive diet, owing to Danville's "well stocked market," the availability of "nurses of the best character," a profusion of "physicians of wide range of learning and desirable skill in practice," an abundance of "medicines of any kind," easy strolls along "well-paved and dry routes," two mails and two trains per day, churches offering "sermons every Sunday from pastors of great learning, eloquence, and piety," and "social intercourse, always convenient in a refined town society" that would induce "habits of propriety" as well as "good manners."[34]

The best opportunity for showing off a young lady's "good manners" and "habits of propriety" came at spring commencement, which was a highlight of Danville's "refined town society." The 1879 commencement was typical. The first day of exercises featured a concert at the Opera House, where graduates presented vocal and instrumental works by composers Mozart, Mendelssohn, and Meyerbeer. The second and final day culminated in the graduation exercises, also at the Opera House. The opening hymn, "A Mighty Fortress Is Our God," preceded musical interludes, graduation essays with such titles as "What Shall a Girl Do After She Graduates?," the commencement address, and the conferring of distinctions and degrees. The affairs were well attended. Everyone in Danville society knew someone who was graduating.[35]

Samuel Wootton Averett helped plan fifteen commencements before he left in 1887 for Judson College in Marion, Alabama. He died there on 20 September 1896. John Taylor Averett planned the next five commencements after 1887 with the new title of president of Roanoke Female College. In 1889 he suffered a stroke which left him wheelchair-bound and by 1892 forced him to retire. The college board of trustees accepted his decision with mixed emotions. The Depression of 1893 loomed on the horizon, threatening to aggravate the problems of declining enrollment and deteriorating facilities. It was evident that new and more decisive leadership was required. Yet Roanoke Female College—John Averett's passion as well as livelihood—was to be his monument. From original trustee to longest presiding administrator, he built, guided, and sustained it. He hired and fired faculty, recruited and

---

[34] *1885–1886 Catalogue*, 23; see also 22.
[35] *1878–1879 Catalogue*, 14–17; *1883–1884 Catalogue*, 14.

graduated students, planned and altered curriculums, bargained with and cajoled vendors, defined and guarded moral values, and carefully managed financial resources so that he and his wife could enjoy a comfortable living after paying 10 percent of the revenues to the other trustees. All of this he accomplished, with time left over for his city, Masonic lodge, church, and veterans' organization. Small wonder that, when he retired, other trustees expressed "sincere admiration and gratitude," "unfeigned regret," and "most cordial and fraternal sympathies."[36] They must have realized that leaders like John Taylor Averett come but once in a generation.

---

[36] Quoted in Gray, "History of Averett College," 156; see also 59.

III. EXODUS AND JUBILEE

1892–1936

5

From the Gay Nineties to World War I

The forty-four years from John Averett's retirement in 1892 to the beginning of Curtis Bishop's presidency in 1936 brought seven presidents and many changes. The board of trustees tried out three names before deciding on Averett College. The curriculum shifted from a combination of preparatory and senior college work to junior college work only. In financial structure the privately owned stock company gave way to a Baptist-controlled corporation. The campus relocated from the Patton Street property on "Baptist Hill" to its present site on West Main Street. In the process the student population grew from seventy-three to over 400. Student life, once restricted to study and devotions, blossomed into many activities: student government, literary groups, honor societies, intercollegiate sports, sororities, a college choir, and student publications. Finally, after experiencing uncertain permanence and heavy debt, the college emerged as an established institution free of financial burden.

Dr. Charles Fenton James, who took the helm at Roanoke Female College after the retirement of President Averett, also taught history, philosophy, ethics, mathematics, and natural science. His wife, Mary Alice Chamblin James, supervised the boarding program. Born in 1844 in Loudoun County, Virginia, Charles James was only fifteen years of age in 1859 when he joined a volunteer cavalry unit raised in response to John Brown's Raid at nearby Harper's Ferry. At the outbreak of Civil War, he joined the 8th Virginia Infantry Regiment and rose through the ranks to captain and company commander. After the war he completed his formal education by earning a baccalaureate degree from Richmond

College in 1870 and a graduate divinity degree from Southern Baptist
Theological Seminary in 1873. A convert both to Christ and the Baptist
faith in one of the many camp revivals of the war years, James was
pastor of churches in Buchanan and Culpeper Counties for sixteen years
after finishing seminary. In 1882 Richmond College elected him a trustee
and in 1884 awarded him an honorary doctorate of divinity. In 1889
Allegheny Institute hired him as president, the position he held before
coming to RFC in 1892.[1]

The James presidency was a period of crisis in enrollment and
obsolescence of the physical plant during the long economic depression
of the 1890s. Enrollment slipped from 108 students in 1885 to fifty-six in
1896. The school year of 1901–1902—James's last full year as
president—saw only a partial recovery, with eighty-five young ladies
enrolled. At the same time the three-decades-old facilities were obsolete
and dilapidated. After all, in 1860 when the Patton Street building on
"Baptist Hill" was erected, Americans were accustomed to outdoor
plumbing, open fireplaces, oil lamps, and washbasins. Urban Americans
in 1895 expected indoor plumbing, central heating, electric lights, and
lavatories.[2]

President James was fully aware of both of these problems. But first
he had to make the college solvent. In December 1892, he informed
trustees the school would face a deficit of $1,000 by summer. Worse,
from his point of view, he and his family would get nothing for labor
except board and lodging. If he could not raise $500 immediately, he
declared, he might have to close the school in two months. As James
hoped, the trustees proffered immediate aid and also amended the college
charter to allow the institution to go into debt for repairs and
modernization. In 1898, after James again threatened to resign, the
trustees borrowed heavily to build a wing onto the main building. The
addition contained modern indoor plumbing, a new president's suite, a
dining room, and eight dormitory rooms. The additional dormitory space
increased the school's boarding capacity from forty to fifty students.[3]

Meanwhile, President James worked hard to make his school more

---

[1] *Religious Herald* 75 (25 December 1902): 9; *1898–1899 Catalogue*, 4; *Headlight: A Journal of Progress and Development* 10 (March 1896): 23; Gray, "History of Averett College," 157–58; Fountain, "Presidents," 11.

[2] Gray, "History of Averett College," 46.

[3] Ibid., 81 (see also 10, 18, 19, 80, 81); *1898–1899 Catalogue*, 8.

attractive to students. Although he retained the existing curriculum, he substituted monthly examinations for midterms and finals. In keeping with the times, he also altered the degree structure. The old system gave way to degrees of Bachelor of Letters, Bachelor of Arts, and Master of Arts. All courses carried weighted points, the number depending upon level and degree of difficulty. For example, Junior I Latin carried two points; Junior II Latin, four points; Intermediate Latin, four points, and Senior Latin, six points. To be eligible for a Bachelor of Letters, students needed fifty points; for a Bachelor of Arts, seventy points; and for a Master of Arts, ninety-one points. The college also began granting three certificates—"Promotion," "Distinction," and "Proficiency"—which denoted either special achievement in an area of study or entitlement to admission to a higher level of study.[4]

Student life changed considerably under James. New "senior privileges" allowed seniors "the company of young gentlemen, under such regulations as the President may prescribe, provided this meets with the approval of their parents, and provided also that their example and influence are always on the side of law and order."[5] Seniors also could leave campus without a chaperon. All girls could shop downtown on Friday afternoons, although all but seniors required a chaperon. All girls could spend the night off campus, if in the home of a relative or family friend, and if parents approved. Student uniforms, which President Averett had introduced "to promote economy and to avoid rivalry in dress," became more attractive under President James.[6] The drab gray cloak, dress, and hat gave way to navy blue serge dress with blue Oxford cap for late fall and winter, and white duck dress with blue Oxford cap for early fall and spring. In keeping with the Baptist disdain of dancing, the president warned: "No pupils will be permitted to attend hops, or germans, so long as they are under the care and jurisdiction of the President."[7] At the same time, students who went home to spend a night were no longer under the "care and jurisdiction of the President" and could dance all they pleased. James even acknowledged that "honest differences of opinion exist among good people on the subject of this

[4] *1898–1899 Catalogue,* 25; *1897–1898 Catalogue,* 26.
[5] *1901–1902 Catalogue,* 28.
[6] *1888–1889 Catalogue,* 32.
[7] *1897–1898 Catalogue,* 11.

popular amusement."[8]

Expansion of extracurricular opportunities kept pace with changes in student life. In 1753, students at Yale University had formed the first literary society/debating club, whose format spread across America to other institutions of higher learning in the nineteenth century. This development corresponded to growing emphasis upon extracurricular activities. Nevertheless, in keeping with Virginia conservatism, students at Roanoke Female College did not found their Philomathean Literary Society until 8 November 1893. Its purpose was to promote an interest in good literature and learned discussion, and its name comes from the Greek word meaning "loving knowledge." The society's members, called Philos, met twice monthly on alternate Fridays until literary societies were abolished in 1971. In 1904 the Philos published a short-lived literary magazine. In 1907 the Mnemosynean Literary Society, named for the Greek goddess of memory, was formed. Its members were dubbed Nemos. For decades Philos and Nemos met new students at the train station and "rushed" them while ostensibly serving as escorts back to campus.[9]

In the 1920s a keener rivalry emerged. Autumn brought the annual Nemo-Philo basketball game; spring, the annual debate. On the day of the event, competition began at a pregame meal in the dining hall. Nemos sat on the right side, which was decorated in black and gold (later lavender and gold); Philos, on the left side, decorated in red and gold. Cheers and songs punctuated the meal. A favorite Philomathean battle hymn went as follows:

We're Philomatheans
We're Philomatheans
We wear the red and gold today
We're going to fight, girls—
With all our might, girls,
And show them we will win the day
Rah! Rah!

---

[8] Ibid; see also *1901–1902 Catalogue*, 10; *1897–1898 Catalogue*, 10; [Averett College] *Chanticleer*, December 1938.

[9] [Averett College] *Pendulum*, 1927, pages not numbered; *1897–1898 Catalogue*, 9; *1928–1929 Catalogue*, 51; *1904–1905 Catalogue*, 29; *1916–1917 Catalogue*, 3; see also Rudolph, *American College*, 137–38.

Now is the time, girls
To show your pep, girls
And may you ever loyal be
And lead the red and gold to victory
So hail, Philomatheans, Hail![10]

From the dining hall the adversaries marched to the court or debate hall. Nemos marched in step to the rhythmic striking of a cowbell. Philos, dressed as pirates on at least one occasion, were led by a Captain Kidd as they sang several verses of "Yo, Ho, Ho, and a Bottle of Rum."[11]

Also in the 1920s, Nemos and Philos adopted initiation rites. Initiates had to dress in outlandish costumes, recite with great pomp and ceremony such literature as laundry lists, propose marriage to a broom, drink a "Chinese concoction" put together by inventive home economics students, present an impromptu folk dance, pass blindfolded through a chamber of horrors, carry on a one-person debate, crawl on hands and knees down four flights of stairs, and eat worms (spaghetti). New students breathed a long sigh of relief when initiation week ended.[12]

The Friday evening meetings were usually more serious. Topics of papers or debates ranged from modern female poets to current agricultural marketing arrangements. Lighter moments occasionally prevailed. A Philomathean meeting in March 1926 featured this debate topic: "Resolved: Men Are Vainer Than Women." After drawing on the world's great literature, as well as abundant empirical knowledge, the judges naturally sided with the affirmative.[13]

President James tried his best to entice young ladies into this uplifting environment. His catalogues highlighted student life with photographs of the president, the class of 1900, and activities in the main building. All suggested a friendly and secure existence under the loving parental guidance of a wise and mature Dr. James. Even liabilities James turned into assets. He defended RFC's outmoded heating system with the following notice, introduced quite without irony:

---

[10] *Chanticleer*, December 1929.
[11] *Chanticleer*, December 1924; ibid., March 1930.
[12] *Chanticleer*, September 1926; ibid., October 1926; ibid., October 1928.
[13] *Chanticleer*, March 1926.

The President has had experience with hot air and steam, and is decidedly of the opinion that the open fire-place or grate is the best for health of body and vigor of mind. The danger of steam heat is that it accustoms pupils to too high a temperature, thus enervating the system and rendering it more vulnerable to attack from exposure, and more liable to collapse in the spring season, when pupils are most in need of physical and mental vigor for the closing work of the session.[14]

One can almost imagine a student shivering before her fireplace in windy February and regretting ever having seen Danville or having believed a catalogue.

Unfortunately, Charles Fenton James died on the verge of success. Nursing the college through the depression of the 1890s and supervising the building program meant late work and worry about budgets, debt, and enrollment. An exhausted leader by 1900, James admitted publicly:

The long continued strain has been too much for my health. Twelve months ago in May, I had a serious collapse. Last October, I had another, followed at Christmas with a severe spell of pneumonia, which made my physician very uneasy. He said that my system was run down and that I needed rest.[15]

The national economic recovery at the turn of the century brought the hoped-for increase in enrollment from eighty-five students in 1901–1902 to 114 in 1902–1903. It never again dipped below 100 students, except in 1919–1920.[16] James's efforts paid off, but the years of struggle took their toll on his heart. On the afternoon of 3 December 1902, James and Professor George Swann were conferring in the president's office. James "complained of having a strange sensation," Swann later remembered, "so the windows were opened that he might have better ventilation. Medical aid was summoned, but to no avail. About three o'clock on Friday morning, December 5, 1902, he died."[17]

---

[14] *1897–1898 Catalogue*, 7–8.

[15] Charles F. James, commencement remarks, 4 June 1900, Averett University Archives.

[16] Gray, "History of Averett College," 46.

[17] Quoted in ibid., 159.

Three days later, grateful trustees and friends dedicated a commemorative plaque in the college chapel bearing the following inscription:

> In Memoriam, 1844–1902; Charles Fenton James, B.A., D.D., Ardent patriot, brave soldier, loyal friend, devout Christian, diligent student, accurate scholar, able minister, skilled educator, true in all the relations of life. We love him. In token of our esteem we have erected this tablet to perpetuate his name.[18]

† † †

Robert Edwin Hatton followed James as president. Reflecting increased professionalism in higher education, he held a Ph.D. degree from the University of Missouri and served as president of three small colleges in the Mississippi Valley before coming to Danville. In addition to being an administrator, the youthful President Hatton was an energetic and able classroom teacher of both philosophy and natural science.[19]

At RFC Hatton instituted extensive and immediate changes. First, he strained the physical and mental constitutions of his eight-member faculty by creating thirteen departments. Such a disparity may seem ridiculous, but the greatest American universities at the turn of the century attempted and performed Herculean labors with tiny faculties. Besides retaining standard offerings, Hatton added courses in teacher training, economics, and business, reflecting the trend toward practical, job-related education. To provide a clinic for teacher education, he added a kindergarten to the preparatory department. Hatton tried to upgrade a good department of music to a conservatory of music, whose quaint motto was, "Music washes away from the soul the dust of everyday life." In keeping with other national trends, he introduced a plethora of new courses in the social and natural sciences, ranging from psychology and physical geography to microscopy and mineralogy.[20]

Like his predecessors, Hatton succumbed to the temptation to

---

[18] Gray, "History of Averett College," 159–60.

[19] *1903–1904 Catalogue*, 6.

[20] Ibid., 8–21.

redefine degrees. Completion of the four-year classical curriculum brought a Bachelor of Arts; the four-year scientific curriculum, a Bachelor of Science; and the four-year literary curriculum, a Bachelor of Literature. Teacher education graduates earned a Bachelor of Didactics and a Virginia teacher's certificate. The Bachelor of Music went to students completing four years in the conservatory, whose expanded offerings now included instruction in organ, violin, violoncello, double bass, and mandolin. The Bachelor of Oratory required completion of a special program in elocution and physical culture. Master of Accounts capped the business curriculum, and Master of Arts applied to students completing a fifth year of study beyond baccalaureate degrees of arts, science, or literature. For the first time, RFC could offer schooling from kindergarten through master's level.[21]

Applying business methods to education, President Hatton convinced his trustees that a school must spend money to make money. With their financial support, he doubled the size of the library to 2,500 volumes and the faculty to twenty-two teachers.[22] One new teacher served as part-time librarian. Seven others taught in the new conservatory of music. Other expensive additions included eight new pianos, gas lighting in all buildings, an elevator, and instructional supplies and equipment such as business machines.[23]

Hatton promised the trustees increased revenue to offset increased expenses. For this he relied on new programs. In touting the new commercial program, for example, Hatton warned parents that "any given girl may some day have herself and family to support." Parents, he said, must "fortify [their] daughters against the possible danger of want by giving them such an education that they can, if need be, earn their own living."[24] Hatton also set up the college's first correspondence school to serve new clients: teachers who needed to upgrade a teaching certificate, students above college age, students needed at home, and those unable to afford residential college work. The minimal overhead offered potentially great profits. Furthermore, at Hatton's insistence, the State Corporation Commission approved an amendment to the school charter removing the word Female and abbreviating the name to

---

[21] Ibid., 22, 27.

[22] Ibid., 28.

[23] *1904–1905 Catalogue*, 8, 21, 29.

[24] *1903–1904 Catalogue*, 33–34.

Roanoke College, thus enabling the institution to attract male day students and new revenue.[25]

Unfortunately, the anticipated new revenue did not materialize. Only fifteen more students matriculated in 1904 than in 1903, raising the student body to 132. In fact, a looming economic recession threatened to depress, not increase, enrollment. Only 116 students entered in 1905 and 112 in 1906.[26]

To avoid additional expenses, the trustees had no choice except to convert the institution from a proprietary school whose trustees received 10 percent of the revenues into a nonprofit corporation affiliated with and managed by Baptists in the Southside. Accordingly, in low-gear emulation of a J. P. Morgan–style reorganization of an industrial giant, in 1904 trustee J. H. Hargrave purchased the school's debt of $6,500, foreclosed on its property, and lent $6,500 to trustee H. L. Boatwright, who bought the property for the Roanoke and Dan River Baptist Associations. The charter change of that year set the number of trustees at twenty-one—eleven selected by Baptist churches in Danville, seven by Roanoke Baptist Association, and three by Dan River Baptist Association.[27]

Student life changed for the better, even if monetary resources did not. The college added tennis, basketball, baseball, and fencing facilities. The first glee club of twenty-one voices was also formed. In an effort to create tradition, Hatton added a Class Day in spring, for seniors to enjoy hearing a guest speaker, partaking of refreshments, and planting a class tree. He enhanced the appearance of academic respectability by changing the uniform to Oxford cap and gown, which students were thrilled to wear off campus. Finally, in 1904 Hatton introduced the first yearbook, called *Echoes* until 1923, when it became *Pendulum*. Noland Hubbard Bowling, class of 1905, worked on the first *Echoes* staff and recalls that their most difficult decision was the dedication. The student body held all instructors and administrators in such high esteem that choosing one was impossible, while choosing all would be meaningless. They resolved their dilemma by dedicating the yearbook to two faculty children who served as student body mascots.[28]

---

[25] *1904–1905 Catalogue*, 45–49; Gray, "History of Averett College," 11–12.

[26] Gray, "History of Averett College," 46 and 160.

[27] Gray, "History of Averett College," 11, 19–20.

[28] *1904–1905 Catalogue*, 26, 30; *1905–1906 Catalogue*, 30–31, 39; Noland Hubbard

A glance at the 1905 *Echoes* reinforces the impression that students changed little before the 1960s. Eating candy and chewing gum were listed as principal amusements. Typical complaints about fellow students included "vanity," "fickleness," "feeling stuck-up," and "thinking only of herself." Common aspirations included "to flirt," "to strike it rich," "to travel," and, of course, "to get married soon." Typical reasons for marriage were "fun," "wealth," "convenience," "love only," and even "revenge."[29]

The 1905 *Echoes* also offers the first glimpse of the "rat" system. Shortly after her arrival, each new girl found under her dinner plate an invitation to a reception. It looked innocent enough, except for the skull and crossbones embossed at top center. On the Saturday evening of the event, the new girls quickly discovered that a rite of initiation preceded the reception. Upper-class students led each "rat" individually into a dark "Room of Horrors and Ghosts" filled with groans and moans. The "rat" was forced to drink a "magical" potion of coffee laced with quinine. Then she had to kneel and promise to share all food from home and love letters from sweethearts. Finally, the poor girl favored the upper-class students with a solo, walked a bedstead, and spent what must have seemed like hours locked in a dark wardrobe. Fortunately, this memorable evening ended with a real reception, where faculty and students munched salmon and ham sandwiches, cakes, peanuts, pickles, fruit, frappé, and candy kisses.[30]

Despite his unfulfilled promises of increased revenue, Hatton was allowed to remain at Roanoke College until 1907, when he resigned to accept the presidency of Liberty College in Glasgow, Kentucky. He at least had the satisfaction of knowing the college in Danville was improved, if not enlarged, by the changes he brought.[31]

† † †

Not surprisingly, the trustees of Roanoke College turned to an older and more seasoned educator, John B. Brewer, for leadership from 1907 to

---

Bowling, letter to author, 25 October 1982.

[29] *Echoes from R. C. 1905*, hereinafter cited as *Echoes [Year(s) Given]*, pages not numbered.

[30] Ibid.

[31] Gray, "History of Averett College," 46, 160; Bowling, letter to author.

1914. Brewer was born on 26 August 1846, at Wake Forest, North Carolina. He was the first of ten children born to merchant-planter John Marchant Brewer and Ann Eliza Wait Brewer. After an early education that included private instruction by grandfather Samuel Wait, the first president of Wake Forest College, and graduation from Bethel Hill Academy in nearby Person County, he joined the Confederate army in May 1864 for service in the battles of Kinston and Bentonville. He farmed for a year after the war before entering Wake Forest College for his bachelor's (1868) and master's (1871) degrees. In the next half century, Brewer became a leader in higher education for Baptists and women. From 1870 to 1881 he served as co-principal of two women's colleges in Wilson, North Carolina. From 1881 to 1896 he was principal of Chowan Baptist Female Institute in Murfreesboro, North Carolina, and from 1901 to 1907 he directed Franklin Female Seminary in Franklin, Virginia. At Roanoke College in Danville, President Brewer taught philosophy and mathematics in addition to his administrative duties.[32]

Because he inherited a school of declining enrollment, financial difficulty, dilapidated facilities, and academic overextension, Brewer made retrenchment and consolidation the hallmarks of his early years. He reduced the faculty to thirteen, cut back course offerings in music, and abolished the teacher education program, kindergarten, and correspondence school. Although he streamlined academic organization by lumping all collegiate departments into one Literary Department, Brewer initially retained the four-year collegiate curriculum and Hatton's academic degree structure. As a result, a typical four-year schedule, which led to breadth of knowledge and a B.A. degree, looked as follows:

Freshman Year	*Sophomore Year*
Algebra	Latin
Latin	English Literature
American Literature	French or German

---

[32] *Religious Herald* 102 (27 June 1929): 10; Commercial Association, *The City of Danville [1913]* (Danville VA: Waddill Printing Co., 1913) 25; *1907–1908 Catalogue*, 3; Gray, "History of Averett College," 160–161.

French or German   French History
Physics   Chemistry

Junior Year   *Senior Year*
Latin   Moral Philosophy
American History   Modern European History
Geometry and Trigonometry   Solid Geometry and Spherical
French or German   Trigonometry
History of the English Language   Astronomy and Botany
                                    Senior Review (Geography,
                                        Arithmetic, Physiology,
                                        Grammar) [33]

Three later academic changes improved the tone of Brewer's campus. As a requirement for admission, he instituted passing an entrance examination or presenting a certificate of completion for fourteen units of high school work. He also added a program in home economics, in keeping with current academic trends. Finally, he adopted an elective system that allowed each student a modicum of freedom in choosing classes. Since its inception in the 1870s at Harvard University, the elective system had been hotly debated. Proponents said all educated citizens need not possess the same body of knowledge. They argued also that the process of learning is as important as the subject matter and that students may be motivated by a curriculum they have a hand in designing. Opponents chose as their model the prescribed curriculum at Princeton University. They complained that an elective system consisted of unrelated, easy courses that rarely encompassed essential classics. Roanoke College consciously followed the Princeton system until Brewer accommodated to the national trend favoring electives.[34]

Although these academic alterations were judicious, Brewer's reputation for farsighted leadership rests more firmly on financial and physical accomplishments. In particular, he affiliated the college with the Baptist Education Commission of Virginia and moved its campus to the

---

[33] *1907–1908 Catalogue*, 8–9. *1909–1910 Catalogue*, 38–39; *1913–1914 Catalogue*, 43.

[34] *1907–1908 Catalogue*, 43–44; *1912–1913 Catalogue*, 35, 41; *1913–1914 Catalogue*, 6; Rudolph, *American College*, 294–306.

current location on West Main Street. Before Brewer, balancing the college budget depended on fickle demand and swings in the national and state economy. It was no news to college administrators that increased revenue was necessary for survival, new students were necessary for increased revenue, and an attractive campus was prerequisite to attracting new students. President Brewer recognized that affiliation with the Baptist Education Commission of Virginia not only could provide a steady source of support, free from economic swings, but also might enable the college to undertake major capital improvements, even including a new campus.

Of course, a renewed commitment to Baptist ways was essential. First, Brewer tightened social rules. He then persuaded the Reverend J. E. Hicks, pastor of First Baptist Church in Danville and an influential member of the Baptist Education Commission of Virginia, to join the college as first chaplain and first Professor of Bible. The college catalogue began to stress that any college calling itself Christian "should be positively Christian." By definition, "positively Christian" meant not only encompassing scriptural instruction but also assigning as much importance "to Paul as to Plato."[35] Brewer established on campus a chapter of the Young Women's Auxiliary (YWA) of the Baptist Women's Missionary Union and exhorted members to live up to their motto, found in Daniel 12:3: "They that be wise shall shine as the brightness of the firmament; and they that turn many to righteousness [shall shine] as the stars for ever and ever."[36] Finally, to avoid the appearance of competition with more academically respectable institutions such as Richmond College, Brewer reduced the curriculum to three years and substituted for Hatton's seven undergraduate degrees the Junior Diploma for two years and the Senior Diploma for three years of work.

Essential Baptist support soon followed. In 1910 the Virginia State Corporation Commission approved an amendment to the college charter changing the name to Roanoke Institute and giving the Baptist General Association of Virginia the right to nominate all trustees. The amendment also entrusted supervision of the school to the thirteen-member Baptist Education Commission, to which Professor Hicks

---

[35] *1907–1908 Catalogue*, 17.
[36] *Pendulum*, 1963, 73; *1910–1911 Catalogue*, 28; *1908–1909 Catalogue*, 7.

belonged.[37]

With financial support from Virginia Baptists now assured, Brewer moved quickly to relocate the campus. On 4 April 1908, the Board of Trustees evaluated a fifteen-acre tract of land on West Main Street near the outskirts of the city. Much of it was gully that sloped from West Main Street toward the Dan River. But the view of the Blue Ridge Mountains in the distance was magnificent. When the Mountain View Land Company reduced the $6,000 asking price by $500, the trustees bought immediately. In April 1909, they approved architectural plans by the firm of Pettit, McLaughlin, and Johnson for a large multipurpose building. Initial high bids for construction led to redrawing the plans, which the firm of Harwood and Moss offered to execute for $40,670. After the Baptist Education Commission agreed to give $15,000 if the trustees raised the remaining $25,000 locally, a contract was signed. Because they were unable to raise more than $10,000, the trustees issued thirty bonds of $500 each at 6 percent interest and maturity in eight years.[38]

In April 1911, Main Hall, as it later was named, was completed. Obviously conscious of new beginnings inherent in that season, Brewer arranged to move from "Baptist Hill" to West Main Street at Easter. President Brewer instructed students to have everything packed and ready for the move before leaving for Easter vacation. Students, trustees, and faculty were proud of their new campus. J. E. Hicks, by then a trustee, wrote glowingly:

> Our magnificent new building on West Main Street is the best college building for girls the Baptists have in the State, and one of the most complete and up-to-date school buildings to be found anywhere. It has first-class dormitories for one hundred pupils and accommodations for as many day students. A splendid new gymnasium is being fitted up; students in Science will have the advantages of large and well equipped laboratories; there are two elegant society halls; the beautiful auditorium, with stage lights and scenery, is the best in the city, and one in which

---

[37] Gray, "History of Averett College," 13–14; *1909–1910 Catalogue*, 3; *1910–1911 Catalogue*, 4, 6.

[38] Gray, "History of Averett College," 20–23, 82–83.

the people take a special pride; the elegant library room is excellently furnished, many new books being added, with all the leading magazines; the music department has been furnished with new pianos throughout…. The building is equipped with the most modern fire escapes, and with large fire doors on the interior is practically fireproof. Every part of the building is thoroughly sanitary. New stationary washbasins are being installed in every dormitory.[39]

The students were equally proud. Because the new auditorium had no seats, a casualty of redrawn architectural plans in 1910, the class of 1911 decided to raise enough money to purchase the first row before graduation in two months. They staged a fair with booths for entertainment and stalls for sale of candy and lemonade. On top of one booth was a sign that read "For Men Only." The one-cent price of admission seemed a cheap price for what patrons imagined they might see inside. Of course, all they saw was a pair of men's suspenders and trousers. Lottie Hundley Coleman, class of 1911, recalls, "Each man paid the penny and came out laughing but would tell no one so every one, through curiosity, had to go see for himself."[40]

President Brewer's gamble paid off. The student body of 107 in 1912–1913, swelling to 147 in 1913–1914, topped 193 in 1915–1916. In 1912 Brewer sold the Patton Street campus for use as a downtown hotel and banked the proceeds. This surplus of funds, ballooning enrollment, and splendid new campus clearly made Brewer the most successful leader in the school's fifty-five years.[41]

Student life in Brewer's seven years was a mixture of more stringent rules and more varied extracurricular opportunities. Senior privileges, instituted under James, disappeared. So did Sunday afternoon visitation from friends outside the college. Instead, students had a two-hour period of quiet and meditation to reflect on the morning sermon. Brewer demanded ladylike behavior at all times. He did not tolerate boisterous conduct, absences from meals or worship, or unchaperoned contact with young men. Also forbidden were unchaperoned trips off campus and

---

[39] *1914–1915 Catalogue*, 5; see also Gray, "History of Averett College," 22–23; Bessie Moses Wooding, letter to author, 23 October 1982.

[40] Lottie Hundley Coleman, letter to author, 3 November 1982..

[41] Gray, "History of Averett College," 46.

debts to fellow students.[42]

Brewer had his rules; his students had theirs. "Obedience when convenient" led the list. Brewer's rules "were pretty strict and I often tried to observe them when they met with my approval," wrote Edna Henderson Lipscomb, class of 1916.[43] Another student remembered, "Sneaking out to meet boys was done often."[44] The student body even published a mock list of rules and regulations. Included were the following:

1. All young ladies must receive no fewer than five gentlemen callers each month.
2. Students should never sweep in corners, along baseboards, or under beds.
3. Teachers who report rule infractions will be punished.
4. Students with a grade average of *below* 93 are exempted from examinations.
5. Trash belongs on the campus and not in the wastebasket.[45]

Plentiful extracurricular opportunities made Brewer's rules more palatable. Social and special-interest clubs abounded. Social clubs included Tau Delta Delta, whose motto was "Might is better than right"; the Jolly Seven, whose favorite pastime was "stuffing keyholes"; the Yankee Club for Northern girls; the Campus Club for boarding students; the Cupid Club, whose aim was "to wield our darts skillfully, when the right man comes along"; the Tar-Heel Club for North Carolina girls; and the Virginia Club for Virginia girls. Special-interest clubs included, in addition to two literary societies and glee club, the Kodak Club (whose motto was "If you love me, smile"); the Dramatics Club for theater buffs and aspiring actresses; the Fudge Club for candy lovers; and the Book Club. At Roanoke College (later Roanoke Institute), Brewer ensured that each girl had a niche. Elitism, ostracism, and social exclusiveness had no

---

[42] *1908–1909 Catalogue*, 22; *1911–1912 Catalogue*, 25–26.
[43] Edna Henderson Lipscomb, letter to author October 1982.
[44] Wooding, letter to author.
[45] *Echoes 1909–1910*, pages not numbered.

place.[46] In fact, it is probable that Brewer's vigorous encouragement of social clubs was a substitute for elitist and exclusive Greek-letter sororities that were becoming the rage elsewhere.

School spirit abounded. Each class, club, and team claimed a flower, colors, motto, and yell, which members proudly wore, practiced, and chanted as badges of membership. The motto of the 1913 freshman class was *Nihil sine labore.* The tennis team yell promised:

Tutti Frutti! Punch and Judy!
The tennis team will do its duty.
Why do you worry? Why do you fret?
The tennis team will get there yet!

The Yankee Club answered with

Boom-a-lacka, Boom-a-lacka,
Sis! Boom! Bah!
Chick-a-lacka, Chick-a-lacka.
Here we all are!
Yankee! Yankee!
Rah! Rah! Rah![47]

When students were not participating in a club activity, they were often observing birthdays and holidays. April Fool's Day was a favorite because students could get by with insolent behavior. Occasionally, however, they went too far. One student hid all day in the attic to make President Brewer think she had absconded. Brewer was not amused. He made the young woman memorize and recite the 119th Psalm, at 176 verses the longest psalm in the Bible. Its theme is the necessity of obedience.[48]

Holidays, birthdays, team competitions, and club meetings may have been fun-filled, but they paled into insignificance beside the excitement, lapsing into hysteria, of the fire in the main building at the

---

[46] *Echoes 1909–1910, 1914–1915,* pages not numbered.
[47] *Echoes 1909–1910, 1914–1915,* pages not numbered.
[48] Wooding, letter to author.

Patton Street campus on 30 October 1909. One student called it "a Hallowe'en party, Fourth of July parade, All Fool's Day, Old Soldier's reunion, Merry Christmas and Happy New Year all mixed into one."[49] When the fire broke out, hysteria temporarily gripped everyone. Hiking up her long skirt, Professor Jessie Brewer raced to the front of the building, where a telephone pole held a fire alarm box. So excited was she that "instead of ringing the alarm, she was seen to dance variations of a war dance around and around the pole, her hat in one hand, her umbrella in the other, uttering shrieks that would outclass any fire bell."[50] Another teacher, Mary Blount, frantically tied her valuables in a sheet, lowered the bundle from a window, and then fled the building. Only Professor Sadie LeGrande, true to her name, kept her wits and "with her usual elephantine grace," quietly descended the stairs of the burning building.[51]

Hysterical students made orderly evacuation impossible. "With a shriek and a wail and a torrent of tears," they ran from the building and threw themselves into the protective arms of young men who assembled on the sidewalk to watch the spectacle.[52] Some observers suspected in these actions more feminine calculation than feminine hysteria. Other students who remained in the building "were rushing around wildly, brandishing wash pitchers on high and flourishing closed umbrellas with energy unsurpassed."[53] Girls threw clocks, pillows, clothes, pitchers, pennants, and even bowls of goldfish from upper-story windows.[54]

Chivalry also reigned. Entering the burning building to help with the evacuation, one Danville lad offered his arm to a young lady, who naturally spurned his advances—after all, the two had not been formally

---

[49] *Echoes 1909–1910,* pages not numbered.
[50] Ibid.
[51] Ibid.
[52] Ibid.
[53] Ibid.
[54] Wooding, letter to author.

introduced. Fearing for the young lady's safety, the boy shoved her through the front door, but at the very moment firemen turned hoses in that direction. Aware that no excuse to the young lady would suffice, the young gallant quietly and quickly disappeared.[55] Firemen were able to confine serious fire damage to the cupola, although the top floor was flooded with water.

---

[55] *Echoes 1909–1910*, pages not numbered.

6

Cross Currents,
1914–1927

In 1914 at the age of sixty-seven, President John B. Brewer retired from Roanoke Institute. His successors would be W. W. Rivers, Clayton E. Crosland, and James P. Craft. Unfortunately, the sum of their achievements would scarcely equal Brewer's. Their thirteen years from 1914 to 1927 were years of drift rather than mastery, a time of conflicting decisions and uncertain direction, and a period of difficult reconciliation between tradition and modernity. It is true that in 1914 the institution acquired an identity that would last until the late 1960s. It also achieved freedom from debt, enabling it to withstand the Great Depression. But Brewer's decisions and a healthy national economy in the 1920s, and not the distinction of Brewer's successors, made these accomplishments inevitable.

Brewer's immediate successor, W. W. Rivers, was born in 1863 at Oxford, Mississippi, where he earned bachelor's and master's degrees from the University of Mississippi. He also studied at the University of Chicago. After a seven-year term as superintendent of schools at Helena, Arkansas, he served as president of three colleges before coming to Danville: Central College in Arkansas, Mississippi Women's College, and Orangeburg College in South Carolina. As did most presidents, Rivers taught classes (Latin and philosophy), while his wife, Georgia Thurston Rivers, supervised the boarding program. His legacy was creating Averett College, a four-year preparatory school and two-year junior college accredited by the Virginia State Department of Education.[1]

---

[1] *1914–1915 Catalogue*, 10; Gray, "History of Averett College," 161; Fountain, "Presidents," 14.

The Junior College movement began in 1892 at the University of Chicago when president William R. Harper separated the first two years from the last two years of collegiate study. In 1896 Harper coined the term "junior college" to apply to an institution offering only the first two years. He also suggested at least two hundred senior colleges with substandard facilities and academic credentials drop the last two years and call themselves junior colleges. The idea caught on immediately. California led the way in public education, while Missouri headed the vanguard in private education.[2]

Rivers was an early convert. Many students, he argued, wanted education beyond high school but without a four-year commitment of time, money, and energy. At the same time many professional schools required only two years of undergraduate education as prerequisite for admission. In addition, large universities were always overcrowded on the freshman and sophomore levels, while many freshmen lacked adequate study habits, emotional maturity, and self-discipline, which the friendly environment, intimate teacher-student relations, and small classes of a junior college could develop. Moreover, since social custom demanded that the "finished" or "complete" young woman master both ornamental courses and collegiate work, gender equity à la 1914 required a junior-college education with extensive ornamental training for young women and a senior-college education for young men.[3] Therefore, Rivers persuaded the trustees to designate the school "Roanoke Institute: A Junior College for Young Women." State accreditation as a junior college came in 1917.[4]

Not surprisingly, because Brewer had undertaken curriculum retrenchment, academic innovations for the new junior college were few. Rivers condensed all preparatory work into four years and all collegiate work into two. The music curriculum, considered ornamental rather than collegiate, remained unchanged. Since accreditation standards prevented

---

[2] Walter Crosby Eells, *Present Status of Junior College Terminal Education* (Washington DC: American Association of Junior Colleges, 1941) 15; Leland L. Medsker, *The Junior College: Progress and Prospect* (New York: McGraw–Hill, 1960) 170; Kelley and Wilbur, *Junior College Teaching,* 14; Carl E. Seashore, *The Junior College Movement* (New York: Henry Holt, 1940) 14.

[3] W. W. Rivers, "The Present Status of the Junior College," *Bulletin of Roanoke Institute* 1 (March 1916): 2–3.

[4] *1914–1915 Catalogue*, title page; *1920–1921 Catalogue*, 24.

awarding degrees, Roanoke Institute granted a Full Course Diploma, a Junior Course Diploma, a Piano Diploma, an Art Diploma, or an Expression Diploma.[5]

While redirection of the school's identity from senior college to junior college proved satisfactory, the name Roanoke Institute was a hindrance. "Roanoke" suggested the city of Roanoke; "Institute" implied high school. The initials "RI" were too close to the "RMI" of Randolph-Macon Institute, which was also located in Danville and later became Stratford College. In December 1916, Rivers suggested Roanoke Institute become Averett College in order to honor the family so closely associated with the school's early years. Surprisingly, a majority of trustees opposed the change, alternatively suggesting Mountain View College. They finally compromised on Danville College for Young Women. After the new name had been in use for only a month, the college alumnae association, founded in May 1908, showed both its mettle and maturity by firing off a letter to the board requesting the change in name to Averett College. If trustees wanted alumnae "to patronize the institution," they wrote, then trustees must honor the family who "wove their lives into the fabric of the school for twenty-five years." [6] Jane, Janie, John, Joseph, Martha, and Samuel Averett had taught there. Samuel and John served as co-principals, John as first president, and John and son William as trustees. In June 1917 the trustees gave in and officially adopted the name Averett College.[7]

Perhaps aware that change in name and mission was change enough, Rivers left student life much as he found it. World War I raged in Europe, and Averett College girls fell in step with "Keep the Home Fires Burning" and "It's a Long Way to Tipperary." Romance, always popular, was difficult at the strict college. Girls daydreamed to the strains of "Let Me Call You Sweetheart" and "When You Wore a Tulip and I Wore a Big Red Rose." Uniforms for students—abolished during the Brewer years—now reappeared, perhaps also a product of the war. On campus, girls wore identical middy blouses and skirts. Off campus, they wore white dresses in warm weather and navy blue suits with stiff corsets in cold weather. By 1916 the college also had a school song, which pledged

[5] *1915–1916 Catalogue,* 1–14, 76; *1916–1917 Catalogue,* 31–49.
[6] Quoted in Gray, "History of Averett College," 15–16.
[7] Gray, "History of Averett College," 15–16.

eternal love and devotion to alma mater "'til echoes roll and rend the sky."[8]

In 1917 President Rivers left academic administration for a career in business. Circumstances surrounding his resignation were so amicable that he bought a bust of Minerva for the college auditorium as a parting gesture of affection.

† † †

Quite the opposite would be true for his successor, Clayton E. Crosland, who was forced to resign in 1921. Crosland was misplaced in Danville. After graduation from Howard College (later Samford University) in Alabama, Crosland earned bachelor's and master's degrees from Oxford University as a Rhodes scholar. He further studied at the universities of Munich, Marburg, Göttingen, and Paris before returning to the United States to become educational secretary of the Baptist Sunday School Board in Nashville. Stints as president of Southwest Alabama Agricultural School and Fork Union Military Academy in Virginia followed. At the new junior college in Danville, President Crosland taught Latin, French, German, and philosophy.[9]

The Crosland years were a time of repose and consolidation. In fact, his presidency was without legacy. Crosland gave his successor the same curriculum he inherited, with only slight and mainly cosmetic modifications. Student life changed little. Uniforms disappeared again, and students looked forward to a newly instituted annual spring trip to Richmond and Washington for music festivals.[10]

The era, not the president, governed life at Averett College from 1917 to 1921. Student enrollment fluctuated wildly. Uncertainty associated with America's entry into World War I in 1917 caused a drop from 193 students in 1916–1917 to 123 in 1917–1918. Wartime prosperity brought a jump to 147 students in 1918–1919, before a

---

[8] *1916–1917 Catalogue,* 4; *1914–1915 Catalogue,* 28; *Echoes 1915,* 83; Lipscomb, letter to author.

[9] Gray, "History of Averett College," 162; *Bulletin of Averett College* 1 (June 1917), hereinafter cited as *Averett Bulletin,* 7; *1918–1919 Catalogue,* 7; Fountain, "Presidents," 15.

[10] *Averett Bulletin* 1 (June 1917): 15, 22–32; *1918–1919 Catalogue,* 5, 17, 22–23; *1920–1921 Catalogue,* 19–26; Gray, "History of Averett College," 46.

postwar economic depression drove down the figure to ninety-one in 1919–1920. The gradual return to prosperity in 1920 brought enrollment back to 137 in 1920–1921. As a result, planning a budget was maddening for Crosland. In addition, the influenza panic of 1918–1919 sparked uncertainty. More than twenty-one million people died of influenza worldwide. Almost 700,000 of them were Americans. Crosland promised parents of potential students that Averett College suffered only one case of the flu in 1918–1919 and "not a class-hour was missed" on account of the epidemic.[11] He rightly attributed the good health of Averett students to a variety of factors: the high quality of food grown in the garden at the rear of campus, "individual plumbing in each room," absence of a "common drinking arrangement," general cleanliness of the new building, and "frequent inspection of each girl's physical condition."[12]

More worrisome for college presidents in 1920, the automobile made American girls mobile, the telephone made them loquacious, and dress styles made them bold. Crosland dug in his heels. Gentlemen callers walked, or more aptly sat, with dates in the parlor. Chaperons were required at all occasions. The college had but one telephone—Crosland's. And "low-cut dresses and expensive jewelry" were forbidden at the college.[13]

In 1921 President Crosland's personal differences with the board of trustees came to a head when he allowed girls to dance with one another during afternoon recreation. The board demanded his resignation. Faculty, students, community, and alumnae came to Crosland's defense, but to no avail. Crosland left Averett for Ward Belmont School for Women and Girls in Nashville, where he would serve as associate president.[14]

† † †

His replacement was James P. Craft, who led Averett College from 1921 to 1927. Craft was born in 1885 at Hartwell, Georgia. After earning a B.S. degree from Mercer University, where he served as senior class

---

[11] *1919–1920, Catalogue*, 18–19.

[12] Ibid., 20; see also 18–19; *1920–1921 Catalogue*, 20.

[13] *1919–1920 Catalogue*, 60; see also 12.

[14] News clippings, scrapbook of Aline Hutchinson, in possession of Mary Conner, Danville VA; Gray, "History of Averett College," 162–63.

president, he studied philosophy at Harvard University as a Thayer scholar and received an M.A. degree. Following a year of teaching in public schools, Craft earned the degree of Graduate in Theology (Th.G.) from Southern Baptist Theological Seminary. Between 1912 and 1919 he was pastor of several Georgia churches before becoming professor of biblical literature and social sciences for two years at Shorter College in Rome.

Precise, confident, scholarly, and tall, Craft looked every inch a successful leader. Often the only male figure on campus, he took seriously his responsibilities as protector of both students and teachers, especially the single females. Late one night Craft thought he discovered prowlers in the college kitchen. Acting first and asking questions later, he fired his pistol into the dark room, only to learn that the strange figures were students breaking strict rules by "raiding the icebox."[15] Fortunately, no one was hurt.

Averett's ability to change with the times was sorely tested in the 1920s, a decade when Americans became materialistic, cynical, and worldly, and less idealistic and innocent. Women were emancipated. Sexual mores changed. The use of tobacco and alcohol by women gained acceptance in many circles.

On the one hand, Averett College under President Craft was aptly described as "a place where the twenties never roared." It grasped the new material fruits of prosperity while retaining many nineteenth-century ideals. Women might be emancipated and chaperonage passé, but Averett girls were more interested in responsible lives as homemakers and career women than in flaming youth. For them, Anne Morrow Lindbergh and tennis star Helen Wills Moody were greater heroines than Zelda Fitzgerald or Gloria Swanson. Not surprisingly, an Averett girl was still forbidden to "color her lips, eyebrows, or eyelashes in any way."[16] Sentimentality, not cynicism, inspired Averett poets. "We two" by two roommates is a good example.

---

[15] Margaret Lanham, "The Fugate Years—1924–1969," typescript, 1, Averett University Archives; *1921–1922 Catalogue*, 6; Gray, "History of Averett College," 162–63.

[16] *1923–1924 Catalogue*, 84; Lanham, "Fugate Years," 1.

We two
Met in September
In Averett's front hall.
Ah, sure we remember
The greetings by all,
And ours to the room
Where we'll stay till June,
We two.

We two
Have studied together,
Quarreled in vain,
In fall and winter weather
For we made up again;
And laughed all the more
Because angry before
We two.

We two
Will look back and sigh
In the years to come
For the days gone by,
For the friends and some
Of the happy hours
In that room of ours,
We two.[17]

But in other respects, Averett reflected the decade. In 1926 the college began annual May Day celebrations with pageantry, May Court, and coronation. No doubt some Averett students were conscious of the mating rituals, flourishing female fertility, and phallic symbol—the May pole—inherent in the celebration. In addition, many rules governing student behavior were modernized. President Craft accommodated to the times by granting privileges to date, shop, and use the telephone. College students could date on Monday afternoons and at least two Sunday afternoons each month. Dates in cars were permissible, provided they

---

[17] *Chanticleer*, April 1925.

were chaperoned. Both preparatory and college girls could shop downtown on Monday afternoons without chaperons. First-year students in the junior college enjoyed one additional free afternoon of shopping each week; seniors, two. Students could sign out for visits to the South Main Lunch or West End Drug Store, and they could take walks in Ballou Park. On designated days they could even attend a movie theater. A dormitory telephone was available from 4:00 to 6:00 P.M. daily and on Saturday and Monday afternoons. For the first time, a student government association and not the president directed student affairs, while an honor system controlled student behavior in the classroom. Happy with these newfound freedoms, the *Chanticleer* warned that a future "conservative trend" might "check [the Averett girl's] progress but it will not subdue her because she has tasted the sweetness of liberty, and like Patrick Henry will suffer no compromise."[18]

Averett students enjoyed the Craft years. A new and expanded Athletic Association and Modern Languages Club provided additional extracurricular opportunities. The growth of intercollegiate athletics perked up school spirit. So did the appearance of a new school song entitled "Tribute to Averett." Sung to the tune of the Welsh national anthem, the song went as follows:

March the hosts of Averett College
Dear to us, our home of knowledge,
March and sing, with praises ringing
        Ever to A.C.!
Raise it high, our banner o'er us,
Blue and gold are e'er before us,
Bow and kneel with tribute bringing
        Ever to A.C.!
Name we conquer under,
Ne'er we fear nor blunder,
Blast nor knell, nor shot, nor shell,
Shall rend our ranks asunder;
Onward, ever onward pressing,
E'er our love to thee confessing

---

[18] *Chanticleer*, December 1924; see also ibid., September 1926, March 1925; *1922–1923 Catalogue*, 68–69; *1923–1924 Catalogue*, 82–83.

Seeking but to be a blessing
    Ever to A.C.!
    II
Hail, the hosts of Averett College,
Alma Mater, source of knowledge,
Shout and cheer, our homage bowing,
    Honor to A.C.!
Love and adoration bringing,
Come we hither, praising, singing,
Work and toil with valor vowing.
    Honor to A.C.!
Loyal are we ever,
Daunted are we never,
Friend nor foe, nor weal nor woe,
Shall cause our bonds to sever;
We with spirit e'er victorious,
Underneath our banner glorious,
Raise and swell our one grand chorus,
    Honor, old A.C.![19]

Perhaps because the world was changing so rapidly around them, Averett students held fast to things immutable, such as lasting friendship. A young history teacher named Mary C. Fugate joined the faculty in 1924. Fresh from a baccalaureate degree at Westhampton and a term as assistant principal at Wakefield High School, she quickly won the affection and admiration of a student body. Inside the classroom she combined patience, knowledge, and a sincere desire to help students learn. Outside the classroom, wrote one alumna, "she was so kindhearted and seemed to love all the girls as if we were her family."[20]

Friendships meant dormitory life, too. During the Craft years, dormitory students enjoyed an informal camaraderie, strengthened by new likes and dislikes. They spent endless hours playing bridge, grumbling about rules and skimpy Sunday suppers, and finding out who just received a food package from home. They laughed about the new

---

[19] *The Handbook of Averett College: 1926–1927* (Danville VA: Averett Student Government Association, 1926) pages not numbered, hereinafter cited as *Student Handbook.*

[20] Gertrude Hodnett Wilson, letter to author, October 1982.

student who fainted because she thought the cotton balls put down her back really were mice. Students kept up with Walt and Phyllis in the comic strip "Gasoline Alley" each week. They hummed or sang "Baby Face," "My Blue Heaven," "I'll See You in My Dreams," and "My Buddy."[21]

Craft's influence on the academic life and financial condition of Averett was also salutary. He added a separate science department and hired a full-time librarian.[22] In 1922 the college built the Annex, later called North Hall, containing twenty-four dormitory rooms, a new gymnasium, and a twenty-by-sixty-foot tiled swimming pool with dressing rooms, showers, and filtration and heating systems. The cost was $60,000. Jubilee finally came when the college cleared its debt by paying off the mortgage.[23] As validation of these improvements, student enrollment increased from 157 in 1921 to 213 in 1927. In the latter year, when President Craft left Averett College for the presidency of Hardin College in Missouri, the junior college finally enjoyed a sound financial footing.[24]

---

[21] Mary Lou Martin Barr, letter to author, October 1982; Dorothy E. Goodman, letter to author, October 1982; Mrs. L. J. Morgan, letter to author, October 1982; Mrs. Robert F. Dove, letter to author, October 1982; Miss Roy Land, letter to author, October 1982; Mrs. Lord Beveridge, letter to author, October 1982.

[22] The science department was certainly needed, since one Averett student in 1924 defined an oyster as "a fish built like a nut" (*Chanticleer,* December 1924).

[23] *1922–1923 Catalogue,* 3; *1923–1924 Catalogue,* 7; *1926–1927 Catalogue,* 6; Gray, "History of Averett College," 163.

[24] Gray, "History of Averett College," 46.

7

A Happy Issue out of Many Difficulties, 1927–1936

The euphoria over declining expenses and increasing revenue ended abruptly with the Great Depression in the 1930s. The president who saw Averett College through these difficult years was Craft's successor, the Reverend John Walter Cammack. Born in 1875 in Orange County, Virginia, Cammack was educated at the University of Richmond (B.A., M.A., and honorary D.D.), Southern Baptist Theological Seminary (Th.M.), and the University of Virginia (Ph.G.). He taught history and English at Rawlings Institute in Charlottesville before joining the *Religious Herald* as associate editor. In 1915 Cammack became secretary of the Virginia Baptist Education Commission. In 1924 he joined the Education Board of the Southern Baptist Convention as corresponding secretary, the post he left to accept the call to Averett College in 1927.[1]

President Cammack became well known in Danville for his outspoken conservative social views. He championed prohibition and shuddered at the thought of repeal—views diametrically opposed by the local newspaper. On one occasion as Cammack was driving his car on a Danville street, he took his eyes off the road long enough to get a handful of popcorn from a bag on the seat beside him. Before he could look back at the road, his car collided with a telephone pole. The *Danville Register* could not resist the headline: "Noted Prohibitionist Wrecks Car Reaching for Corn."[2]

President Cammack faced a financial and spiritual depression like no other in Averett's history. Two years after his inauguration, the stock

---

[1] *1927–1928 Catalogue*, 8; Gray, "History of Averett College," 164.
[2] Lanham, "Fugate Years," 8.

market crashed. In Danville and throughout America, bankruptcies mounted and entrepreneurs lost their savings. Unemployment increased, breadlines formed, and fear gripped everyone. Soon banks began to fail. One Averett commuting student, whose mother worked in a local bank, remembers the winter of 1931–1932 this way:

> One morning I entered the main building to find the floor jammed with dormitory girls completely out of control, screaming and crying over telegrams ordering some to pack and get on the way home. I inched my way to within a few feet of Miss Fugate and asked permission to call the American National Bank. My mother answered. Her voice was faint.... People were four abreast at the tellers' windows and lined outside in a similar manner, extending for a city block. Fred Leggett, Sr., owner of Belk's Department Store, had pushed a $30,000 deposit in cash through one of the windows in an effort to stay the mass withdrawals. He was ignored. Nights followed at my home when we left the door unlocked for Mother until the wee hours.... The First National Bank made a big deal of flying in One Million from the Federal Reserve.... The Commercial Bank closed permanently and later was found solvent. Fear had taken its toll.[3]

President Cammack fought the Great Depression with a combination of what he called "rigid economy and cautious progress," the effects of which were both retrenchment and advancement.[4] Remarkably, enrollment increased from 234 students in 1927–1928 to 411 students in 1935–1936, but only because Cammack accepted students "on whatever financial terms their parents could meet."[5] Cammack reduced faculty salaries but never missed a payday. Averett meals were nourishing but not fancy; the college cook, Bea Totten, even became famous locally for her delicious "Depression rolls" and "Depression pies." When beets and peaches graced student tables meal after meal, everyone suspected Cammack's lenient financial terms included barter.[6]

---

[3] Sara L. Wells Nixon, letter to author, 28 October 1982.

[4] Lanham, "Fugate Years," 7.

[5] Ibid.

[6] Ibid; Gray, "History of Averett College," 46.

For President Cammack, a period of economic uncertainty was not the time to give up building for the future. Since 1922 the Southern Association of Colleges and Secondary Schools had recognized Averett as a junior college but withheld full accreditation because of lack of adequate science facilities. As soon as he became president, Cammack began raising $100,000 for construction of a music and science building. At the 1928 commencement exercises, Sue Averett, daughter of "Captain Sam," poured the first shovelful of cement into the foundation of the new building. Completed in November and named Danville Hall to honor the city whose citizens subscribed over $40,000 for construction, the four-story building housed departments of chemistry, biology, business, home economics, and music. The Southern Association responded with full accreditation for the junior college.[7]

Other capital improvements followed. Dr. T. L. Sydnor of Danville donated $1,000 for construction of Sydnor Athletic Field. The class of 1928 built the Lingernook, an eighteen-by-twenty-foot log cabin, nestled in the woods near the athletic field, where students could go for private parties, solitude, or meditation. In 1930 the college spent $10,000 from its building fund for construction of a president's home on fashionable Mountain View Avenue. This nine-room Colonial Revival dwelling was useful for entertaining trustees, alumnae, and potential donors.

In academics, Cammack reinstituted the teacher education program and opened a summer school primarily for public school teachers who wished to upgrade certificates. He also expanded athletics to include golf, soccer, hockey, swimming, basketball, hiking, tennis, and horseback riding. Cammack discontinued all but the last two years of the preparatory school, recognizing that improvements in public education throughout Virginia made the lower grades at Averett superfluous. During his tenure national honorary societies were introduced to recognize outstanding students in forensics, dramatics, and general scholarship.[8]

Students during the Great Depression had little money—but fortunately, friendship with teachers and classmates came free of charge. Although alumnae are rarely unanimous, teacher Mary Fugate stands out

---

[7] *Chanticleer,* December 1928; Gray, "History of Averett College," 24–25.

[8] *Chanticleer,* February 1939; *1928–1929 Catalogue,* 62–63; *1933–1934 Catalogue,* 35, 53; *1934–1935 Catalogue,* 63; *1935–1936 Catalogue,* 23; Gray, "History of Averett College," 25.

in everyone's memory. Sensing her strength of character and high esteem in which the student body held her, President Cammack made her dean of the college. Titles meant little because Dean Fugate also served as social science teacher, housemother, dean of women, and registrar.[9] These professional responsibilities put her in daily contact with scores of students, who adored her "wise counsel," "excellent teaching," "compassion," "serene Christian living," and "quiet understanding way."[10] Her interest in students extended to the homesick, for whom she invented special tasks to distract them and reasons for them to accompany her in birdwatching on the back campus. Dean Fugate also understood how sad and neglected some individuals felt on weekends. She issued a standing invitation to join her Sunday Evening Story Hour in the Radio Room, followed by refreshments. To students dressed in pajamas and bathrobes and sitting helter-skelter on furniture, cushions, and rugs, she read favorite short stories. Fifty-three years later, one of Dean Fugate's Story-Hour girls was still sharing with friends one of her mentor's favorites—*The Story of the Other Wise Man* by Henry Van Dyke.[11]

Small wonder that students wrote poetry to Dean Fugate. A good example, published in *Chanticleer* in 1934, is the following:

A finer woman never lived,
    Or trod this earth below
Than that one whom we love so dearly
    And have the joy to know.

She is always kind and sweet to us,
    As patient as can be,
If we're heartsick, blue or burdened
    This she can plainly see.

---

[9] Lanham, "Fugate Years," 5.

[10] Mildred Frances Hale Gardy, letter to author, October 1982; Mrs. David Gladstone, letter to author, October 1982; Mrs. Carl T. Walker, letter to author, October 1982; Mrs. Winfred I. Viele, letter to author, October 1982; Mrs. Harvey Edmund Dunn, letter to author, October 1982; Mrs. Kathryn B. Thompson, letter to author, October 1982; Mrs. Jerome H. Simonds, letter to author, October 1982.

[11] Mrs. Coleman B. Edmunds, letter to author, October 1982; Shirley Marie Whittington Crute, letter to author, October 1982; Frances De Dan, letter to author, October 1982.

So do you wonder why we love her?
  Why our praises ring true?
God made only one Mary Fugate—
  A real woman, true-blue.[12]

Other members of the Cammack faculty also enjoyed high esteem. One was future president Curtis V. Bishop, then vice president and English teacher, who was "never too busy to listen," always "reasonable" in his expectations, and ever "the epitome of the perfect Southern gentleman—so wise and so gentle, yet so firm."[13] Demanding excellence from his students, he carefully corrected mistakes with appropriate notes in the margins of written work. On one occasion he returned an English theme with a note the student could not decipher. Asked about the message, an embarrassed Bishop translated, "Please write more legibly."[14] Another favorite professor was Margaret Matheny in the business department. One of her students remembers having to babysit instead of socialize, and having to walk five miles to Averett instead of taking the streetcar, so she could scrape together enough money to complete freshman year. She felt misplaced from the start, because for many Averett students

> a major disaster consisted of a rained-on hair-do, [or] a broken fingernail.... Had it not been for Mrs. C. A. Matheny (Margaret), I probably would have never made it through the first week.... She looked right through the home-made and bargain basement wardrobe straight into the troubled soul of a frightfully scared little girl. With no fan-fare she quietly and lovingly took me under her wing and into her heart.[15]

With Margaret Matheny's encouragement, she went on to teach, write, and encourage others.

The Great Depression governed social life at the college. With the

---

[12] *Chanticleer*, 4 December 1934.

[13] Dot Sturdivant McAdams, letter to author, October 1982; Louise Williams Griffith, letter to author, October 1982.

[14] Griffith, letter to author.

[15] Mrs. Cecil Buckner, letter to author, October 1982.

repeal of prohibition, President Cammack declared off-limits every establishment that sold beer. This action proscribed Danville restaurants and teashops and left only three drugstores open to students. Dates, therefore, consisted of sitting in one of the two college parlors or auditorium, or going chaperoned to a movie. Cars were few, forcing students, dates, and chaperons to ride a streetcar to the theater. The Schoolfield Theater was popular because it showed reruns at two-thirds the regular price. Unfortunately, West Main Street from theater to college passed by Ballou Park, which was very dark at night. After movies like "The Bride of Frankenstein," all dignity and station were forgotten as students, dates, and faculty chaperons ran for the last streetcar. Even loss of reputation was preferable to the dark walk home.[16]

Occasionally, young men with sweethearts in one of the social clubs would save gasoline money, borrow cars, and have a party at a cabin in the country. Cammack, of course, had to know and approve every detail. Needless to add, faculty chaperons were present. The ten or so couples loaded Model A's with picnic food, ice cream, and radios or record players and sped twenty miles to relative freedom. After the picnic they turned on the radio or played the phonograph to provide informal accompaniment to "Singing in the Rain," "My Blue Heaven," "Red Sails in the Sunset," "Let Me Call You Sweetheart," "Goodnight, Sweetheart," "Little White Lies," "Stardust," "Ain't She Sweet," and "Love Letters in the Sand." In the parlance of the 1930s, everyone had a "swell" time.[17]

For occasions such as cabin parties, Averett girls wore their nicest dresses, or blouses, skirts, and sweaters. Because of the Depression, "nicest" often included homemade. On campus the dress code specified type if not quality of apparel. Dormitory halls required at least a bathrobe. Public areas required decent street wear or classroom wear of either dresses or skirts and blouses. Dinner required a change of street wear with perhaps jewelry; church, a best suit or dress; recitals, an evening gown; and "gym," black bloomers and white blouses. Silk hose went everywhere except to gym.[18] Proper dress was an annoyance only at

---

[16] Mildred Frances Hale Gardy, letter to author, October 1982.

[17] Mrs. Henry T. Law, letter to author, October 1982; Mrs. Charles G. Eastwood, letter to author, October 1982; Mrs. Clifton W. Jenkins, letter to author, October 1982, Mrs. Raymond Ridgeway, letter to author, October 1982; Mary Creath Colston, letter to author, October 1982; De Dan, letter to author, October 1982; *Chanticleer*, May 1929.

[18] Lillian Smith George, letter to author, October 1982, Griffith, letter to author; Mrs.

breakfast. Sometimes a student who slept past the first call for breakfast was forced to bound out of bed, roll up pajamas legs, throw on a dress, and sprint to the dining room. Sometimes, too, to the giggles of peers and frowns of President Cammack, the student felt her pajamas unroll with each step across the dining hall to her seat.[19]

Despite the shortage of contingency funds, the college usually was able to help students attend retreats and conventions. Averett College had a rich religious life. Morning Watch and daily chapel, though compulsory, seemed to be popular with students. The faculty strived to set an example of Christian living, and the Averett chapters of YWA and Baptist Student Union (BSU) frequently planned activities. Accordingly, a large Averett contingent attended annual BSU conventions at such sites as First Baptist Church in Richmond (1931) and Virginia Polytechnic Institute (1932). Averett also had an excellent newspaper, *Chanticleer*. In 1929 the Virginia Intercollegiate Press Association decided to include junior-college newspaper staffs at their annual convention at Virginia Polytechnic Institute. Cammack consented to send the *Chanticleer* staff, provided they published a paper of journalistic excellence. The plucky editor wrote President Herbert Hoover and received in return an advance copy of his forthcoming 1929 Thanksgiving Proclamation. The proclamation and accompanying presidential letter were page one, center. The staff attended the convention and won first place for best junior-college newspaper.[20]

Not only did Averett girls travel more under Cammack's presidency, but they also exhibited political awareness for the first time. The occasion was the presidential election of 1928, which pitted Democrat Alfred E. Smith against Republican Herbert Hoover. Averett students were Democrats by birth because most hailed from the Old Dominion. But Al Smith was not a Virginia-style Democrat. A Roman Catholic from the sidewalks of New York, he was a "wet" and a product of Tammany Hall, New York's corrupt political machine. With what degree of presidential or faculty prompting no one knows, Averett students stepped back, swallowed hard, and embraced the Republican

---

Carl T. Walker, letter to author, October 1982; Jenkins, letter to author; Ruth T. Dunn, letter to author, October 1982.

[19] Colston, letter to author.

[20] De Dan, letter to author; Mary Mustain Kirk, letter to author, October 1982; Griffith, letter to author.

Hoover. Even the Democratic *Chanticleer* agreed. On election night students marched downtown in small groups singing college and Hoover songs. They went from ice cream parlor to ice cream parlor to sample wares, listen to election returns, and rejoice with other Hoover partisans.[21]

In 1936 John Cammack left Averett, purportedly to return to the ministry. The college he left was better off than the one he inherited. Indeed, seven presidents and forty-four years of hard work since John Averett's retirement in 1892 put the institution on firm financial footing, relocated its campus, changed its name, redirected programs in academics and student life, reduced the collegiate emphasis from four to two years, won support from Virginia Baptists, and secured necessary accreditations. It remained only for a new president to lead the junior college into a Golden Age.

---

[21] *Chanticleer*, November 1928.

IV. THE BISHOP YEARS

1936–1966

8

The Lengthened Shadow of One Man

Ralph Waldo Emerson observed in *Self-Reliance*, "An institution is the lengthened shadow of one man." Of no institution is this observation more appropriate than Averett College under President Curtis V. Bishop. In a personal style of administration some have characterized as benevolently dictatorial, he assumed many of the supervisory responsibilities of academic dean, business manager, director of admissions, dean of students, director of public relations, director of development, and even college architect, while also serving as president. Regardless of how his leadership is characterized, certainly the financial and academic strength of Averett College at his death in 1966 bore testimony to his singular competence, fortitude, vision, and charm—the hallmarks of his remarkable leadership.

Curtis Bishop was born on 8 July 1894, at Inman, South Carolina. Like many South Carolinians, his parents were farmers who raised cotton and peaches. His father tried to instill self-reliance and industry in his children by giving each of them an acre of land to farm. So industrious was young Curtis that he won first place for his corn crop in county-fair competition.[1] Despite the prevalence of red clay, pine trees, and Methodists in the area around Inman, in later years he liked to remember the rural environment of his youth as Ben Robertson did in *Red Hills and Cotton*. It was a land "of deep dark pools" and "old Confederates and tenant farmers and colored people and swarms of politicians and preachers." His white neighbors were "Democrats and Baptists—a strange people, complicated and simple and proud and religious and

---

[1] James Arnold Davis, "Dr. Curtis V. Bishop: Focus on a Junior College Career, 1930–1966" (Ph.D. diss., University of Florida, 1973) 8–9.

family-loving" and "emotionally quick on the trigger."[2] They practiced self-improvement and self-reliance, total immersion and total abstinence. These particular South Carolinians valued honor, modesty, frugality, loyalty, and good manners. They insisted upon separation of church and state, congregational polity, freedom of conscience, free will in the matter of salvation, and the Bible as the only infallible guide to life on earth and in the hereafter. They distrusted the federal government but participated in local and state politics with a passion. With over 50 percent of the state's population black, his white neighbors practiced what political scientist V. O. Key called "the politics of color," encompassing not only the thought and rhetoric of racism but undeviating disfranchisement and segregation.[3]

While this complex environment in the South Carolina upcountry produced Curtis Bishop the man, extensive formal schooling developed Curtis Bishop the scholar. After graduation from Spartan Academy at Welford and a tour of duty in the Navy in World War I, he attended the University of Richmond for two years. When money ran out, he returned to Spartan Academy to teach and work weekends at the J. O. Jones Clothing Store in Spartanburg, using the money he earned to pay tuition at Furman University in Greenville. In summer 1923, the young Furman graduate became principal of Spartan Academy and hired a beautiful young history teacher named Helen McDowell. She became his wife in 1924, the same year he joined the Furman faculty as associate instructor of English. During his six years at Furman University, Bishop flourished. In addition to room, board, and a respectable starting salary of $1,200, he received intellectual stimulation from its president, William McGlothlin, and from some of the state's best students. McGlothlin encouraged Bishop to earn a master's degree in English at the University of Texas during the summers. In the 1920s a master's degree was considered sufficient for college teaching, and Bishop's future at Furman seemed assured.[4]

However, in 1930 President John W. Cammack of Averett College

---

[2] James Arnold Davis, "Bishop," 9; Ben Robertson, *Red Hills and Cotton* (New York: Grosset and Dunlap, 1942) 5–9.

[3] James Arnold Davis, "Bishop," 10; V. O. Key, Jr., *Southern Politics in State and Nation* (New York: Alfred A. Knopf, 1949) 130–31.

[4] James Arnold Davis, "Bishop," 10–12; see also folder marked "Bishop, Curtis, 1936–1966," Curtis V. Bishop Papers, Averett University Archives.

offered Bishop the vice presidency and a teaching position in English. Bishop accepted the Danville post and never regretted his decision. In the next six years he added to his responsibilities the supervision of extension courses offered on the Averett campus by the University of Virginia. He also directed the Danville Local Forum, which secured eminent scholars to lecture on international relations, history, economics, and the arts.[5] In 1934–1935, when President Cammack took a study leave of absence, he left Bishop in charge as interim president. The following year Cammack suffered domestic and health problems that gave Bishop the responsibilities, though not the titles, of office. The teetotaler Cammack also made an injudicious statement in the *Religious Herald* about excessive drinking at public universities, sparking a public controversy that increased his unpopularity. In March 1936, Cammack resigned the presidency, ostensibly for the purpose of returning to the ministry. The board of trustees chose as his successor acting president Curtis Bishop.[6]

The man who became ninth president of Averett College in 1936 was a complex individual. A Southern gentleman by choice, he stressed values of tradition, courtesy, dignity, integrity, Christian virtue, and personal honor. In his usual dark suit, white shirt, and conservative tie, he lived up to his own definition of a gentleman as "a man whose dress is always appropriate and whose address is always courteous."[7] An optimist by nature, he fostered a strong esprit de corps during trying times in the Great Depression and World War II. Friend and English professor Margaret Lanham observed, "Face him with absolute proof of Doomsday tomorrow, and he would somehow get by you with his hope."[8] A man of boundless energy, he seemed to be everywhere at once. He would pop into classrooms for a quick greeting, stroll through "the Spot" (the student center) for conversations with students, or tour a college building under construction to chat with workers. Like other Virginians, he was a

---

[5] The Danville Local Forum kept students and the public well informed on current events. In 1937, for example, lecture topics included the causes of the Spanish Civil War (then in progress), the US Supreme Court, Southern culture, Social Security, and the public power industry. *1937–1938 Catalogue*, 18–19.

[6] James Arnold Davis, "Bishop," 12–13, 57–59.

[7] Margaret Lanham, "In Memoriam," *Pendulum*, 1966; see also James Arnold Davis, "Bishop," 3.

[8] Lanham, "In Memoriam," *Pendulum*, 1966.

conservative Democrat who had no difficulty supporting national Republicans after the Democrats turned leftward in the late 1930s. In 1952 Bishop energetically campaigned for Dwight Eisenhower, introduced the general to other local "Eisenhower Democrats," and rode the "Eisenhower Special" through Virginia and North Carolina. In addition, Bishop was a skillful conversationalist who could relate to any audience or individual. He was equally at home among college freshmen, Rotarians, academic administrators, politicians, construction workers, scholars, and visitors to campus such as movie idol Randolph Scott.[9]

Southern politicians often enjoy only moderate success as administrators. Certainly, their forte is the ability to converse and listen. Betty Jefferson, who served as Bishop's secretary for fifteen years, observed, that he "was the closest thing to a father confessor the college had."[10] In addition, his optimistic nature prompted faculty and trustees to trust his assurances that money for this or that venture was sure to come. Yet Southern-style administrators have their faults. Unaccustomed to limitations on power, they often lapse into paternalistic or arbitrary administration. Bishop was no exception. He enjoyed his role as "the boss" and seldom delegated authority. Sometimes his high energy level led him to undertake too many projects, thereby reducing the quality of his work. Not infrequently, he failed to control his anger and lived to regret impulsive comments. As most men of his era he was a product of his environment on racial issues. Bishop grew up in South Carolina at a time when governors Benjamin R. Tillman and Coleman L. Blease praised lynchers and referred to African Americans as animals. Although Bishop did not accept the meanness of their attitudes or the excesses of their rhetoric, he fully accepted racial segregation and white supremacy. In these views, however, Bishop was in virtual agreement with all the governors of Virginia during his tenure as president.[11]

Yet Bishop's philosophies of life and education, more than his personality or prejudices, guided his actions as college president. He never tired of extolling the virtues of higher education and proclaiming

---

[9] *Chanticleer*, 28 October 1952, James Arnold Davis, "Bishop," 3–5.

[10] Quoted in James Arnold Davis, "Bishop," 5.

[11] Lanham, "In Memoriam," *Pendulum*, 1966; James Arnold Davis, "Bishop," 17–18; see also Francis Butler Simkins, *Pitchfork Ben Tillman* (Baton Rouge: Louisiana State University Press, 1967 [1944]) 396; C. Vann Woodward, *Origins of the New South, 1877–1913* (Baton Rouge: Louisiana State University Press, 1967 [1951]) 394.

the importance of the Christian junior college for women. Education perfects the individual, Bishop was fond of explaining. It guides the individual to know himself, practice consideration for others, be dependable, and appreciate God. As a foundation of liberty, democracy, and republican government, education breeds good citizenship. Bishop loved to quote the Jeffersonian dictum, "If a people expect to be ignorant and free, they expect what has never been and will never be."[12]

Likewise, he felt that the role of the junior college was essential. Junior-college students, he professed, have a greater opportunity than senior-college students to receive instruction of high quality in a small class or tutorial setting at a time in their lives when they are most impressionable. This experience breeds self-confidence and maturity by allowing younger students to assume leadership roles in student government, honor court, and campus organizations. At senior colleges these positions are reserved for upperclassmen. Private Christian schools for women, he believed, could restrict student-body size more easily than public institutions. Their residential nature encourages responsible living, social interaction, and leadership development. In addition, they offer an education not only free from immodesty and temptations of coeducation but one that will outfit the woman to assume her role as "the backbone of the Christian home and the chief teacher of morals to children."[13] Bishop's motto for Averett College affirmed his belief in the importance of Christian higher education: "As good as the best academically; frankly, aggressively, unapologetically Christian."[14]

After his inauguration as president of Averett College, Curtis Bishop was determined to make it one of the best known and most admired junior colleges in the East. His influence on physical facilities was immediate. By summer 1938, he raised $10,000 to enlarge and modernize the dining room and kitchen. Next came renovation of the President's House to make that dwelling more useful for social and academic affairs. This included redecoration of the living areas and conversion of the basement into a classroom and small gymnasium. Turning his attention to the grounds, Bishop converted a swampy and

---

[12] Quoted in James Arnold Davis, "Bishop," 40; see also 18.

[13] Quoted in James Arnold Davis, "Bishop," 5.

[14] Lanham, "In Memoriam," *Pendulum*, 1966; see also James Arnold Davis, "Bishop," 23–33, 61; Curtis V. Bishop, "Mutual Responsibilities of the Local Church and the Christian School," *Religious Herald* 138 (28 January 1965): 9.

wild back campus into an amphitheater and landscaped lawns to serve as sites for May Day pageants, commencement exercises, receptions, and a Daisy Chain ceremony.[15]

World War II delayed construction but not planning. Bishop envisioned a new multipurpose building combining dormitory space for fifty girls, classrooms, and an auditorium. In 1943 he opened the campaign to raise $100,000 for the project. Three handsome contributions from newspaper publisher Stuart James Grant and local trustees P. F. Conway and C. B. Clements signaled an auspicious beginning. Yet the war effort took precedence over expansion. Bishop had to wait for 1945 and generous contributions from Dr. C. W. Pritchett and the estate of C. L. Davenport, Averett's longtime trustee and board secretary for whom the new building would be named. The five-story Davenport Hall absorbed the Annex (built in 1923) and included the necessary dormitory and classroom space. Yet because contributions totaled only $75,000, construction of the auditorium was deferred. Prior to completion of Davenport Hall, the college housed extra dormitory students in two houses at 345 and 439 West Main Street. The new residents labeled the houses East Hall and West Hall, and the names stuck.[16]

President Bishop's next project was a new gymnasium-auditorium complex. Unfortunately, construction was delayed by declining student enrollment, budget deficits, and economic recession in the early 1950s. By 1955 Bishop had raised enough money to put a gymnasium under contract to English Construction Company. Built into the hillside of Mountain View Avenue at a cost of $127,000, it had temporary roofing to allow for future construction of an auditorium at street level above the gymnasium. The facilities allowed for an enlarged intramural program, intercollegiate competition in basketball, volleyball, and badminton, permanent seating for 350 spectators, and modern shower, locker, and training rooms. Meanwhile, at a cost of $23,000, Bishop converted the old gymnasium in Davenport Hall into classrooms, dormitory space for

---

[15] James Arnold Davis, "Bishop," 66; Gray, "History of Averett College," 25.

[16] *Chanticleer*, October 1943; December 1943; October 1944; October 1945; October 1946; James Arnold Davis, "Bishop," 96–98; Gray, "History of Averett College," 25–26; *Averett College Institutional Self-Study: 1976* (Danville VA: Averett College, 1976; hereinafter cited as *1976 Self-Study*) 155.

twenty-four girls, and a new and larger student center called the Spot.[17] Three years later another fundraising campaign raised $262,000 for construction of Pritchett Auditorium, named for Dr. C. W. Pritchett, whose generous contributions made the facility possible. The building boasted a radio studio, five piano studios, offices, storage for the drama and music departments, modern sound and lighting equipment, two dressing rooms, a large stage, and seating for 660 spectators.

The college dedicated Pritchett Auditorium on 15 November 1959, during a week-long Centennial Celebration. Alumnae from throughout the United States came for the occasion. Sixty-three colleges and universities sent representatives. Students, faculty, and local citizens mingled with alumnae, dignitaries from other institutions, and Baptist leaders from throughout Virginia to hear addresses by distinguished visitors and attend many cultural events. These included a concert by famed Metropolitan Opera soprano Eleanor Steber; a play, *The Chalk Garden*, by the Averett Players under the direction of Elizabeth (Betty) Smith; an art exhibit by Carson Davenport; and a Delius musicale by college musicians.[18]

The Centennial Celebration gave Averett the opportunity to portray itself as a center of culture and learning. The celebration was both alpha and omega because Bishop used it as a vehicle for more fundraising. Although he preferred to concentrate on a restricted list of potential donors, he bowed to trustee pressure and combined outside professional assistance with local leadership. The consultants gave the new Averett Centennial Fund-Raising Campaign a professional appearance by organizing a working staff that included three campaign chairmen, nine section chairmen, twenty-seven colonels, over three hundred Big Brothers, a host of Little Sisters, and a Special Gifts Committee. On 18 November 1959, as the Centennial Celebration was ending, state senator and Averett board chairman Landon R. Wyatt announced the beginning of the fundraising campaign to insure "that the future may keep pace with the past."[19] Wyatt announced a goal of $350,000 for construction of

---

[17] *Chanticleer*, 20 October 1955; James Arnold Davis, "Bishop," 98; Gray, "History of Averett College," 26; *1976 Self-Study*, 160–61.

[18] News clipping, scrapbook donated to Averett College by Frances Hallam Hurt, Averett University Archives, hereinafter cited as Hurt scrapbook; *Danville Register*, 1 November 1959, 1-B, 2-B.

[19] News clipping, Hurt scrapbook.

two buildings. One would be a multipurpose structure combining a new library, a student center, and a creative and performing arts center. The other would be a residence hall with kitchen, dining room, and dormitory space for fifty students.[20] Within a month the several hundred campaigners were able to raise $125,000, prompting a proud Curtis Bishop to tell the *Danville Register* that the stalwart campaigners "stand for everything that is good in Danville civic life."[21] Within three months pledges stood at $213,000. Yet the number of pledges fell off dramatically for every month thereafter, and the $350,000 goal was never realized. Bishop began to regret choosing the public campaign with expensive professional consultants over quiet contacts with wealthy donors.[22]

Nevertheless, in 1960, with money generated by the Averett Centennial Fund-Raising Campaign, Bishop was able to construct Danville Hall Extension and transform Danville Hall into dormitory space for sixty-two students, four classrooms, and modern research facilities. In 1963 the college raised $500,000 for construction of a multipurpose building with fallout shelter, kitchen, dining hall, and dormitory space for one hundred girls. Completed in September and named Bishop Hall in honor of the president, the building was joined to Danville Hall Extension, Davenport Hall, and the gymnasium-auditorium complex. This arrangement allowed President Bishop to assure parents their daughters need not be exposed either to the elements or to urban turmoil from September when they entered Averett until May when they left. Quaint as this inducement might sound, it was taken seriously during the mid-1960s in the aftermath of civil rights protests in Danville. After demonstrations in 1963, for example, 130 students cancelled reservations at Averett. The completion of Bishop Hall allowed for an increase in resident population to 400 girls.

Finally, in 1965 President Bishop added a three-story administrative wing and a two-story dormitory-classroom wing to the southwest and northeast faces, respectively, of Main Building. With its main entrance on Mountain View Avenue, the administrative wing of 3,600 square feet contained fifteen offices that would serve the president, the academic

---

[20] Ibid.

[21] *Danville Register*, 31 December 1959, 1-B.

[22] James Arnold Davis, "Bishop," 99–101; Gray, "History of Averett College," 26–27; *Chanticleer*, 25 February 1959; October 1959.

dean, the dean of students, and the business manager. After completion of this structure, President Bishop had the satisfaction of knowing he would leave to his successor a college over two and one-half times larger in square footage of buildings than he inherited. Indeed, it was Curtis Bishop who built the modern Averett (junior) College.[23]

Bishop's influence on the curriculum was also pronounced. Shortly after his inauguration, Bishop abolished the preparatory school. This decision allowed him both to concentrate efforts and avoid problems of mixing immature girls with mature young women. Under Bishop the library almost tripled its collection. Of equal importance, Bishop followed the trend in junior-college education and added preprofessional programs to the curriculum. New or reemphasized programs included fashion merchandising, medical technology, nursing, physical therapy, occupational therapy, dental hygiene, religious education, journalism, education, library science, law, and medicine.[24]

New programs required new diplomas. In 1937 the college began granting a Junior College Literary Diploma, a Junior College Home Economics Diploma, a Junior College Commercial Diploma, and a Junior College Diploma in Fine Arts. With minor variations these diplomas were awarded until 1957. The most prestigious of the four was the Junior College Literary Diploma. Requiring sixty-four hours of course work, it was given to students majoring in liberal arts, general culture (the terminal two-year program), or preprofessional work. Then, in 1957, the Virginia General Assembly authorized junior colleges to grant degrees, and Averett quickly shifted from diplomas to the degrees of Associate in Arts and Associate in Science.[25]

Faculty and students gave meaning to new buildings, programs, and degrees. Of Bishop's relations with the Averett faculty, biographer James A. Davis wrote:

---

[23] James Arnold Davis, "Bishop," 101–2; *1976 Self-Study*, 159; *Chanticleer*, 25 October 1960; 4 May 1963.

[24] *1937–1938 Catalogue*, 15; *1944–1945 Catalogue*, 15; *1951–1952 Catalogue*, 3; *1960–1961 Catalogue*, 3, 13; *1966–1967 Catalogue*, 22.

[25] *1936–1937 Catalogue*, 23–24; *1938–1939 Catalogue*, 25–26; *1940–1941 Catalogue*, 25–26; *1956–1957 Catalogue*, 27–28; Gray, "History of Averett College," 33–38.

Bishop enjoyed an advantage many college presidents did not have—that of having been a college professor. His success as an instructor of English literature was recognized by hundreds of students and other professional persons with whom he worked. He, therefore, understood and demanded measures of quality performance; knew the demands on an instructor's time; realized their financial plight; and praised their work as being the real measure of success of the college.[26]

The continuity of Averett's faculty was a source of great strength to the college. In 1959 the twenty-four faculty members had taught at the college a combined total of 310 years. Another source of strength was the high quality of both faculty and programs. As an example, President Bishop worked with Chairman of the Music Department Carimae Hedgpeth to develop one of only a handful of fully accredited music programs among junior colleges nationwide. In addition, Bishop was able to attract and retain professors of the caliber of nationally known artist Carson Davenport.

Davenport's acclaim as an artist and that of Bishop as a junior college president rose together. Davenport's participation in the PWA Art Project during the 1930s attracted the attention of Eleanor Roosevelt, who hung one of his paintings, "Pioneer Women," in the White House. Davenport studied at the New York School of Fine and Applied Arts, Grand Central School of Art in Manhattan, Corcoran School of Art (Washington), and the Ringling School of Art at Sarasota, Florida. He won prizes for works in national competition in six states and staged one-man exhibitions at the Virginia Museum of Fine Arts in Richmond and Ferargil Galleries in Manhattan. His works also were selected for display at the 1939 World's Fair and in group exhibitions at three Manhattan galleries. Davenport's works currently are in the Virginia Museum of Fine Arts, the Rosenwald Print Collection in Philadelphia, the Knoedler Galleries in New York, and the Reynolds Aluminum Company Collection.[27]

In the 1960s, however, friction grew between the aging president

---

[26] James Arnold Davis, "Bishop," 103.

[27] Carson S. Davenport File, Averett University Archives; Gray, "History of Averett College," 39; *Chanticleer*, 3 April 1980.

and his faculty when dramatic growth and changes in higher education demanded less paternal and more collegial governance. The faculty came to this realization before the president did. Areas of conflict included salaries, contracts, perquisites, and arbitrary administration. Although salaries at Averett were, in fact, competitive with those at comparable institutions until the 1960s, there was no official salary scale. President Bishop paid each teacher according to perceived needs without regard to earned degrees. Complaints of underpayment were not allayed by knowledge that Bishop's own salary was low. When faculty contracts did not appear until a month after classes began each fall, uncertainty outweighed understanding.[28] Perhaps more serious was the president's arbitrariness. For example, after a faculty self-study committee wrestled for weeks to define Averett's mission, the president casually substituted his own off-the-cuff formulation. The committee chairman promptly resigned, and the committee voluntarily disbanded. Fifteen minutes later Bishop sought out the former chairman, praised the committee's efforts, and accepted its statement of mission in place of his own. Here, flexibility tempered arbitrariness, although the impression of arbitrariness was not erased.[29]

Nevertheless, faculty ambivalence toward President Bishop did not outweigh their appreciation of his executive abilities, especially in areas of student recruitment and external relations. Here he used charm, attention to detail, and perseverance. Typically, Bishop drove "25,000 to 30,000 miles annually" to talk with parents and prospective students.[30] He also penned handwritten letters to applicants. Bishop preached or lectured at Baptist churches with high school seniors, and attended Baptist district association meetings to lobby ministers. He arranged to have dinner in many homes of prospective students to cement bonds of friendship and trust, and he even chartered a Pullman car each year to bring prospective students from New York, New Jersey, Pennsylvania, Delaware, and Maryland. As a result, by the 1950s New York ranked second, New Jersey third, and Maryland fifth in number of students at Averett.[31]

---

[28] James Arnold Davis, "Bishop," 103–6; David Gray, interview with author, Averett College, 20 January 1983.

[29] James Arnold Davis, "Bishop," 103–6.

[30] *Danville Register*, 26 May 1959, 3.

[31] James Arnold Davis, "Bishop," 63–65, 92–95.

Accepting the town-gown relationship as complementary rather than antagonistic, President Bishop became an esteemed community leader. He was reared with the idea that men of talent and position have an obligation to improve their community. His education reinforced his rearing. He loved to quote English philosopher Francis Bacon: "In this theater of man's life, it is reserved only for God and angels to be lookers on."[32] In his first year in Danville, Bishop became an active Rotarian and was club president the next year. In 1945 he was elected Rotary district governor for forty-four clubs in Tennessee and Virginia. The Danville Chamber of Commerce named him vice president in 1945 and president in 1946. His service on the boards of trustees of Memorial Hospital and Community Chest was further testimony that the educational, cultural, commercial, and professional leadership of Danville merged in one man.[33]

It was only natural for a man like Bishop to enter politics. In 1950 local civic leaders persuaded him to offer for city council. In the tradition of Old Virginia, he "stood" for election and thus did not campaign actively. His reputation for responsible leadership guaranteed victory. His warmth and charm gave him first place in the balloting. To no one's surprise, Bishop was the new council's unanimous choice for mayor and president of council. As a councilman, Bishop used his influence on behalf of bond issues for electric power and schools. He also supported a change of Danville's government to the council-manager form. His position was not surprising, since this system copies the trustee-president form of collegiate administration. He also took his place in the leadership structure of southside Virginia that included such Byrd machine stalwarts and personal Bishop friends as State Senator Wyatt and Governor William M. Tuck. In 1956 Bishop was re-elected councilman and mayor, although a severe heart attack the following year forced his resignation as mayor. He declined to seek a third term on council.[34]

Danville appreciated his many contributions. At a banquet in Hotel Danville on 20 December 1951, he received the Kiwanis Club's coveted Outstanding Citizen of Danville Award. Bishop's response was characteristic and gracious. The tribute, he said, was less "an award for

---

[32] Quoted in ibid., 263.

[33] James Arnold Davis, "Bishop," 68–69; *Religious Herald* 139 (2 June 1966): 20.

[34] James Arnold Davis, "Bishop," 69–70, 73–74.

what I have done" than it was "a challenge to do something worthy of the honor shown me."[35]

Given Bishop's paternalistic administrative style and deep personal Christian commitment, which was demonstrated by his long service as deacon and men's Sunday school teacher at Danville's First Baptist Church, it was ironic but perhaps inevitable he would cross swords with the leadership of Virginia Baptists. In 1953 the Virginia Baptist Board of Missions and Education in Richmond threatened to eliminate Averett's annual subsidy, amounting to about 6 percent of the college's annual budget, unless something was done about deficits of over $50,000. Yet deficits clouded deeper concerns. Some Baptists worried that Bishop's civic and political activities interfered with recruiting and fundraising. Others complained Averett was trying to recruit out-of-state students to the exclusion of Baptist girls in Virginia.[36]

Bishop was fortunate to have on the executive committee of his board of trustees two personal friends—State Senator Wyatt and president of the University of Richmond George M. Modlin. Bishop convinced them that not only were his political and civic activities performed during his free time, but also that they generated revenue for the college. He pointed out that day-student enrollment was climbing, local gifts were increasing, and city leaders supported Averett's program of physical expansion. Bishop acknowledged a decline in enrollment caused the deficits—yet he claimed fewer births during the Great Depression were alone responsible. He argued that a temporary deficit, high standards, and an improved physical plant would better serve the college than a balanced budget, lower standards, and obsolescent facilities. Bishop also insisted that projected increases in enrollment would convert deficit into surplus in 1953–1954. With help from Wyatt, Modlin, and the executive committee, Bishop's arguments won the day in Richmond. His predictions soon proved correct. Increasing enrollment brought a surplus, the short-term debt was paid off, and the crisis ended.[37]

---

[35] *The* [Danville] *Bee*, 21 December 1951, 1-B.

[36] Minutes of the Board of Trustees of Averett College, 9 January 1953, 1–3, Averett University Archives, hereinafter cited as Averett Board Minutes; see also James Arnold Davis, "Bishop," 76–78.

[37] Averett Board Minutes, 9 January 1953, 2–5; James Arnold Davis, "Bishop," 77–81.

Bishop also fought the Baptist leadership over tuition fees. In 1946 the Board of Missions and Education expressed concern that Averett's high tuition kept away deserving but poor Baptists. It compared Averett's fees unfavorably with those of Baptist junior colleges in North Carolina and South Carolina and particularly with Bluefield College in Virginia. A disgusted Curtis Bishop met these complaints in a six-page reply that hardly concealed his anger. He attacked the assumption that quality education might be had cheaply. The Southern Association of Colleges and Schools accredited Averett College, he noted, but not Bluefield College and most Baptist junior colleges in the Carolinas. Bishop could not resist adding that for twenty years Bluefield College had received three times as much Baptist money from Richmond as Averett. Denying the view that Baptist junior colleges existed for lower-income students, Bishop insisted that scholarships and work-study money made certain no Baptist girl in Virginia was turned away from Averett College "because she lacked the money to pay her fees."[38] Switching to the offense, Bishop suggested that substandard facilities and furnishings chased away more students than did high tuition. Persuaded and perhaps abashed by the cogency of these arguments, Baptist leaders decided to drop the issue.[39]

In large measure Averett College became well known and widely respected outside of Danville and Virginia because of Curtis Bishop's national reputation. Bishop was active in junior-college circles throughout the South. In 1938 the Southern Association of Colleges and Schools organized its junior college division; Curtis Bishop was elected secretary-treasurer in 1939. The following year the group organized the Southern Association of Junior Colleges, of which Curtis Bishop became

---

[38] Curtis Bishop, Report to the Virginia Baptist Board, 4 November 1946, Averett University Archives, 2.

[39] James Arnold Davis, "Bishop," 79–83. "This little barrage indicated a deep-seated but non-personal controversy that existed among Baptist junior college educators in the state. Bluefield had a 'preferred status in funding' because Dr. Charles Harmon, President, maintained a broader religious requirement in curriculum, social practice, and life of the college. Each year he expounded upon this philosophy which was very popular within the Baptist Association. This appeal to the emotions of Baptists gave Averett and Virginia Intermont the image of being less in line with Baptist beliefs since they sought to broaden the purpose and clientele of their institutions. The conflict eased somewhat in the 1950s after Bluefield College received accreditation and Dr. Harmon became active in the educational world outside of Virginia" (James Arnold Davis, "Bishop," 84–85).

president in 1942. Meanwhile, Bishop remained active in the Southern Association of Colleges and Schools by helping with initial accreditation of four junior colleges in Virginia, chairing important association subcommittees, and in 1960 serving as the only junior-college president who chaired a committee for revision of standards.[40]

From 1936 to 1966, few educators in junior-college circles throughout the nation were better known. In 1950 Bishop was elected president of the American Association of Junior Colleges (AAJC). Founded at St. Louis in 1920, this organization provided a forum for exchanging ideas and information. It also boosted the junior-college concept among educators and laypersons. Bishop attended his first AAJC annual meeting in 1932 as Averett's vice president. His love of fellowship, conversation, and politicking earned him a seat on the association's board of directors in 1937. For the next twelve years, Bishop was in the thick of a bitter and protracted contest between two factions within the AAJC. Executive Secretary Walter C. Eells led one faction, Western educators with ties to the University of Chicago the other. The conflict generally pitted East against West, private junior colleges against public, the liberal arts against terminal, semiprofessional, and vocational education, and independent junior colleges against institutions combining the last two years of high school with the first two years of college. Although Bishop was a leader of the Eells faction, his political sensitivity and adroitness led him to compromise and conciliate, approaches that helped save and strengthen the AAJC. In fact, Bishop's reputation as a forceful and conciliatory leader gained him another board seat in 1946, vice presidency in 1949, and presidency in 1950. Undoubtedly, the high point of his AAJC involvement was his presidential year, when he welcomed junior college presidents from throughout America to Roanoke, Virginia, for the thirtieth annual AAJC meeting. Musical presentations by the Averett Chorus and speeches by Bishop and Governor John S. Battle brought national recognition to the Old Dominion, its Baptist college in Danville, and its best known junior-college educator.[41]

Despite his time-consuming involvement in regional and national

---

[40] James Arnold Davis, "Bishop," 140–45, 147–48, 153–56. Bishop also was active in the Southern Association of Baptist Colleges and Schools, and he served as its president in 1965.

[41] James Arnold Davis, "Bishop," 164–94.

associations, Bishop still found time for debate on matters of public policy in his beloved adopted state. He advocated and worked for creation of an independent community-college system in the Old Dominion. He foresaw no competition for Averett College because the community college would appeal to a different clientele. To his close friend, Governor Albertis Harrison, Bishop time and again voiced his hopes for public junior-college education in Virginia. Partly as a result of Governor Harrison's labors, just such a system became a reality during the governorship of Harrison's successor, Mills Godwin. Unfortunately, Bishop did not live to see it.[42]

Curtis Bishop died on 19 February 1966, at the age of seventy-one years. All who knew him were proud of his legacy. His wisdom, charm, graciousness, friendliness, dedication to public service, skills as a speaker, willingness to compromise, and Christian commitment were traits that inspired students and friends in Danville for thirty-six years. Bishop's position as a spokesman for the junior-college movement helped bring acceptance of this new concept in higher education. His service as mayor and city councilman prepared Danville for its industrial renaissance in the 1960s. Bishop's term as president brought to Averett an expansion in programs, doubling the size of the faculty and physical plant, and both national recognition and regional respect. Truly, no one in the future would walk the corridors of Averett College without hearing the echoes of his footsteps.

---

[42] Ibid., 133–35.

9

Student Life
From New Deal to New Morality

During the presidency of Curtis V. Bishop, Averett College reached its zenith as a junior college. The addition of extensive landscaping and seven new buildings or wings gave Averett what its overly enthusiastic president called "the only completely landscaped campus in Virginia." The addition of vocational programs enabled the college to meet changing vocational needs of space-age Americans. President Bishop came to enjoy a national reputation among junior-college educators, and the City of Danville gained a renewed appreciation of the college, partly because of the civic contributions of its president.[1] Equally noticeable was a change in campus life, which became more cosmopolitan with the addition of students from New York, Pennsylvania, New Jersey, and Maryland. Students enjoyed more freedom and thus more capacity for growth. Finally, student life became more eventful with the discarding of old traditions, emergence of new ones, and advent of war and student revolution.

The chief tradition abandoned during the Bishop years was the Hiding of the Crook. The crook was a shepherd's staff about five feet in length whose custody was disputed between seniors and juniors. Seniors were responsible for guarding the crook, juniors for wresting it from them. Each autumn the president of the senior class would burst unannounced into the auditorium in the middle of a chapel program. Holding the crook high above her head, she marched down the aisle and out the door, giving the juniors what was supposed to be their only glimpse of the crook until spring commencement. The senior class had

---

[1] *Danville Register*, 26 May 1951, 3.

twenty-four hours to hide the crook somewhere on campus. Rules stipulated that it could not be under lock and key and at least two inches of the staff had to be visible. Should the junior class find it, they in turn had twenty-four hours to hide it from the seniors. The class possessing the crook at spring commencement displayed the trophy before presenting it with due ceremony to the losers. The tradition of the crook was an excellent catalyst for class morale and class identification.[2] It continued until World War II, when a more diverse and nonresident student body lost interest in the tradition.[3]

In this contest the junior class was seldom victorious. Their longest string of annual losses was twelve. But it ended on the afternoon of 24 March 1936, when the juniors stumbled upon the crook in the college furnace room. They kept their discovery a secret until the next morning at breakfast, when a telegram arrived for the senior class president. Ashen faced, she rapped for silence and read the message to the student body. The message was signed "The Crook" and said in part: "This message I bring to my senior guardians. Thanks for a furnace and a warm winter, but March 21 has passed and I no longer fear winter's blast. May the juniors cool me off on the campus."[4] Pandemonium broke out, with juniors hooting and seniors groaning. Since the once-omnipotent seniors were unable to find the crook before year's end, the juniors had the privilege of contemptuously presenting the staff to them at commencement.

While hiding the crook symbolized the rivalry between junior and senior classes, the Daisy Chain Ceremony at spring commencement affirmed both the sisterhood of the two classes and everlasting love of alma mater. Alumnae still rank this ritual as one of their fondest memories. On the day of the event, juniors arose at 4 A.M. and boarded flatbed trucks for the trip to daisy fields near Danville. After several hours of picking daises and numerous verses of "I've Been Picking Daisies, All the Live Long Day," juniors returned to find that senior Big Sisters had cleaned rooms and prepared breakfast for junior Little Sisters. After breakfast juniors met in the gymnasium where they attached daisies to several ropes that stretched the length of a football field. Finishing the

---

[2] *1928–1929 Averett College Handbook*, 34 *Student Handbook*; *Chanticleer*, 4 December 1934, December 1935.

[3] Lanham, "Fugate Years," 9–10, 12.

[4] *Chanticleer*, March 1936.

daisy chains by mid-afternoon, juniors raced for a quick shower and white dresses they would wear in the ceremony. At 4:30 P.M., carrying the daisy chains on tiny pillows on their shoulders, juniors transferred three of the chains to the shoulders of seniors, who used the chains to form the letters "AC" on the field. With the other chains the juniors formed the numerals of the class year. As the chain transfer was completed, both classes sang the daisy-chain song, which went as follows to the tune of "High above Cayuga's Waters":

Fashioned by wee fairy fingers,
Flower with heart of gold,
Whisper in my ear the secret
Which the south wind told.
Has the ever-guarding pine tree
Towering to the skies
Told whence comes, oh chain of daisies,
Strength that never dies?

Love unbounded, love unceasing,
This the south wind told,
Made my petals white as snow-drops,
Made my heart of gold.
Friendship's bond that love has given
Keep it ever true,
Sisters of our Alma Mater.
We pledge our love to you.[5]

The ceremony was memorable and tearful. Seniors reflected upon love, loyalty, and friendship they had known for two years. They also reflected upon a future both certain and uncertain. Juniors, happy to become seniors, realized they were seeing many senior friends for the last time.[6]

Another tradition fostering friendship and kindness between classes in the 1930s was Peanut Week, which began on a Monday in winter when spirits needed boosting. The names of all students were written on

---

[5] *Chanticleer*, May 1938, June 1942, 3 June 1950; Lanham "Fugate Years," 9.
[6] *Pendulum*, 1963, 19.

individual slips of paper, wrapped in peanut shells, and tied with red or yellow ribbons, depending upon the class. After these were put into two fish bowls, each senior drew a junior's name and each junior a senior's name. For six days each student purchased for her "peanut" an inexpensive gift, ranging from a package of bobby pins to a piece of candy or fruit, that mysteriously appeared on bureaus or in desks. Recipients spent the week trying to discover the identity of their donors. At a banquet on Saturday evening, "peanuts" finally were introduced to one another at the climax of a suspenseful week.[7]

Local Greek-letter sororities also played a part in college life during the early Bishop years. A highlight of autumn was sorority rush week in November. The sororities invited prospective members to theater parties downtown, formal dinners in the Gold Room of Hotel Danville, waffle suppers at the college, buffets at the Country Club Inn, and informal get-together parties in members' rooms. However, such practices were inappropriate to Averett's small student body because a girl not pledged felt deeply the sting of rejection. Also, periodic financial mis-management by the sororities caused headaches for the administration. In November 1949, President Bishop issued an ultimatum: either the sororities had to submit to stricter college supervision, or disband. In practice this meant every girl would receive a bid, and most sorority business affairs would be subject to the dean's approval. When the sororities spurned stricter supervision, the administration ordered a plebiscite and the student body voted to disband the clubs.[8]

Despite such pressure from the administration, students found a more relaxed social atmosphere under President Bishop. His liberal-ization of privileges included increases in breakfast cuts, downtown permissions, dating privileges, church cuts, and off-campus weekends. The college even sanctioned dances, which still remained anathema to many Virginia Baptists. "On dorm" in the late 1930s, Averett girls swayed to Glen Miller's "Moonlight Serenade," read *Mademoiselle*, and practiced the Big Apple. They smoked covertly, even though the penalty for smoking on campus remained two weeks of campus restriction. They also enjoyed Kay Kyser's "All the Things You Are," dreamed of "riding in a convertible, madly with the top down," and aspired to be

---

[7] *Chanticleer*, February 1936, April 1938.

[8] *Chanticleer*, December 1928, December 1937, 1 October 1947, 26 November 1949.

"temperamental and to marry four million dollars." Averett girls craved fancy clothes, moonlight, and formal balls. They demanded sincerity above other qualities in friends. They drooled over Rhett Butler in *Gone with the Wind,* and they were quick to adopt the slang of their times, such as "swell," "laudy-dee" and "de-vine." Fashion was changing. Averett girls in the late 1930s dressed in bobby socks, saddle shoes, skirts, and "sloppy Joe" sweaters. But ageless student pranks remained. Girls continued to short-sheet beds, shout down the hall that so-and-so's boyfriend was calling on the telephone (when of course he was not), and snatch bathrobes from the door of the shower stall in the common shower room at the end of each hall.[9]

Searching for the crook, taking part in sorority activities, being kind to one's "peanut," holding the May Festival, making the daisy chain, and participating in five days of commencement exercises consumed only a small part of a full social year in the 1930s. In addition to lectures, concerts, chapel services, plays, and recitals, Averett students attended such student-sponsored events as theater parties, BSU receptions, outdoor barbecues, teas for college guests, athletic events, Nemo-Philo contests, costume parties, Student Government Association stunt night, junior-senior banquet, and three formal dances. Averett girls especially enjoyed producing a multidiscipline, Christmas nativity program of about thirty selections. Open to the public, it featured music by the choral choir, tableaux by the drama department, and recitations of Biblical passages by the verse-speaking choir. Laura J. Fuessel of the music department and formerly of the Metropolitan Opera was director of the affair, while Bonnie J. Alderson had charge of the tableaux.

Madame Fuessel and her choral and verse-speaking choirs were in great demand in the Middle Atlantic region. Each spring the two choirs toured several states, presenting secular programs by day in high schools and religious programs each evening in Baptist churches. These outings also enabled students to see first-run movies and legitimate theater, catch

---

[9] *Chanticleer*, November 1939, March 1940, April 1940; *1938–1939 Averett Handbook*, 22 *Student Handbook*; Mrs. William L. Major, letter to author, October 1982; Marion Beard Proehl, letter to author, October 1982; Mrs. Joseph Frederick Parker, letter to author, October 1982; Mrs. George E. Lawrence, letter to author, October 1982; Mrs. Jacob N. Rohme, letter to author, October 1982; Mrs. O. E. Corder, letter to author, October 1982; Mrs. Peter W. Payne, letter to author, October 1982; Mrs. Bernard F. Fetter, letter to author, October 1982.

up on lost sleep, climb the steps of the Washington Monument, and shop in large department stores.[10]

Other extracurricular influences at Averett were more serious. Many alumnae from the late 1930s remember the college for values it instilled or reinforced. Frances Stiff Appel, class of 1938, came to Averett from a home that frowned on the use of tobacco. President Bishop reinforced this prohibition. A year after graduation she visited New York for the World's Fair. In the lobby of her hotel, curiosity got the best of her and she purchased a pack of cigarettes simply to "see what smoking was like." As she was putting the pack in her handbag, she heard her name called from across the lobby. "I looked up," she recalls, "and there stood Dr. Bishop," who was then recruiting students in the Northeast. "When I got to my room," she added. "I threw away the cigarettes, knowing it didn't matter where you were, you could never get away from those things of value which influenced your life."[11]

American values were never more strongly tested than during World War II. Indeed, the future of freedom and democracy seemed to hinge on American success against Hitler, Mussolini, and Tojo. In the 1930s Averett girls took a keener interest than most Americans in Asian and European conflicts because of periodic exposure to, and exhortation by, Baptist ministers who served as missionaries in the Orient. No doubt Averett students were also aware that fascism made glorification of the state the national religion. They were concerned, therefore, when Japan seized parts of China, when Italy conquered defenseless Ethiopia and Albania, and when Germany seized Austria, Czechoslovakia, Memel, and Poland. After France fell in June 1940, Averett students surpassed most other Americans in extent and depth of pro-British sentiment. The *Chanticleer* declared America should "cast its lot whole-heartedly with Great Britain...for the preservation of civilization."[12] The newspaper endorsed a petition to Congress by Averett's chapter of the National Committee to Defend America by Aiding the Allies. It called for all aid to Great Britain short of war. A year before America entered the conflict, a student poll at Averett revealed that 97 percent of the girls supported the Committee to Defend America by Aiding the Allies, 77 percent

---

[10] *Chanticleer*, May 1938, December 1939, March 1940; *1935–1936 Averett College Handbook Student Handbook*; *1943–1944 Catalogue*, 71ff.

[11] Mrs. E. Wesley Appel, letter to author, October 1982.

[12] *Chanticleer*, October 1940.

favored loans to Great Britain, 86 percent favored conscription, and 89 percent were willing to serve in a supporting battlefield role such as nursing.[13]

These sentiments had not abated twelve months later when Japan attacked Pearl Harbor and America formally declared war. Within hours President Bishop made an inspiring address to the study body. In it he portrayed the war as a clash of philosophies: freedom versus tyranny, democracy versus totalitarianism. With memories of World War I, Bishop affirmed there could be no complete and final victory unless the peace that followed the war secured a worldwide Bill of Rights. He called on Averett students to practice austerity so that fighting men could have necessities. He concluded with a plea for them to set an example for all Americans: "To think without confusion clearly, to love one's fellowmen sincerely, to act from honest motives purely, to trust in God and Heaven securely."[14]

Bishop's message brought out the best in Averett students, who threw themselves wholeheartedly into the war effort. Early in 1942 the girls began knitting helmet caps for soldiers, sweaters for refugees in Europe, and afghans for the wounded in hospitals. They also mounted a "Get in the Scrap" campaign to collect scrap metal for resmelting and old newspapers for wood pulp. The college contributed two kilns from the art department, heavy equipment from the gymnasium, iron ring-stands from the chemistry laboratory, and empty food containers from the kitchen. A "Buy War Bonds and Stamps" campaign followed the "Get in the Scrap" campaign. In 1942 Averett students sold $10,000 in stamps and bonds for the purchase of a barrage balloon for use in air defense. During the drive the campus was plastered with posters containing a drawing of a balloon, checkered into blocks of $100.00 each. One after another of the blocks was colored red as hundred-dollar lots of stamps and bonds were purchased. In 1943 Averett students sold $15,000 in bonds and stamps for the purchase of 100 parachutes at $150 each.[15]

Students involved themselves in the war effort in yet other ways. The choirs abbreviated their spring choral trips to conserve gasoline for the war. They rolled bandages for the Red Cross, wrote hundreds of

---

[13] *Chanticleer*, December 1940.

[14] *Chanticleer*, December 1941.

[15] *Chanticleer*, February 1942, October 1942, January 1943, October 1943.

letters to servicemen overseas to bolster morale, and participated in air-raid drills, conducted by physical education instructor Faye Hill. The library, located below ground level, served as an excellent air raid shelter. When Miss Hill sounded the air raid siren, the girls calmly gathered up shelter blankets and textbooks and headed for the library. With a little practice they completed the drill in four minutes, which was certainly sufficient time to outrun any squadron of German bombers flying in from the Atlantic Ocean.[16]

Averett faculty and alumnae did their part. Lieutenant Colonel Harold McNeely, a member of the class of 1940 and one of the handful of male alumni, was a P-47 (Thunderbolt) pilot in Belgium. He flew one hundred missions and participated in the Normandy invasion in 1944. Lieutenant Ruth Fowler, class of 1934, was an army nurse overseas; Lieutenant Olga Heard, class of 1933, was head dietitian of a military hospital in Australia. Ensign Elizabeth Ender, who taught organ and music theory, even gained national recognition as one of the authors of the official WAVE hymn, "Waves of the Navy."[17]

One of the most annoying aspects of college life in wartime was shortages. By 1943 one student looked back in disbelief at commodities once so plentiful. Sugar was first to become scarce, "and we thought that was bad!" Then the same thing happened to meat and eggs, and "people began to get wrinkles and limp." New shoes vanished, and Averett girls began swapping and selling.[18] Finally, contraband cigarettes disappeared, and Averett girls looked back wistfully on the days "when you walked into someone's room and were immediately not only offered but actually coaxed to take a cigarette." By 1945, they groused, "You now walk into a room, see your best friend take her last drag with the aid of a bobby pin, and pant breathlessly for the next half hour."[19]

Worst of all shortages was lack of men. The draft and surge of patriotic fervor quickly depleted the supply of available dates. The warning "Loose Lips Sink Ships" made parting doubly hard, for Averett girls sometimes suffered in silence rather than mention one boyfriend was bound for North Africa or another for Italy. Averett girls trusted one another, but a girl could never be sure who might overhear a

---

[16] *Chanticleer*, February 1942, November 1942, October 1943.
[17] *Chanticleer*, November 1943, April 1944, 3; February 1945.
[18] *Chanticleer*, February 1943.
[19] *Chanticleer*, February 1945.

conversation. With many males overseas, Averett seniors resorted to cadets from Hargrave Military Academy in Chatham who previously had been thought *infra dig*. Hargrave boys were bused to Averett for Saturday dances, where partners would be decided by lot. Nancy Adnia McDowell, class of 1944, recalls, "When the bus came from Chatham and my number was matched with his, my blind date was almost 5 feet tall; I was 5 ft. 8. [But] we danced the night away and had a lot of laughs."[20] One faculty member recalls that girls such as Nancy McDowell sang the current lament, "They're Either Too Young or Too Old," with great feeling.[21]

With male company in short supply, Averett girls made the most of a boyfriend's leave. Curfews frequently were disregarded. Elly S. Caro, class of 1945, remembers when her future husband came to see her at Averett:

> I thought I would die if I didn't see this man again[, and] so we arranged that I would meet him after bed call. My roommate and I tied sheets together and climbed out the third story window for our clandestine meeting. The entire dorm floor was in on the escapade and it was thrilling, fun, and very scary.[22]

The Big Sister–Little Sister network usually saw to unlocking windows and doors after hours.[23]

Occasionally, however, even carefully laid plans went awry. Dot Weaver, class of 1946, remembers breaking a date with a local fellow in order to see a young sailor—her future husband, Milford Weaver—who was coming to Danville. At the last minute his leave was cancelled. Meanwhile, her local beau had made other plans. Dot was left to repent at leisure.[24]

Writing and joking about the shortage of males seemed to help. The following poem by two Averett girls suggests student interest in the

---

[20] Nancy Adnia McDowell, letter to author, October 1982; see also Mrs. Paul F. Neal, letter to author, October 1982 and Mrs. Annice W. Carneal, letter to author, October 1982.

[21] Lanham, "Fugate Years," 11.

[22] Elly S. Caro letter to author, October 1982.

[23] Mrs. Robert H. Auerbach, letter to author, October 1982.

[24] Mrs. Milford Weaver, letter to author, October 1982.

biology department skeleton, Hubert, was not entirely academic.

Back in the days of his flashing youth,
I'll tell you a tale of the gospel truth,
He charmed the women and made them swoon,
He wooed them all 'til he met his doom.

I've told you this tale about Hubert the Great
So you'll have a chance to acquire a mate.
He's not the Sinatra he was back then
But he's all there is left of our vanishing men.[25]

Despite the shortages and attendant discomfort, Averett students were proud to be involved in America's great crusade for freedom. Helen Kent, class of 1944, penned this recognition of each individual's contribution to victory:

When peace has come to all the world
    And life once more is sane,
I'll wonder why we fought this war
    And what we had to gain.

Are we better now than we were before?
    Have we strived to get ahead?
Or have we fought a war in vain
    For those who now are dead?

They gave their lives on battlefields
    And didn't question why,
They fought in trenches filled with mud
    And watched their comrades die.

When peace has come I want to be
    Among the ones who say,

---

[25] *Chanticleer*, February 1944.

They're worthy of the following words
  Which brought this peace today:

I did my part
  In helping some
Return to home
  Now war is done.

By the help of God
  And my own strong hands
I kept the boys
  In foreign lands

Supplied with food
  And guns and tanks,
For which still echo
  Cries of thanks.

  ...
Though the road was rough
  I dared not rest,
And I'm proud to say,
  "I did my best."[26]

Despite involvement in the war effort, young women at Averett still found time to be students and to be female. They groused about "men around town who have a girl in every school...and get away with it." A perennial complaint was "girls with slim figures who eat and eat and grow skinnier—while others starve and grow rounder." Other annoyances included soda machines that robbed customers, students who swept their room dirt into the hall in front of a neighbor's door, and the classmate who swore she had failed the morning's history test because she did not "crack a book," only to get a grade of A when the paper was returned.[27] Between complaints, Averett students hummed the popular songs of World War II: "I'll Be Seeing You," "Don't Sit under the Apple Tree," "White Christmas," "I'll Be Home for Christmas," "When the

---

[26] *Chanticleer*, May 1944.
[27] *Chanticleer*, November 1942.

Lights Go On Again, All Over the World," and "As Time Goes By." They also enjoyed dressing in Sunday attire for candlelight dinners every Wednesday evening.[28]

Most of all, they enjoyed each other's company in dormitory and classroom. The day of arrival for new students was special because seniors and faculty mingled with them in an informal and chatty manner. On this occasion in 1943, the elderly Bible instructor, Louise Bryan, was present when each frightened new girl gave her name and some identifying fact, such as "My father's a Baptist minister in Roanoke." Then a "wonderful, happy, breezy, outgoing, audacious" youngster from Brooklyn, New York, who gave her name and city, added casually, "My pop's a liquor salesman." Adding insult to injury, she flicked ashes from her cigarette onto the hall floor as she spoke. Students, new and old alike, gulped and blanched. But Miss Bryan sensed the youngster was ignorant of either school rules or professors' specialties. Absorbing the comment, Professor Bryan assured her Averett was delighted to have her. Interestingly, because the young girl "didn't know Noah from Paul," she fell in love with the Old Testament course and its teacher. Her friends would chuckle as she came from Bible class exclaiming, "My God, I never heard this before!" or "Did you know *that* about Moses!"[29]

Another favorite teacher was Margaret Lanham, who joined the faculty in 1943 to teach English literature. After earning a B.A. degree from Converse College and M.A. and Ph.D. degrees from Vanderbilt University, Dr. Lanham devoted her professional life to Averett until retirement in 1978. Students appreciated her dedication to teaching, thorough preparation for class, love of good literature, command of the spoken and written word, and high expectations of students. She made the acquisition of knowledge "a natural part of living," wrote one

---

[28] Mrs. Grady L. Sumner, letter to author, October 1982; Rosemary Dempsey, letter to author, October 1982; Mrs. Ralph L. Forest, letter to author, October 1982; Mrs. Z. B. Ogden, letter to author, October 1982; Mrs. F. L. Owens, letter to author, October 1982; Mrs. John Elliott, Jr., letter to author, October 1982; Mrs. Robert McAlister, letter to author, October 1982; Mrs. Edith A. Barbour, letter to author, October 1982; Mrs. Frederick M. Lyon, letter to author, October 1982; Mrs. R. Stuart Grizzard, letter to author, October 1982; Mr. Burnell Jones, Jr., letter to author, October 1982; Mrs. Ralph Chamberlain, Jr., letter to author, October 1982; Elizabeth Coward Hutton, letter to author, October 1982; Neal, letter to author.

[29] Betty S. Cox, letter to author, October 1982.

alumna.[30] Betty Cox, a student of Dr. Lanham's in 1943–1945 and later professor of English at Gardner-Webb College, summed up Margaret Lanham in one sentence: "She was a lesson in character and manners, as well as English literature."[31]

The period following World War II brought fundamental changes. The most significant was the appearance of male students in large numbers (though full coeducation awaited an even more radical era of change in the late 1960s). Although Averett had had a few men as day students occasionally, the passage of the Servicemen's Readjustment Act, better known as the G.I. Bill of Rights, in 1944 would release a postwar flood of World War II veterans eager to take advantage of a free, full-time college education. When demand outstripped classroom capacity, Averett, like many women's colleges, opened its doors to returning servicemen. In 1946 twenty-five "vets" entered the college, causing its hallowed halls "to echo to the thump of heavy masculine feet."[32] In 1947 forty men attended classes, and twenty-two of them eventually graduated. Several were selected for membership in Phi Theta Kappa, the junior-college equivalent of Phi Beta Kappa. The veterans quickly adapted to college life. In October 1946, they formed a local fraternity, Gamma Phi Nu, and leased a house a mile south of Danville. The *Chanticleer* carried "Those Versatile Vets" and "Male Call," two regular columns in which veterans voiced male concerns, criticized female fashions, and advised girls on how to treat a veteran. These young men also took parts in dramatic productions, assuming male roles once filled by females. Averett girls enjoyed having the veterans on campus. Everyone paid more attention to dress and makeup, and a few girls even began "hitting the bottle" (that is, peroxide) to produce the blonde hair of a Hollywood goddess.[33]

Despite the presence of veterans in the late 1940s, Averett girls had little trouble adjusting to peacetime conditions. New students felt at home quickly because each junior had a senior Big Sister to orient, advise, and comfort her. The use of correct slang was another ticket to acceptance. Inappropriate actions were "tacky," situations were "loads of

---

[30] Hutton, letter to author.

[31] Cox, letter to author.

[32] *Pendulum*, 1948, 51.

[33] *Chanticleer*, 31 January 1948, 8 May 1948, 27 October 1948, 17 November 1948, 26 November 1949, 25 March 1950.

fun" or "loads of laughs," and accomplished people were "O.T.B." (on the ball). Students enjoyed listening to favorite radio programs such as *Inner Sanctum, Amos and Andy, Lux Radio Theater,* and *Voice of Firestone,* as well as comedians George Burns and Gracie Allen, Jack Benny, and Fred Allen. Also fun were the college dances where girls and their dates danced to student favorites such as "Always," "Tenderly," and "I'm in the Mood for Love."[34]

The Fighting Forties soon gave way at Averett to the Fabulous Fifties, a decade that combined conformity and rebellion. In the country at large, conformity reigned. Americans dressed alike and sought fulfillment in look-alike suburban houses, two-car garages, television, washday miracles, and powerful automobiles with tailfins. Popular television shows such as *I Love Lucy, Father Knows Best,* and *Dragnet* emphasized traditional American values of home and marketplace. Dwight D. Eisenhower was president, and Averett students liked Ike. He appealed to middle America in his choice of recreation—golf—and his choice of opponents—egghead intellectuals.

Similarly, in the 1950s the tendency toward conformity and tradition was strong on the Averett campus. Students liked artists and songs that peddled romantic love. Special favorites were Nat King Cole with "Unforgettable," Eddie Fisher with "Wish You Were Here," the Four Aces with "Heart and Soul," Johnny Mathis with "Wonderful, Wonderful," Frankie Avalon with "Venus," and Bing Crosby and Grace Kelly with "True Love." Averett girls enjoyed the security and comfort of "going steady" rather than casually dating. Favorite reading included works from the genre that presented romantic love and traditional values that were violated but in the end re-embraced. Averett students grew more fashion-conscious with the advent of a fashion merchandising program that staged an annual fashion show. Fashion merchandising majors also served as a *Chanticleer* "Fashion Plate of the Month" and

---

[34] Mrs. Gerald Sims letter to author , October 1982; Kathryn R. Jacques, letter to author, October 1982; Mrs. Alfonso Vazquez, letter to author, October 1982; Mrs. Walter R. Holloway, letter to author, October 1982; Mrs. Kurt L. Hirchmann, letter to author, October 1982; Mrs. Warren E. Neubert, letter to author, October 1982; Mrs. Jack M. Barts, letter to author, October 1982; Mrs. W. B. Mosely, letter to author, October 1982; Mrs. Robert N. Kullman, letter to author, October 1982; Mrs. E. Lacy Bowen, letter to author, October 1982; Mrs. Herbert V. Ewell, Jr., letter to author, October 1982; Mrs. Richard H. Reed, letter to author, October 1982.

even wrote an advice column in the *Chanticleer* titled "College Clothes Rack." As late as 1960, when traditional values began to be questioned seriously across America, the *Chanticleer* definition of the Averett Girl was more appropriate to 1950. She demonstrated, the paper said, "pride, a sense of loyalty, a manner of dress and appearance which denotes a lady, a well-rounded personality, and that certain indefinable characteristic—integrity."[35] Also in 1960, postwar conservatism, rather than an echo of anti-Catholicism in the Hoover-Smith contest of 1928, accounted for an Averett preferential ballot choosing Richard M. Nixon over John F. Kennedy by 66 percent to 26 percent. No less a reflection of postwar conservatism was *Chanticleer's* touting of school spirit and keeping the Sabbath, and its lack of interest in issues such as racial prejudice and civil rights.[36]

Perhaps students would have been more conscious of national problems if they had not been so absorbed in their intramural impatience, bordering on rebellion, with out-of-date rules and regulations. After challenges from students, the administration responded with modifications of rules and regulations three times in the decade 1950–1960. In 1950 restrictions on car dates were eased and curfew on Saturday and Sunday evenings was moved to 11:30 P.M. Later in the decade the administration eased the lights-out restriction, permitted students to select their own seats in the dining hall, and reduced required chapel programs to three a week. President Bishop also altered dress codes to allow Bermuda shorts in the library and sweatshirts at breakfast, gave honor roll students expanded dating and curfew privileges, and made attendance voluntary at dinner and church.[37]

After allowing students to ride in cars without chaperons in the 1950s, the administration found it increasingly difficult to enforce old prohibitions such as the one against alcoholic beverages. Although drinking remained a "shipping offense" and the dean of students sometimes sniffed breaths as students came in from dates, many still violated the rule.[38]

---

[35] *Chanticleer*, 25 October 1960.

[36] *Chanticleer*, December 1953, 28 April 1955, 25 February 1959, 26 March 1959, 25 October 1960.

[37] *Chanticleer*, 25 March 1950, 27 February 1958, 26 January 1959; Lanham, "Fugate Years," 14–15.

[38] Mrs. Walter Irvin Henson, letter to author , October 1982; Mrs. Francis S.

These regulations were more liberal than those of many denominational schools in the South. Nevertheless, Averett students demonstrated their impatience by publishing a "Student's Ten Commandments," which encompassed the following:

1. Thou shalt not cut class; take the whole day off.
2. Thou shalt not chew gum; tobacco is more tasty.
3. Thou shalt not run in the halls; yell "FIRE" to clear the way.
4. Thou shalt not talk back to professors; ignore them completely.
5. Thou shalt not write on desks; use a nail file—it's much more penetrating.
6. Thou shalt not borrow homework; don't bother to do it at all.
7. Thou shalt not copy neighbor's answers on tests; use the textbook instead.
8. Thou shalt not walk down stairs; slide down the banister—it's much more sporty.
9. Thou shalt not be late returning from a date—don't even bother to sign out—they won't miss you.
10. Thou shalt not visit thy neighbor during study hour; have a party—you can see more people at once.[39]

In the 1950s Averett students adopted slang that was strange to the ears of their parents and even to friends only a decade older. "Cat" meant boy; "chick," girl; "cool," pretty, handsome, popular or stylish; "crazy," exciting; to "dig," to appreciate; "stoned," ecstatic or captivated; and "square," misfit. Dancing and music carried particular labels for the new decade. The most popular music was rock and roll, epitomized by the Elvis Presley song, "You Ain't Nothing but a Hound Dog," with its bad grammar and crude metaphor. Distinctive dance patterns of the 1950s and early 1960s included the huckle-buck, the bop, the twist, and the mashed potato. The generation gap between parents and youths extended to faculty and students. Alumnae recall the embarrassment of faculty members when students would "scream from the onset to the end" of an Elvis Presley appearance on television.[40]

Swienckowski, letter to author, October 1982.

[39] *Chanticleer*, 30 November 1959.

[40] *Chanticleer*, 22 November 1948, Mrs. Tilmon Chamlee, letter to author , October 1982; Mrs. Robert W. Rice, letter to author, October 1982; Mrs. Howard H. Simms, letter

School-sponsored dances were popular at Averett during the decade. Each September and Christmas the college held a dance with live orchestra in the gymnasium. Male guests included students from nearby schools such as the University of North Carolina. Each fall Averett chartered buses to carry its student body to dances at Duke University, North Carolina State University, and the University of North Carolina. These events gave Averett girls a wide range of acquaintances.[41]

Another innovation of the 1950s was the panty raid. Few were actually held, most were rumored, and the results were more in the nature of boy-meets-girl than of seizing trophies. The male students at VPI Extension in Danville usually organized these tumultuous events. During one panty raid several young men got as far as the first floor of a dormitory before being confronted by Pauline Coll, the popular director of student personnel and a master at controlled ferocity. An alumna recalls that "there quickly followed a mass exodus of about 75 boys!"[42]

In spite of panty raids, everyday dormitory life in the 1950s changed little from previous decades. Bridge became such a fad that some students took part in a "floating bridge game" from breakfast until lights-out. "As one [student] had a class, another sat in and the same game continued all day," an alumna remembers.[43] Several Latinos from south of the border taught their American counterparts to dance the cha-cha, while they learned firsthand about snow. Experiencing their first snowfall, a group of Cuban girls "ran out bare-footed and squealed and giggled—they couldn't understand 'where it went' when they caught it!"[44] Dormitory students liked to "hang out" at the College Shop four blocks up West Main Street. A trip downtown for a movie or shopping usually was followed by apple pie at the GSK or Cavalier restaurants. Usual topics of conversation among students were boyfriends, examinations, weekends, movie stars, popular tunes, and teachers.

In addition to Dean Fugate and Professor Lanham, favorite teachers

---

to author, October 1982; Mrs. Edward Evans, letter to author, October 1982; Mrs. R. Thomas Clark, Jr., letter to author, October 1982.

[41] *Chanticleer*, 30 May 1952, December 1950, December 1950, 20 October 1956.

[42] Mrs. Rene L. Herbst, letter to author , October 1982; Mrs. Robert F. Drewes, letter to author, October 1982; Mrs. Ronald W. Collins, letter to author, October 1982; Mrs. George E. Fulford, Jr., letter to author, October 1982.

[43] Collins, letter to author.

[44] Ibid.

included Charlotte Read, Grace Crenshaw, and Pauline Coll. With baccalaureate and master's degrees from Richmond Professional Institute, Charlotte Read came to Averett in 1955 to teach fashion merchandising. Students found her approachable, understanding, concerned, knowledgeable, and genteel.[45] Grace Crenshaw, a graduate of Emory and Henry College with a master's degree from the University of Virginia, arrived in 1929 to teach courses in mathematics, Latin, psychology, and history. Students praised her patience, her willingness to tutor outside the classroom, and her ability to make difficult subjects fun to learn and easy to understand. They also took delight in her privileged status: because she tutored so many Danville policemen in mathematics, she could park her car anywhere in the city without fear of getting a ticket. In recognition of her contributions to the institution, today Averett annually presents the Grace V. Crenshaw Award to the second honor graduate.[46]

After receiving a B.A. from the Oklahoma College for Women and M.A. from the University of Oklahoma, Pauline Coll came to Averett in 1946 to teach French and Spanish and later serve as director of student personnel. Alumnae recall her accessibility. "Her door was always open...to help with our BIG problems," wrote one former student.[47] They marveled at her ability to match quickly the photographs on applications with the young ladies who arrived on campus in September, most of whom she called by name as she greeted them. Professor Coll could be stern or gentle as the situation required. One former student remembers that when Miss Coll, "with a lift of the eye-brow," called her name, "I quickly knew I was going in the wrong direction."[48] Another remembers, "She gave me unlimited understanding and faith in myself and others.... She even came to my room and gave me pep talks."[49]

The event that generated the most conversation at Averett College in the early 1950s was the Graveyard Episode. In early March 1952, three

---

[45] Mrs. Joan S. Thorp, letter to author, October 1982; Mrs. Robert J. Owens, letter to author, October 1982.

[46] Rice, letter to author.

[47] Mrs. James R. Lockerman, Jr., letter to author, October 1982; Mrs. Stanley H. Rayner, III, letter to author, October 1982; Fulford, letter to author; Chamlee, letter to author.

[48] Clark, letter to author.

[49] Drewes, letter to author; see also Mrs. Ira H. Hurt, Jr., letter to author, October 1982.

male and two female day students were passing the time by discussing bones, relics, ghosts, old graveyards, and séances. One of the five, Jay Heze Ford Pigg—a member of a prominent family in Pittsylvania County—led the others to his family's antebellum graveyard near Danville. They removed several bones and a skull from the grave of a former slave, carried them to the Averett day-students' lounge, and announced that a séance would be held. After complaints from fellow day students, Pigg burned the bones in the college furnace. Four days later President Bishop learned of the episode. Horrified by the macabre prank and its identification with spiritualism, Bishop took testimony from each of the five individually and then expelled four and suspended the other.[50]

Meanwhile, President Bishop became the least of the students' worries. On March 17, Dennis Jones, whose family owned the property surrounding the graveyard, noticed the desecration and notified authorities. On March 27, a grand jury indicted the students for violating the state's grave-robbery law. Conviction on this felony carried a five-to-ten-year prison sentence. Worse was to follow. The Associated Press picked up the story, which quickly became front-page news across America. Newspapers as far away as the *Spokane Daily Chronicle* carried the tale, and not all of the papers chose to see the incident as a prank, which prompted W. Carrington Thompson, the local commonwealth's attorney and later a Virginia Supreme Court justice, to confide in Bishop: "Never in my life have I witnessed such an orgy of cheap sensationalism by the press."[51] Finally, on March 29, President Harry Truman's announcement he would not seek another term pushed the story to the back pages. Despite the timely intervention of Truman's news, letters and telephone calls denouncing the grave desecration continued to pour in to President Bishop, who simply assured each complainant the five individuals "ceased to be students the moment I found out about the incident."[52] Public attention finally subsided after a trial on May 23 in which Judge John D. Hooker reduced the charges

---

[50] News clippings and statements, folder titled "Grave Episode," Averett University Archives; *Danville Register*, 28 March 1952, 1, 5B, 6; *Commercial Appeal*, 28 March 1952, 1.

[51] W. Carrington Thompson to Curtis V. Bishop, 28 March 1952, "Grave Episode," Averett University Archives.

[52] Copies of correspondence, "Grave Episode," Averett University Archives.

from grave robbery to trespass and fined each student fifty dollars.[53]

In many ways, the Bishop years of the 1960s were simply a continuation of the 1950s. Averett students were uneasy over turmoil caused by the Bay of Pigs invasion, the Berlin Crisis, and developments in Southeast Asia. They reacted with horror to the assassination of President John F. Kennedy. But, products of a traditional political and social environment, they avoided causes and crusades. Dances and hall decorations for holiday seasons always took precedence over national issues. The *Chanticleer* even warned of communist involvement in the nation's social and political unrest.[54]

Stylish dress was deemed essential in the early 1960s. Averett students insisted on clothing with labels like Vanity Fair, McMullen, Villager, London Fog, and Bass. They liked weejuns, oxford-cloth blouses with button-down collars, cardigan or crew-neck sweaters, madras dresses, tweed or plaid woolen skirts, and stockings or knee socks. Blouses were always thought to look best with a fraternity pin attached to the front, even though getting pinned meant a girl might be thrown into the shower by roommates. And the outfit always looked best on an Averett girl at a university fraternity party. There she and her date strolled with an arm around the back of each other's waist, the free hands holding refreshments as both conversed with other couples—equally stylishly attired—and swayed or foot-tapped to music by the Lettermen, the Beatles, the Righteous Brothers, Bo Diddley, Ray Charles, Little Stevie Wonder, the Supremes, the Beach Boys, or the Rolling Stones. The look was strictly "collegiate."[55]

The word "collegiate" perhaps best describes Curtis Bishop's impact on student life as well. Although not accorded the measure of freedom they desired, by 1966 Averett students were no longer regarded as children who must be told where to sit for dinner, how to worship, where to shop or relax, how to dress, where to date, and what to do on

---

[53] *Commercial Appeal*, 23 May 1952, 2.

[54] *Chanticleer*, 20 May 1965, 16 December 1965.

[55] Martha H. Lester, letter to author , October 1982; Mrs. Richard A. Hevenor, letter to author, October 1982; Mrs. Charles D. McManus, letter to author, October 1982; Mrs. R. Kenneth Tonning, letter to author, October 1982; Mrs. James S. Moore, letter to author, October 1982; Mrs. Bruce Griffith, letter to author, October 1982; Mrs. Lawrence L. Layman, Jr., letter to author, October 1982; Mrs. William Charles Davison, letter to author, October 1982; Mrs. Samuel R. Theal, letter to author, October 1982.

dates. What rules remained were calculated to induce behavior appropriate to females in all ages. No longer did the president try to shut the college off from the outside world. In fact, traditions to that end, such as hiding of the crook, were discarded. Ever-present chaperons, a disapproval of dancing, and a president who was literally quick on the trigger to discourage prowlers were replaced by unsupervised car dates, formal and informal hops, student-body road trips to North Carolina universities, and panty raids. A politically naive student body gave way to one concerned with foreign and domestic affairs, albeit from a conservative perspective. And a largely local and provincial student body somehow managed to integrate Northerners and Latin Americans in large numbers to the edification of all three groups. In short, Averett College seemed to grow up during the Bishop years.

V. PROMISE AND FULFILLMENT

1966–2001

10

Metamorphosis,
1966–1973

To its faithful supporters Averett College seemed to possess a destiny. Founded in the uncertain antebellum period, the institution was able to survive the lean times of Civil War and Reconstruction. Only two months away from economic ruin in 1892, it was able to weather the depression of the 1890s that forced the closing of other colleges. Beset by slumps in enrollment and tuitions often paid in barter, Averett was able to hang on through the Great Depression of the 1930s and even prosper. Averett College survived because its presidents insisted the school meet the needs of its patrons. Therefore, in the nineteenth century, it provided intellectual and cultural growth with a Christian flavor for daughters of local men of prominence. In the early twentieth century, the school prepared young women for Christian family life and the marketplace. In the middle years of the twentieth century, it offered a junior-college education with a Southern flavor that protected "virtue," developed genteel qualities, provided vocational skills, and stressed the liberal arts and sciences necessary for transfer to a senior institution. When Americans in the 1960s began to assume that young people were entitled by birthright to a senior-college education, Averett was ready to complete its destiny. Promise would be fulfilled at last.

Curtis Bishop's death in February 1966 created a vacuum in the sense that an institution does not easily replace thirty years of forceful and energetic leadership. Yet this vacuum was more seeming than real. Averett still had a respected, capable, and conscientious leader whose association with the college predated Curtis Bishop's by six years. This person was Mary C. Fugate, who assumed the acting presidency until a permanent successor could be found. Born on 7 October 1901, in Grayson County, Virginia, she was the eldest of five children of Henly Mitchell Fugate and Eliza H. Roberts Fugate. Her father was an ordained Baptist minister and a graduate of both the University of Richmond and Southern Baptist Theological Seminary. Brothers, sisters, and relocation came quickly in Mary's early life. Brother Henly was born in 1903, sister Henrietta in 1905, and twins Elizabeth and Watkins in 1910. The family moved to Tazewell in 1904 and to Farmville only three years later. In Farmville Mary started her elementary education in the training school of the Farmville Normal School, later to become Longwood College. Partly owing to the excellence of instruction there, she decided to become a teacher. As a seven-year-old she held regular play-school sessions for younger brother Henly, who later was able to complete the first and second grades in only one year.[1]

During her father's four-year pastorate in Norfolk (1911 to 1915), Mary Fugate entered Maury High School. Shortly thereafter, the Fugates moved to Waynesboro, Georgia, where the father was pastor of the town's Baptist church. World War I disrupted local life in Waynesboro with high cotton prices, calls for voluntary war work, and growth of both the armed forces and war industries. The proximity of the Army's Camp Gordon bought an endless stream of soldiers and sweethearts to Waynesboro to be married by Parson Fugate.[2]

The family's move to Macon, Georgia, in 1918 coincided with Mary's matriculation at Westhampton College of the University of Richmond. Her parents had chosen Westhampton for Mary as early as 1914, when Henly Fugate, Sr., helped raise money to found the school. Mary's first year at Westhampton was exciting. Because the University of Richmond lent a part of its campus to the US Army for use as a military hospital and discharge center, students were housed first in St. Luke's Hospital on Grace Street and then in private homes in an area of downtown stretching for twenty-five blocks. This inconvenience was compounded by the influenza epidemic of 1918, which struck the college community as severely as it struck the nation. Although Mary was bedridden for days during the epidemic with a less serious viral infection,

---

[1] Mary C. Fugate, interview with author, Averett College, 12 April 1983, hereinafter cited as Fugate interview.

[2] Ibid; Mary C. Fugate, handwritten personal reminiscences, in possession of author, hereinafter cited as Fugate reminiscence.

she recovered in time to celebrate the Armistice on 11 November 1918. She and several friends hopped atop a coal truck and, like other ecstatic citizens, rode up and down Richmond streets, shouting for joy.[3]

Mary Fugate was an excellent and popular student. She thrived in the nurturing, small-college atmosphere that characterized Westhampton in 1918. The importance of close relationships between teachers and students, which she learned in Farmville, was reinforced there. She was elected class president her sophomore year, a council member of the YWCA her junior year, and president of the Student Government Association her senior year. She also was tapped for membership in Mortar Board in recognition of her high standards of scholarship and collegiate service.[4]

Upon graduation in 1922 she applied to the State Department of Education to be listed on its roster of available teachers. The Superintendent of Schools in Sussex County, Virginia, consulted this list to select an assistant principal who could teach history, English, and mathematics. Partly because the superintendent had been a friend of Mary's father at the University of Richmond in the 1890s, Mary landed the job at Wakefield High School in the Sussex County system. Her college roommate also was hired to teach in Sussex County, and the two girls roomed together for two more years.

Among the many other friends of Henly Fugate, Sr., was the Reverend James P. Craft, once a pastor in Georgia and now president of Averett College. Mary Fugate remembered that her father "had never been modest in talking about his children," and it was not long before Craft invited her to Averett College to teach English, history, mathematics, and biology in the high school department.[5] In 1924 she moved to Danville and discovered that her duties also included teaching a course in Sunday school pedagogy and, for six weeks, Latin. Despite the extra work, she enjoyed Averett. Its congenial faculty contained three Westhampton friends, and its front lawn doubled as a croquet field in warm weather. She spent the school year of 1926–1927 at Columbia University earning a Master of Arts in history. In spring 1927, she accepted Craft's offer to return to Averett as acting dean. In 1928

---

[3] Fugate reminiscence; Fugate interview.

[4] Fugate interview.

[5] Ibid.

President John W. Cammack made her permanent dean and registrar.[6]

Dean Fugate was a capable and admired administrator. She was a model of integrity and seemed incapable of deviousness, petty motivation, or dishonesty. She also was a model of discretion, dignity, self-control, and dedication to job, superiors, and subordinates. Reserved and fair-minded, she measured her words carefully and never tried to play favorites among colleagues, which meant not granting exceptions to policy. Faculty, for instance, were expected to meet each class for the allotted time, give all final examinations as scheduled, and leave for vacation only after the work of the semester was completed. A famous Fugate memorandum asking that the dean's office be notified if a faculty member planned to miss class for any reason, including illness, led to a long-remembered joke that faculty were even expected to advise Dean Fugate whenever they planned to be ill.[7]

Yet Dean Fugate's devotion to her job never spoiled her sociable nature. She was always good company, well informed, gentle in her opinions and humor, and able to converse with anyone. A part of this sociability derived from her spontaneity. On one hectic day a visitor to her office happened to express curiosity about feather-stitching. Professor Margaret Lanham remembers that, "pressed as she was, the dean sent out for a needle and thread and gave a demonstration of feather-stitching." Another part of her sociability derived from an interest in collecting. Almost all of the pre-1966 material in the archives of Averett College was preserved by her and given to the school when it could house them properly. Perhaps without trying, she collected in her mind the maiden names, married names, majors, personal triumphs, and clever statements of former students. Perhaps again without trying, she forgot their faults.[8]

Not surprisingly, Dean Fugate was called upon for civic and professional leadership. An active member of the National Association of Women Deans and Counselors, she served as chairman of its junior-college section and president of its regional association. She was also

---

[6] Ibid.

[7] Pauline Coll and Margaret Lanham, interview with author, Averett College, 13 April 1983, hereinafter cited as Coll-Lanham interview.

[8] Ibid; Margaret Lanham, "Mary C. Fugate: A Sketch toward a Portrait," typescript, 31 May 1969, Averett University Archives, hereinafter cited as Lanham, "Fugate Portrait."

president of the Virginia Association of Collegiate Registrars and Admissions Officers. In addition to serving on numerous local boards, she served on the boards of directors of the Virginia Foundation for the Humanities and Public Policy and the Virginia State Division of the American Association of University Women. Quite naturally, honors were bestowed on her by grateful recipients of her time and energy. Selected for alumni membership in Phi Beta Kappa, she also was among nine recipients of the Distinguished Alumna Award during the celebration of Westhampton's golden anniversary, and she received one of eight Distinguished Service Awards from the University of Richmond. Honored with her were A. L. Philpott, speaker of the House of Delegates of Virginia; Harold F. Snead, chief justice of the Supreme Court of Virginia; Warren M. Pace, president of the Life Insurance Company of Virginia; and Robert T. Marsh, president of First and Merchants National Bank.[9]

Mary Fugate's acting presidency at Averett College from January to September in 1966 proved to be business as usual. For several previous years she had shouldered the burden of administration while President Bishop was in declining health, preoccupied with civic work, and increasingly out of touch with changing student mores. Although Dean Fugate had not established policy, salaries, curriculum, or institutional direction, she quietly and effectively attended to matters at hand. Trustees, faculty, and students alike knew what Fugate leadership meant and were optimistic.

As acting president she lost no time in helping to locate a successor. The board of trustees appointed a search committee of trustees headed by President George Modlin of the University of Richmond. Although not a trustee, acting president Fugate interviewed each candidate. For several months the committee searched in vain. Finally in July, when members learned the former president of Judson College, Conwell A. ("Connie") Anderson, might be available, an interview was hastily arranged. Mary Fugate supported his candidacy from the start. The board offered Anderson the position, and he assumed the presidency, effective 1 September 1966.[10]

---

[9] Biographical resume of Mary C. Fugate, Averett University Archives; *Spider Football Magazine*, University of Richmond, 22 October 1977, 72–73.

[10] Coll-Lanham interview; Mary Joan Davis, interview with author, Averett College, 13 April 1983; Fugate interview.

In some respects, Conwell Anderson was an unlikely choice to head a Southern women's college. A Midwesterner by birth and rearing, he was born in Sister Bay, Wisconsin, on 24 May 1926. Unlike the heritage of Averett predecessors, his background was Swedish Baptist. Fearing discrimination, if not persecution, at the hands of Lutherans in Sweden in the 1860s, his great-grandfather had fled with his family to Wisconsin, where he founded the local Baptist church in which several generations of Andersons would be reared. The Anderson family was proud of their Swedish heritage and their family's devotion to religious liberty. The great-grandson, "Connie," spoke Swedish before he spoke English and naturally assumed that every American family was bilingual.[11]

Church and the family dairy farm and cherry orchard were prominent influences in Anderson's early life. As the only son, he was counted on to do several shares of the farm labor. Winter days meant chores at the dairy; summer days meant picking and loading the cherry crop. Yet there was also time for downhill skiing and for fantasizing feats of athletic skill. While hurling a baseball against a large rock in his yard, young Anderson imagined major league baseball games in which he was the pitcher. The ricocheting balls became grounders or pop flies hit by opposing batters. "I would go through the entire White Sox batting order several times in an afternoon," he recalled. Free time indoors often meant participation in activities at church, especially in the Baptist Young People's Union and orchestra.[12]

Anderson was a typical, well-rounded youngster of the Midwest during the Great Depression. He was an above-average student who preferred athletics to academics. Although no subjects really fascinated him, he did enjoy history and social studies. Fictional stories of adventure and intrigue, rather than textbooks, struck his fancy. A popular student, he was elected president of his senior class. Although he admired his quiet and hard-working father, he had no special childhood heroes. His political orientation was Republican, since there were no Democrats in Sister Bay.[13]

The most prominent influence in Anderson's later teen years was World War II. Anderson graduated from high school in 1943. He

---

[11] *Pendulum*, 1979, 124; Conwell A. Anderson, interview with author, Averett College, 11–12 January 1983, hereinafter cited as Anderson interview.
[12] Anderson interview.
[13] Ibid.

yearned for high adventure and also felt an obligation as a patriotic American to get into the fray. On the other hand, he had planned for years to attend college. He resolved his dilemma by attending Bethel Junior College in St. Paul, Minnesota, for one year before enlisting in the Navy. He was posted to Boston for service aboard the USS *Emmons,* a destroyer-minesweeper. In November 1944, the ship left for the Pacific to take part in operations off Okinawa in March and early April 1945. While screening for radar pickets on April 6, the *Emmons* was attacked and sunk by kamikazes. With a shrapnel wound in his leg, Anderson was lucky to get aboard a life raft and lucky that darkness kept the desperate Japanese from strafing the survivors more than once. The wounded sailor was put aboard a troop ship and taken to the United States for a survivor's leave. He was awarded the Purple Heart and the Naval Unit Citation. The war's end found him assigned to a naval hospital in Banning, California.[14]

After the war Anderson re-enrolled at Bethel Junior College and graduated in 1947. There he met his future wife, Marjorie Erickson of Erie, Pennsylvania, who asked his sister to introduce them after she saw his picture on her desk. Theirs was a storybook romance. They met at a watermelon party at the beginning of school. He traded in his car to buy an engagement ring on Valentine's Day, and they were married six months later. After graduation, their wedding, and a short stint in Chicago, the young couple moved to Tuscaloosa, Alabama, where he became a history major at the University of Alabama. Anderson selected the school because aunts, uncles, and grandparents who wintered in southern Alabama praised the region. Receiving a B.A. in 1949 and master's degree in 1950, he aspired to a career of teaching history at the senior-college level. His quest for a doctorate in Latin American history was interrupted by two years of teaching at the University of Alabama Center at Gadsden and on the Tuscaloosa campus. He finally earned his Ph.D. degree in 1954. The university offered him an assistant professorship in history, which he was on the verge of accepting when called elsewhere.[15]

In December 1953, during his last year in Tuscaloosa, Connie and Marge Anderson traveled to Dallas to watch the Alabama football team

---

[14] Ibid.
[15] Ibid.

play in the Cotton Bowl. One of his students, football hero Bart Starr, had given them tickets. At a New Year's Eve party in Dallas, Anderson met and impressed a trustee of Mary Hardin-Baylor College in Belton, Texas. The following summer officials from Mary Hardin-Baylor telephoned to ask if they could consider him for their academic deanship, since he was so highly recommended by an influential trustee. The surprised young professor consented, landed the position, and moved his family to Texas. Mary Hardin-Baylor proved to be an excellent training ground for a young administrator. Because the president was interested in fundraising and public relations, he turned over much of the daily administration to Dean Anderson. At this time also, the Southern Association of Colleges and Schools began requiring detailed reports on all phases of college life, a task which also fell to Anderson. Between 1954 and 1960, he came to know his institution in particular, and college administration in general, as few deans ever do.[16]

In 1960 former faculty of Mary Hardin-Baylor who relocated to Judson College at Marion, Alabama, recommended Conwell Anderson for Judson's presidency. He was offered and accepted the position, remaining there until 1965. The transition from dean to president was easy, even though he was initially awed by the realization there was no one to whom he could refer decisions.[17] A mutual affection developed between the Andersons and the Judson community. He was particularly impressed by the fact that students expected "close relationships" and "exciting experiences" with faculty and administrators, but also "accepted authority."[18]

Although happy at Judson, Anderson grew increasingly uncomfortable in Alabama in the mid-1960s. Friends in the community abandoned him when he persuaded the trustees to integrate the college. He saw in his elder daughter unhealthy tensions springing from racial attitudes in the Deep South. He yearned for a new college whose academic, administrative, and student life he could fashion. Thus in summer 1965, when Baptists in Maryland approached him with an offer to preside over a new college that existed only on paper, he left Judson College for the presidency of Maryland Baptist College.

---

[16] Ibid.

[17] *Pendulum*, 1979, 125.

[18] Ibid; see also Anderson interview.

Anderson quickly realized his mistake: Denominational support was not as extensive as the board of trustees led him to believe. The level of trustee commitment to the college was not high. Worst of all, two months after Anderson took office, the trustees voted to build a junior college instead of a senior one. Resigning in January 1966, Anderson accepted a position as associate director of the Institute of Higher Education at the University of Georgia. From this position he was called to the presidency of Averett College in August 1966.[19]

Conwell Anderson brought twelve years of administrative experience, good credentials, and an awareness of how treacherous it was in the 1960s to steer a course between race and finance, institutional needs and denominational wishes, and the prescribed curriculum and student demands for relevancy. As past president of both the Southern Association of Colleges for Women and the Division of Higher Education in the Alabama Education Association, he had earned modest recognition and gave solid promise for the future. Anderson also brought the courage to take sizeable risks, a philosophy appropriate to the times, and a personality that proved to be pleasing to students, alumnae, faculty, and trustees. The forty-year-old Anderson was handsome, articulate, informal, and dryly humorous. His dislike of snobbery and stuffiness was symbolized by proficiency at billiards and a navy tattoo on his left arm. He was attentive to student needs, a characteristic that sometimes reduced tension. Sensing his special qualities, the *Chanticleer* found him

> a gentle, sweet, handsome, intellectual man with vast qualifications, experience, and enthusiasm for his work.... His subtle sense of humor and tactful, yet easy-going mode of expression have already captured our hearts, demanded our respect, and challenged our most reluctant potentials toward constructive womanhood.[20]

---

[19] Anderson interview; see also Averett Board Minutes, 11 August 1966.

[20] *Chanticleer*, 13 October 1966; see also author's interviews with Stephen C. Ausband, 11 April 1983; Russell C. Brachman, 29 April 1993; Mary Elizabeth Compton, 29 April 1983; Mary Joan Davis, 13 April 1983; John Dever, 15 April 1983; David Gray, 29 April 1983; Richard M. Inlow, 29 April 1983; Carol S. Kushner, 29 April 1983; Robert C. Marsh, 29 April 1983; Charles Postelle, 28 April 1983; and Charlotte Read, 28 April 1983, Averett College.

Although President Anderson provided dynamic leadership, he sometimes displayed the all-too-human weakness of being quick-tempered and appearing disrespectful of those who requested explanations or opposed policies. His dry humor occasionally carried enough bite to alienate, while some people perceived his self-confidence as arrogance.[21]

The Andersons arrived in Danville in late August 1966. They took up residence in the college infirmary while the president's house was redecorated, remodeled, and enlarged. Meanwhile, President Anderson took pains to assure the several constituencies of the college that his changes would be gradual and not precipitous. "A wise president," he assured them, "is one who spends much of his time learning about the institution before he plunges in and makes any rash moves."[22] But circumstances have a way of forcing quick and dramatic changes. When Averett's neighbor, Stratford College, announced plans in fall 1966 to become a senior college, it was evident that Averett's very existence was threatened and a response was unavoidable. With a senior-college program, Stratford would certainly become the more prestigious of the two Danville schools and siphon off Averett's population of day students and some of its financial support from local contributors. A concerned Anderson confided to his faculty in November, "I would fear for the local status of Averett in comparison with Stratford a generation hence."[23] Anderson began steering the several Averett constituencies toward adoption of four-year status as the only way for the college to remain competitive.

Still other concerns were forcing Anderson's hand earlier than he would have liked. The open-door admissions policy of newly created public community colleges created an unfavorable impression of junior-college education among confused laypersons. At the same time, recruitment and retention of faculty were becoming more difficult. The Baby Boom of the 1940s nearly swamped colleges with students in the 1960s and created a seller's market for Ph.D.'s at the same time community colleges entered the bidding for M.A.'s. The former attraction of private junior colleges was simultaneously eroded. In

---

[21] Ausband interview, Brachman interview, Compton interview, Davis interview, Dever interview, March interview, Postelle interview, and Read interview.

[22] News clipping, 4 September 1966; Development Office files, Averett University.

[23] Faculty Minutes, 11 November 1966, Averett University Archives, 3

addition, seniors in high school were becoming aware of the difficulty in transferring from a junior college to a newly crowded senior college, while those who once sought a "practical" diploma after two years were lured to cheaper community colleges. Fundraising was also more difficult for a junior college. Foundations and even alumni preferred to help universities and senior colleges. These concerns soon were shared by Averett's faculty. But how could a change be effected?[24]

In autumn 1966, President Anderson began discussing with subordinates the feasibility of making Averett once again a senior college. He carefully used the wording "to reinstate baccalaureate degrees" rather than the phrase "to add baccalaureate degrees" in hopes of defusing opposition to steps not in keeping with the school's heritage. By November, Anderson was able to advise trustees, a "consensus had emerged" among his subordinates that "conditions had changed so markedly" as to require "consideration of a senior-college program with majors in selected disciplines."[25] Before the month was out, the executive committee of the board of trustees authorized Anderson to appoint a committee of eighteen trustees, administrators, and faculty to study the feasibility of creating a senior college. President Anderson chaired that committee.[26]

The group met for the first time on 19 January 1967. A frank discussion of the changing educational environment quickly led to the conclusion that senior college status was desirable. The members agreed the three initial priorities should be faculty improvement, library improvement, and dormitory additions. Anderson then appointed two subcommittees to investigate possible curriculums and calendars. At the next meeting of the full committee in early February, members approved B.A. degrees in seven areas and B.S. degrees in four areas, with enough hours offered in education for state certification. The committee projected an optimum student body of seven hundred to eight hundred

---

[24] Ibid., 2–3; Conwell A. Anderson, "A Proposal [to the Board of Trustees] to Reinstate Baccalaureate Degrees," in "Annual Report of the President to the Board of Trustees, October 20, 1967," hereinafter cited as Anderson, "Baccalaureate Proposal."

[25] Anderson, "Baccalaureate Proposal."

[26] Ibid; Averett Board Minutes, 21 November 1966. The Committee of Eighteen included trustees Landon Wyatt, Charles Easley, Clifford Gaddy, L. H. Kernodle, O. Lewis Roach, and Julian Stinson: faculty members Russell Brachman, David Gray, Margaret Lanham, Elnora Light, Terry Pettit, and Charlotte Read; and administrators Mary Fugate, Carolyn Pulley, Nancy Sindon, Ralph Dorr, and Mary Joan Davis.

students. Most attractive for the eighteen planners was an innovative academic calendar. The Calendar Subcommittee recommended a 4-4-2-1 academic year that comprised a four-month fall term ending before Christmas, a four-month spring term ending in late April, a May-June term, and a summer school. The Averett Option, as it was called, offered graduation in four years using only the fall and spring terms and left plenty of free time for employment in spring and summer. By using the two terms from April through June, students could graduate with a single major in three years or double major in four years.[27]

Armed with unanimous recommendations by the Committee of Eighteen, Anderson began soliciting the views of members and officials of the trustees, the faculty, the denomination, and the Southern Association of Colleges and Schools. All responded positively. Anderson then scheduled the topic for discussion by the full board of trustees on 20 October 1967. A vote by the trustees for four-year status was by no means a certainty, since several trustees had strong reservations. What helped galvanize support was a speech against it by board member and president of the University of Richmond, George Modlin. Under different circumstances his arguments would have been compelling. But the majority of board members were Danvillians who refused to surrender their college to the views of an outsider. With a smile President Anderson recalled the outcome of the vote: "It was parochialism in its grandest form."[28]

The board even went beyond Anderson's recommendations. In addition to reinstating baccalaureate degrees and admitting senior-college students beginning in September 1969, thereby giving the college two years in which to strengthen faculty and library, the board voted to reinstate coeducation. This decision was only natural because males had attended Averett in small numbers as day students before President Bishop excluded them in 1960. This decision was also wise because many local men wanting a bachelor's degree would choose to stay in the area and commute to Averett. Anderson, who had lost the battle for coeducation at Judson College, sat silently but delighted as trustees brought to bear many of the same arguments for coeducation at Averett

---

[27] Anderson, "Baccalaureate Proposal"; Averett Board Minutes, 21 November 1966.

[28] Anderson, "Baccalaureate Proposal"; Averett Board Minutes, 16 October 1967; Faculty Minutes, 9 November 1967, 2; Anderson interview.

he had mounted in vain at Judson.[29]

The new four-year program was comprehensive. Anchored in the liberal arts and sciences, it included a core curriculum of sixty to sixty-six hours. Required fields of study were English, fine arts, foreign languages, history, mathematics, religion, natural science, social science, and physical education. This core reflected the faculty's conviction that no person could be considered educated without exposure to the spiritual and intellectual components of the Western heritage. Initial plans called for a degree requirement of 126 semester hours, later reduced to 120 semester hours. Interestingly, while other colleges and universities in America were proclaiming the necessity of "relevant" courses, Averett College was proclaiming the relevance of the liberal arts and sciences.[30]

By 1969, Averett College was evolving into a senior institution with the Anderson stamp upon it. Beyond the college's walls, the president led in seeking to change Averett's local and statewide identity from a junior to a senior college. He did so by clever advertisements in both print and broadcast media, personal contacts with guidance counselors, and recruiters to tell the Averett story. Within the college, Dean Mary Fugate's retirement gave Anderson an opportunity to name his own person to this key administrative post. Dean Fugate graciously submitted her resignation in 1966 when Anderson became president, but he persuaded her to stay until planning for the senior college could be completed. Her expertise and the immense respect accorded her by faculty and alumnae were a great help to Anderson. When she reiterated her desire to retire in 1969 after forty-two years of service, Anderson accepted. He then hired R. Kirby Godsey, who had earned a B.A. degree from Samford University, theological degrees from New Orleans Baptist Theological Seminary, the M.A. in philosophy from the University of Alabama, and the Ph.D. in philosophy from Tulane University. In September the college added the junior academic year. Enrollment figures continued to prove the wisdom of the decision to become a senior college. In anticipation of baccalaureate opportunities in 1970, day-student enrollment increased from ninety-six in 1966–1967 to 155 in 1968–1969.[31]

---

[29] Anderson interview.

[30] Faculty Minutes, 9 November 1967, 3, appendix; see also Rudolph, *American College*, 455.

[31] *1969–1970 Averett Bulletin*, 24; *Chanticleer*, 3 March 1969; Conwell A. Anderson,

Construction of a library and dormitory for upperclassmen were two prerequisites for accreditation by the Southern Association of Colleges and Schools. To realize this goal, in November 1968 the board of trustees authorized a capital improvements program of $1.3 million. The following year trustee Curtis English of Altavista agreed to construct the dormitory for $500,000, which was at least $100,000 less than the total cost-per-bed projection. Completed in 1970 and named Fugate Hall in honor of Mary Fugate, the three-story building housed 150 students in fifteen suites of ten students each. Each suite contained a living room, five bedrooms, a large bathroom, and storage closets. Fully carpeted and fully air-conditioned, the building used furniture designed by Averett's inventive business manager, Ralph Dorr. Parlors, decks for sunbathing, and a recreation room offered ample diversions.[32]

The Mary B. Blount Library came the following year. In a casual conversation in 1968 with Baptist leader Frank Voight, President Anderson despaired of ever meeting the library prerequisite for accreditation. Ruefully, he admitted the trustees would not go into debt for that purpose. After a moment's reflection, Voight replied that he knew someone who might be willing to help: Mrs. David S. Blount, a member of Roanoke's Grandin Court Baptist Church, where Voight formerly was pastor. Mary B. Blount, a schoolteacher, appreciated the value of education and was a generous Christian who wanted her contributions used for a Christian purpose. Voight arranged for President and Mrs. Anderson to have lunch with Mrs. Blount at Hotel Roanoke. She soon visited the campus, decided that Averett was worthy, and added a codicil to her will pledging to cover the projected construction cost of $600,000. When the trustees agreed to borrow on the strength of the codicil, President Anderson persuaded Mrs. Blount to allow the library to bear her name.[33]

In September 1971, the Mary B. Blount Library was ready for

President's Annual Report, 20 October 1967, 3 June 1968, 30 May 1969. Retiring from the Averett faculty in 1969 were Grace Crenshaw with forty years of service, Carson Davenport with twenty-five years of service, and Eleanor Moore with fourteen years of service.

[32] Averett Board Minutes, 31 October 1969; Anderson interview; 1975 Averett Self-Study, 162. Averett University Archives

[33] Anderson interview; Averett Board Minutes, 2 July 1970; *Chanticleer*, 8 September 1970; 1975 Self-Study, 107–26, 163. The John W. Daniel Construction Company constructed the library at a cost of $661,200.

occupancy. To give students a sense of ownership, the college scheduled September 14 as Moving the Library Day. Beginning at 10:00 A.M., Mrs. Blount joined hundreds of students, faculty, administrators, and trustees to carry armloads of books from the old library in the basement of Bishop Hall to the new building on West Main Street. Faculty wags could not resist noting that they saw many upperclassmen carrying books for the first time. The workers moved 34,000 volumes by early afternoon and then repaired to the athletic field for a faculty-student picnic and softball game. Alumni from this period remember the day as one of their most memorable at Averett College.[34]

With a library and a dormitory for upperclassmen in place, the college community eagerly awaited full accreditation. At commencement exercises on 24 April 1971, Averett College conferred 175 degrees, including ninety-six baccalaureates. The evaluation committee of the Southern Association of Colleges and Schools (SACS) completed its favorable review a month earlier, and in the fall President Anderson and Dean Godsey attended the meeting of the SACS Commission on Colleges to outline steps taken to improve faculty credentials and library. Finally, in December the association fully accredited Averett College as a senior college. A five-year odyssey was ending.[35]

Because senior colleges are expensive to operate, President Anderson coupled planning for senior-college status with new initiatives in public relations and fundraising. In 1967 the board of trustees approved the creation of the board of associates. This group of approximately twenty-five professional and business leaders assisted the board of trustees and administration in efforts "to promote the present and future programs of the College."[36] This service involved long-range planning, consultation, fundraising, and public relations. On several occasions the associates were the difference between success and failure in both fundraising and community understanding.[37]

Equally important was the creation of an office to coordinate fundraising, public relations, and alumni affairs. In October 1967, the board of trustees approved creating a development office and hiring Dr.

---

[34] *Chanticleer,* 22 September 1971.

[35] *Chanticleer,* 22 April 1971; Anderson, President's Annual Report, 31 April 1971.

[36] News release, 18 December 1979, Development Office files.

[37] Anderson, President's Annual Report, 20 October 1967; Faculty Minutes, 11 November 1966.

O. Wendell Smith, a former professor of economics of Judson College as director. Smith created an annual fund drive and aggressively pursued support from alumni, parents, foundations, associates, trustees, friends, government, faculty, staff, businesses, civic organizations, and Baptists. He stressed deferred giving and conducted seminars on estate planning so the college could enjoy sustained income. Smith wrote scores of grant proposals to foundations. He spoke to civic, business, and professional groups about the monetary and cultural value of Averett to city, state, and region. His efforts soon began to pay off. Exclusive of funds received from the denomination and various governments, annual contributions to the college increased more than 2,000 percent between Smith's arrival in 1967 and his departure in 1978.[38]

Averett College came to enjoy increased revenue partly through the efforts of Smith and the board of associates and partly through federal aid to education. Because of concerns about separation of church and state, President Bishop had never applied for federal aid. In November 1967, the Baptist General Association of Virginia determined that acceptance of federal aid did not threaten the independence of a denominational college. The following month Anderson persuaded the board of trustees to sign the Assurance of Compliance with the Civil Rights Act of 1964, which was a prerequisite for application. This action effectively integrated the student body. It also enabled the college to apply for and receive for the 1968–1969 session $36,000 in federal student aid through national defense loans, work-study funds, and economic opportunity grants. This money enabled 180 students, representing 28 percent of the student body, to earn a degree. Federal student aid increased from the original $36,000 to almost $1.5 million by 1981–1982. In that academic year more than 500 Averett students, representing 53 percent of the student body, received federal student aid.[39]

By December 1967, Anderson became aware that a number of Baptists were uncomfortable with the compromise to separation of church and state. He was aware also that Averett's relations with its denominational parent had become strained during Bishop's presidency.

---

[38] Ibid.

[39] Howard W. Lee, President's Annual Report, 5 June 1981; Averett Board Minutes, 31 October 1969.

Accordingly, in 1968 Anderson appointed a Ministerial Advisory Committee of twenty influential ministers from central, southside, and southwest Virginia for the primary purpose of interpreting the college to the denomination. Secondarily, they would advise the college on collegiate religious life and plan an annual spring conference for ministers. The conference, it was thought, would give the college an opportunity to show off its faculty, bring up-to-date Baptist speakers of national reputation, and encourage fellowship through a ministers' golf tournament at Danville Golf Club.[40]

The consequent improvement in relations between college and denomination came none too soon. In November 1968, the Committee of Twenty-four, composed of eminent Baptist leaders from throughout the Commonwealth, recommended to the Baptist General Association of Virginia that it gradually discontinue financial support of Averett College and four other denominational schools. The recommendation called for continuation of support to Bluefield College and the University of Richmond. The committee's vice chairman, Howard W. Lee, was minister of West Main Baptist Church adjacent to Averett and a friend of the college. He was, however, in the minority of the committee in wishing to fund programs at all denominational institutions. The majority report contrasted the request by all Baptist schools for $4 million in denominational support with the fact the Baptist General Association had only $4.5 million to spend, not only for schools but two homes for the aged, one home for children, and the *Religious Herald*. Dr. Lee lamented: "To do anything adequate for the schools, we would have to quit everything else and go into the school business."[41] He offered the small consolation that the cutoff would be gradual and federal funds soon would replace Baptist dollars.[42]

The committee's report would have affected more than 6 percent of Averett's annual budget. In October the executive committee of the trustees at Averett labeled the report "unacceptable": "Its discrimination is too unreasonable" and "its consequences are too far-reaching," the committee stated.[43] Thus armed, Anderson and influential trustee W. Curtis English set out to contact Baptist leaders across Virginia to

---

[40] Averett Board Minutes, 15 January 1968.
[41] News clipping, 10 November 1968, Development Office files.
[42] Ibid.
[43] Averett Board Minutes, 14 October 1968.

explain the Averett position. They found allies among supporters of
Virginia Intermont College, Hargrave Military Academy, Fork Union
Military Academy, and Oak Hill Academy—the other four schools slated
to lose financial support. Resulting grassroots opposition defeated the
committee's recommendations when the Baptist General Association
met. Instead, the association adopted the safer formula of funding
programs that contributed to a school's Christian witness, such as
Christian counseling and a department of religion, rather than giving
undesignated grants to schools. Anderson enthusiastically supported this
formula because it retained aid for Averett College and at the same time
softened Averett's sectarian personality. The latter outcome was
desirable because it diminished chances the constitutionality of federal
and state aid to the college would ever be successfully challenged in
court.[44]

With denominational relations secure, the college shifted its focus
inward. The old library in Danville Hall was converted into dormitory
rooms. A 200-car parking lot was constructed on the lower campus at the
corner of Surry Lane and Woodland Drive. Built at a small fraction of its
worth by the paving company of Robert Thompson, a member of the
board of associates, the parking lot solved a perennial and festering
problem with homeowners adjacent to campus. The board of trustees
voted to make dormitory space available for male students in September
1970. However, since Fugate Hall was not ready for occupancy at that
time, female students had to be housed in the male dormitory and male
students in the Hotel Danville. With the hotel over a mile from campus,
the fifteen young men proved impossible to supervise. In the absence of
close control the group soon took predictable risks: female company in
their rooms, alcohol abuse, and a total disregard for curfews.[45] After
completion of Fugate Hall, the male students were moved into Second
Main Hall. But misbehavior came too, and for several weeks the young
men managed to elude dean of students Mary Jo Davis and get into the
women's dorm rooms on Third Main Hall. Dean Davis finally
discovered a concealed stairwell and trap door from the days when these
dormitories were part of the auditorium. Although a carpenter's crew

---

[44] Averett Board Minutes, 31 October 1969.
[45] Averett Board Minutes, 24 April 1970; *1970–1971 Averett Bulletin*, 9; Mary Joan
Davis, interview with author, Averett College, 8 March 1983.

quickly removed the temptation, she spent the rest of the year trying to corral guilty parties.[46]

The faculty, the curriculum, and the schedule also underwent change and improvement. Saturday classes were abolished and an evening college opened. New majors such as law enforcement, social work, and business were added to reflect Averett's continuing commitment to career education grounded on the liberal arts. The college established a chapter of the national honorary fraternity, Alpha Chi, in order to recognize and reward exemplary character and academic excellence among Averett students. The college set up the Reading Center to offer specialized training to students majoring in education and provide diagnostic, tutorial, and corrective services for children in southside Virginia. The academic degree structure changed slightly when the trustees approved the awarding of honorary doctorates.[47] Faculty salaries were raised to a level above the average paid by Baptist colleges and universities in the South, and a faculty study-leave program was instituted to upgrade faculty credentials. As a result, 35 percent of the faculty held earned doctorates by 1972. The faculty was organized into five divisions under rotating division chairs: fine arts, humanities, science and mathematics, social sciences, and professional studies. The board of trustees approved a faculty tenure policy following guidelines laid down by the American Association of University Professors.[48]

The president's difficulty managing capital improvements, denominational relations, fundraising, public relations, and curricular change paled to insignificance beside the difficulty of controlling student behavior during the period from 1966 to 1973. Revolt and change were everywhere as undergraduates participated with vigor in movements to alter society. The civil rights movement and feminism challenged an outmoded and restrictive social structure in place for three centuries. The youth movement, with its insistence that no one over thirty years of age could be trusted, altered both the intellectual and leadership structure.

---

[46] Faculty Minutes, 12 April 1973, 30 August 1973; Anderson, President's Annual Report, 5 May 1972 and 4 May 1973; *Chanticleer*, 9 February 1973.

[47] In 1973 the college awarded the first honorary doctorate to Joseph M. Taylor, the former director of the Danville division of Virginia Polytechnic Institute and later a president of Danville Community College.

[48] See Anderson, President's Annual Report, 20 October 1967, 3 June 1968, 10 May 1969, 13 April 1970, 31 April 1971, 5 May 1972, 4 May 1973.

The peace movement and opposition to the war in Vietnam confronted the American tendency to become involved in the affairs of other nations and settle disagreements through resort to military force. Men demonstrated a youthful disdain for conformity by wearing beards, long hair, sandals, and denim jeans; women burned their bras and wore miniskirts, jeans, and revealing blouses. Destruction of property and seizures of buildings on college campuses nationwide symbolized a disdain for authority. The new sexual revolution—with the Pill, cohabitation, and abortions on demand—showed contempt for traditional sexual mores. Rebellion in the name of spontaneity, honesty, equality, and sensitivity to needs replaced middle-class manners and concern for social status. Radical solutions gained favor over "working within the system."[49]

Yet students at Averett College were more *in* the era of change and revolt than *of* it. Political liberalism and social activism never made much headway. An attempt to establish an Averett chapter of the National Student Lobby (which worked in legislative halls across America for such liberal issues as the Equal Rights Amendment, an end to the war in Vietnam, and mandatory student representation on college boards of trustees) met with no success. By a vote of 369 to 87, Averett students overwhelmingly endorsed Richard Nixon over George McGovern in the presidential election of 1972. The faculty vote of fifteen for Nixon and fifteen for McGovern manifested the only moderate-to-liberal sentiment.[50] While undergraduates on other campuses often made a college president's life miserable, Averett students designated 4 February 1970, as Anderson Appreciation Day. Student-originated and student-led, the celebration began with an assembly in the auditorium where a drama about the president's life was presented, and ended with a dinner for the Andersons and their guests.[51]

Part of the motivation behind this event was the mature way in which the administration at Averett College handled the National Vietnam Moratorium Day on 15 October 1969. While many campuses witnessed confrontations between students and administrative

---

[49] See Tom Wicker, "Arcadia and Aquarius," in *Great Songs of the Sixties,* ed. Milton Okun (New York: New York Times, 1970) 12–14.

[50] News clipping, 2 November 1972, Development Office files; *Chanticleer,* 5 April 1972.

[51] *Chanticleer,* 23 February 1970.

establishments, at Averett College there was mature and responsible discussion. President Anderson suspended classes for the day and scheduled seminars and public forums to discuss America's involvement in Indochina. The day began with students, and even interested parents, meeting in small groups with faculty moderators. History Professor Charles P. Postelle, who chaired a discussion group, recalls how for the first time he became aware of the "generation gap." The parents, most of whom were veterans of World War II, assumed a "my-country-right-or-wrong" attitude. The students, being of an age to be affected by the draft, were more skeptical. A combat veteran himself, Postelle remained neutral but reminded parents that adult memories become dim, noting some of his World War II comrades-at-arms detested the flag-waving jingoism that glossed over horrible realities on the battlefield. Although the moratorium day produced no agreement, all had an opportunity to speak until a student-body assembly in the gymnasium concluded the proceedings.[52]

Perhaps the most familiar image of the 1966–1973 period is the drug scene. The use of drugs was present but never widespread at Averett College. Students were satisfied with beer for informal occasions, mixed drinks for formal ones, or nothing at all. In fact, the major confrontation with the administration during this period involved regulations against drinking on campus. Many students complained that they could vote, pay taxes, and die for their country but were not considered responsible enough to consume alcoholic beverages on the Averett campus. After all, they added, as citizens of the Old Dominion, they could legally purchase and consume beer. A poll of 468 students by the *Chanticleer* in December 1972 revealed 77 percent favored drinking at special campus events, 72 percent wanted a designated area on campus where drinking was allowed, and 55 percent voted for drinking in the dormitories.[53] A mass meeting of students to protest the rules against

---

[52] *Chanticleer*, 31 October 1969; Charles Postelle, interview with author, Averett College, 17 February 1983.

[53] *Chanticleer*, 14 December 1972. An analysis of the views on a day-student–versus–dormitory-student basis reveals the following sentiments: in favor of drinking at special events (82 percent of dormitory students and 71 percent of day students); in favor of a designated area on campus for drinking (77 percent of dormitory students and 63 percent of day students); and in favor of allowing drinking in dormitory rooms (66 percent of dormitory students and 40 percent of day students). Averett Board Minutes, 13 December 1972.

drinking forced the administration and trustees into a dilemma.

Their own personal convictions aside, Anderson and the trustees were aware of the potentially serious consequences of a shift in policy. The University of Richmond had recently dropped its ban against campus drinking, and coupled with public statements on theological matters from liberal professors at the university, the change resulted in negative responses from Baptist churches in Virginia. Specifically, local churches decided to earmark money for use by the Baptist General Association with the stipulation that none of it go to the University of Richmond. With millions of dollars flowing in from pharmaceutical magnate E. Claiborne Robbins, the University of Richmond could afford to be cavalier in its attitude toward Virginia Baptists. Averett College could not. Anderson had worked hard to build stronger denominational relations in his six years at Averett. On the other hand, he respected student opinion and believed students to be responsible individuals. The controversy at Averett ended with a pragmatic trustee decision to reaffirm the policy against drinking on campus, coupled with an equally pragmatic administrative decision not to engage in snooping.[54]

Although Averett students belonged more to the silent majority than the counterculture, they did enjoy the cultural trappings of the 1966–1973 period. Dress styles of the period caught on, more as a result of characteristic youthful rebellion than any attempt to make a political or social statement. The typical male "radical" at Averett College wore faded but laundered jeans and long but shampooed and stylishly combed hair. The music of the period, with its themes of revolution and change, held a particular fascination. Student favorites included "Aquarius," which proclaimed a new age where "peace will guide the planets / and love will steer the stars."[55]

And yet the 1960s also brought environmental degradation, population explosion, and the threat of nuclear destruction. Students began to look not to the future but to the past, when life was simple and problems seemed to have easy solutions, as evoked in the Beatles' ballad, "Yesterday":

---

[54] Averett Board Minutes, 13 December 1972; Anderson interview; Anderson, President's Annual Report, 13 April 1970.

[55] James Rado and Gerome Ragni (words) and Galt MacDermot (music), "Aquarius," in *Great Songs of the Sixties*, 37.

Yesterday, all my troubles seemed so far away,
Now it looks as though they're here to stay,
Oh, I believe in yesterday.[56]

Other songs with less social commentary also were popular at Averett College in the 1960s. The love song remained popular, although it became realistic and ceased to be sentimental. One student favorite was John Denver's "Leaving on a Jet Plane," with its theme of the pain of separation from a lover. One alumna recalled that the song "would always bring tears to our eyes when we sang it in small groups with someone playing a guitar."[57] Folk music continued to be popular. Students liked folk artists Bob Dylan and Peter, Paul, and Mary, whose music dealt with revolution, death, despair, love, injustice, and the futility of war. Black music got a new name in the 1960s: soul, a music described as having "gospel intensity," a "rhythmic freedom and drive," and "real gut emotion."[58] Averett favorites included Otis Redding's "Respect" and "Sittin' on the Dock of the Bay" and James Brown's "Papa's Got a Brand New Bag." Rock music changed in the 1960s but remained the most popular of all the varieties of music at Averett College. The major change was discarding all instrumental accompaniment except an electronically amplified rhythm section—drums, guitar, bass, and keyboards. Averett students "dug" rock music, they "dug" it loud, and they "dug" it by such groups as the Beatles and the Rolling Stones.[59]

To say that Averett students from 1966 to 1973 were more a part of the silent majority than the counterculture is not to suggest that change—much of it student-initiated—was absent from the campus. When Conwell Anderson became president in 1966, rules and regulations were strict. The Honor Code pledged a student not to drink alcoholic beverages and to report other students who did. Dormitory

---

[56] John Lennon and Paul McCartney, "Yesterday," in *Great Songs of the Sixties*, 322–23; see also Wicker, "Arcadia and Aquarius," 14; Mrs. Allen T. Pugh, letter to author , October 1982; Michelle Scott, letter to author, October 1982.

[57] Mrs. Jack A. Mayes, Jr., letter to author , October 1982.

[58] Milton Okun, "The Sixties: Song and Sound," in *Great Songs of the Sixties,* 7.

[59] Ibid., 7–10; James C. Green, letter to author , October 1982; Mrs. George Mahler, letter to author, October 1982 , Mrs. Eduardo J. Trinidad, letter to author, October 1982 , Mrs. Vigen Gurdian, letter to author, October 1982.

students were not allowed to spend the night away from the residence halls except when parents visited the campus. Curfew was 10:00 P.M. Mondays through Thursdays, 11:30 P.M. Fridays and Sundays, and 12:00 midnight on Saturdays. Lights-out every night was 1:00 A.M. Those leaving campus after 7:00 P.M. during weekdays needed the dean's permission and at least two companions. Overnights to other colleges required a written invitation from the hostess in the home where the Averett student would stay. First-year students were limited to three overnights the first semester and four overnights second semester. Students could not keep cars, and those riding in automobiles beyond a ten-mile radius of Danville needed the housemother's approval. First-year students had to double date during their first semester. A rigid dress code specified that "male visitors are required to wear coats and ties at all times."[60] The same code dictated acceptable student dress for class, church, mixers, town, Christmas Dance, Sweetheart Dance, May Day Dance, concerts, forums, dress-up dinners, travel, and even sunbathing on the sunroofs. Attendance was mandatory at chapel, assembly, concerts, forums, dormitory meetings, and weekday meals except breakfast. Housemothers even conducted weekly inspections to ensure rooms were clean and neat.[61]

President Anderson heeded student demands for change. Gradual modifications of the curfew finally culminated in open hours for senior women and all men in 1971. Gradual modification of the dress code for campus visitors finally gave way to "anything goes" in 1971. Similarly, by 1970 the dress code for Averett students specified "neat jeans"—but disallowed "grubby jeans." The distinction between "neat" and "grubby" was so subjective that the administration gave up trying to dictate fashion altogether in 1971–1972 and stated simply: "Averett College students…are expected to dress in a manner suited to the occasion and to the place."[62] In 1968 Anderson removed drinking from the Honor Code and altered the no-drinking policy so the prohibition applied only on campus and to college-sponsored activities. Also in 1968 he allowed students to keep automobiles on campus. Required attendance at chapel, which was reduced from two days a week in 1968 to one day a week in

---

[60] *Averett Student Handbook, 1966–1967,* 33. [*Student Handbook?*]

[61] Ibid., 14, 27–35, 41–43.

[62] *Averett Student Handbook Student Handbook, 1971–1972,* 28; Linda Hawks Walker, letter to author, October 1982.

1970, was made voluntary in 1971.[63]

Other modifications accompanied changes in rules and regulations. In the late 1960s, the appearance of Libra Day (replacing May Day) announced that Averett was adopting traditions more appropriate to a co-educational senior college. Held on a Saturday in mid-October, Libra Day featured an outdoor carnival on the athletic field where each class and organization set up booths to sell food and beverages or offer games of skill or chance. A picnic in late afternoon and an informal dance in the evening climaxed the day's activities. Moreover, in 1971 the male population had grown large enough to support a local fraternity, Lambda Phi Omega. In 1973 another was added, Kappa Sigma Phi. The "frats" hosted parties, sponsored sweethearts, "rushed" freshmen, held Byzantine initiation rites, and raised money for charitable projects. Also in 1971 the old library in the basement of Bishop Hall was converted into a student center, named by students "the B.I." for Bottom Inn. Students met there to munch burgers at the grill; try their skills at billiards, table tennis, and foosball; pick up mail; watch *Happy Days, M.A.S.H., The Young and the Restless,* and *All My Children* on television; play hearts, spades, or Spite and Malice; or just chat about the school year.[64]

By mid-1973, Averett College had progressed further in the previous seven years than in any other definable period in history. The junior college had given way to the senior college. The former women's college was now co-educational. Reflecting the growing bureau-cratization of American colleges in the 1960s, the skeletal administration of Curtis Bishop gave way to Connie Anderson and a host of registrars, deans, coordinators, and directors. Enrollment increased more than 80

---

[63] *1967–1968 Student Handbook*, 14, 16, 18, 23; *1968–1969 Student Handbook*, pages not numbered; *1969–1970 Student Handbook*, 20–28; *1970–1971 Student Handbook*, 19–22; *1971–1972 Student Handbook*, 20–29; *1972–1973 Student Handbook*, 20–29.

[64] The Big Spot became the College Bookstore, while the Baby Spot became the Trustees Dining Room (*Chanticleer*, 26 January 1972, 13 October 1972, 7 December 1973); Carolyn E. Odenheimer, letter to author , October 1982; Christine Riley Bettencourt, letter to author, October 1982; Bridus G. Voss, letter to author, October 1982; Alger Robbins, letter to author, October 1982; Jane L. Owen, letter to author, October 1982; Polly Milliner Ransome, letter to author, October 1982; Mrs. Leo A. Napoleon, letter to author, October 1982; Dorothy M. Putney, letter to author, October 1982; Mrs. Hylah Horton Lohr, letter to author, October 1982; D. Fred Willis, letter to author, October 1982.

percent, to 1,024 students. A new dormitory, a new library, and a new fine arts building expanded the physical facilities. The evening college and Reading Center inaugurated a new era in community service. An innovative calendar and functional curriculum of liberal arts and career education provided an educational experience of high quality. A new office of Institutional Development and federal student aid guaranteed sustained revenue. Academic freedom and faculty tenure were firmly established. Averett's Christian heritage and concern for the individual was retained and even highlighted. Finally, the century-old promise of academic excellence at the baccalaureate level in a Christian setting was being fulfilled.

11

Conwell Anderson's "Second Term,"
1973–1979

Although establishment of the senior college temporarily completed the educational evolution of Averett College, the institution lacked maturity by 1973, the halfway point in Anderson's presidency. Absent were senior college traditions, institutional self-confidence, a loyal body of senior college alumni, a permanent and stable faculty, a flexible but finished curriculum, clarification of institutional mission, and a definition of institutional identity. Between 1973 and 1979 the college acquired these things, and academic adulthood was achieved at last. Yet these six years were a period of failure as well as achievement. President Anderson, who seemed to have a Midas touch during the first half of his presidency, saw his hopes for a union with Stratford College and a new campus for Averett College evaporate during the second half. Stratford instead closed; Averett proved unable to raise $9 million required to relocate the institution to land donated by Dan River Mills; and the same president who energetically participated in student, faculty, and civic life during his first six years in Danville was laid low by a heart attack and finally forced by poor health to resign.

The 1973–1974 academic year began as one of the most hopeful in history. Averett and Stratford coordinated their academic programs with a view toward possible union. Stratford College was an excellent institution with a history as interesting and significant as Averett's. Founded in 1854, the Methodist-affiliated school was located at the corner of Loyal Street and Tazewell Alley, not far from the first site of Averett. Although curricular offerings at the two schools bore a close resemblance, the Methodist institution had always displayed fewer resiliencies in hard times. Reconstruction caused it to close in 1876. Seven years later it reopened as Danville College for Young Ladies on fashionable Main Street. After a decade the depression years of the 1890s forced the trustees to recognize their inability to maintain facilities necessary for a first-class collegiate education. Accordingly, they transferred ownership and control to the Randolph-Macon school system within the Methodist Church, which already oversaw two colleges and two preparatory schools. The Danville College for Young Ladies thus became Randolph-Macon Institute, the third preparatory school in the system. In the late 1920s, when the trustees of the Randolph-Macon system decided to close the school, several Danvillians bought it, renamed it Stratford, and created a four-year preparatory school (Stratford Hall) and a two-year junior college (Stratford College).[1] The connection with the Methodist church ceased, and Stratford became a private, nondenominational institution.

Strong leaders have a way of altering an institution's history. In 1963 W. Hugh Moomaw became president of Stratford College. A graduate of Washington and Lee University (B.A.) and the University of Virginia (M.A. and Ph.D.), Moomaw taught history at Randolph-Macon College in Ashland before heading the Fulbright Scholarship Program in England. As president of Stratford College, he launched an ambitious building program that resulted in the construction of five major buildings in six years and a sixth building four years later. More importantly, he pushed the school toward senior-college status and higher standards. In 1964 Stratford discontinued Stratford Hall, and in 1966 the institution decided to become a senior college with plans to admit a junior class in 1967 and award bachelor's degrees in 1969. Although enrollment shot up from 250 students in 1963–1964 to 566 students in 1968–1969, it plummeted to 320 students in 1973–1974. A recent decision by the University of Virginia to admit undergraduate women partially dried up the pool of female applicants at Stratford, which unwisely had chosen to remain a single-sex institution. This decline in Stratford's enrollment prompted the college to undertake a serious reevalution.[2]

Anderson and Moomaw first discussed coordination between the

---

[1] Robert Russell Neely, "A History of the Private Secondary Schools of Danville, Virginia" (master's thesis, University of Virginia, 1938) 181–245; Alvin L. Hall, *The History of Stratford College* (Danville VA: Womack Press, 1974) 30ff.

[2] Hall, *Stratford*, 61–65.

two schools in 1970–1971. The next year they initiated a series of logical and limited steps by sharing two faculty members and the two libraries. They designated 1973–1974 as a transitional year leading to eventual union or confederation, during which the two student bodies used both campuses for courses, meals, research, and fraternization. Buses ran between the campuses every fifteen minutes. Coordination seemed to students a natural course of action, since only six blocks separated the two schools and since Averett had the larger student body, while Stratford had the larger physical plant.

Indeed, to cost-conscious administrators, coordination aiming toward confederation offered many advantages. Combining faculties would strengthen both institutions by eliminating duplication, which would allow for a reduction in sixteen faculty positions for an immediate savings of $150,000 over a two-year period. Because of Stratford's declining enrollment, tentative plans called for it to terminate twelve faculty positions at once for a savings of $122,950, while Averett lost two faculty members by retirement and two by nonrenewal of contract. Similar savings would accrue from combining all purchasing, maintenance, housekeeping, accounting, record-keeping, and infirmary, student, and library services. Caught in a pattern of declining enrollment and an inability to maintain facilities or liquidate debt on its projected income, Stratford needed Averett's increasing enrollment. Too cautious to go into debt in order to expand, Averett needed Stratford's excellent facilities and wide array of academic majors.[3]

Great as the benefits were, there were still problems. For students who insisted on parking next door to the building in which they attended classes, six blocks seemed like six miles. In addition, Averett's curricular philosophy was based as much on career education as on the liberal arts, while Stratford's was based almost entirely on the latter. Not only was there a long-standing rivalry between the two student bodies, but also each faculty considered itself far superior to the other and suspected that the other school's primary motive for coordination was mercenary.

---

[3] Copy of memorandum from Dean O. Lawrence Burnette to President W. H. Moomaw, 28 May 1974, file titled "Coordination Averett Stratford," Averett University Archives, hereinafter cited as Coordination file; Kenneth R. Erfft, Report to the Board of Trustees of Averett College and of Stratford College, Coordination file; Faculty Minutes, 22 February 1973, 1–3; Conwell A. Anderson, memorandum to the Executive Committee of the Board of Trustees, 19 February 1973, Coordination file.

Interscholastic faculty relations and meetings were not always cordial. Another issue was the future structure of the coordinated or confederated institution. Although never finalized by the two presidents nor agreed upon by their boards, tentative plans called for one faculty under Averett's dean, Kirby Godsey, one office of development under Averett's Wendell Smith, and one business office under Averett's Ralph Door. So far as the office of president was concerned, Anderson advised Moomaw he did not expect to step aside. Thus, the prominence of Averett personnel in the future confederated institution posed problems for Stratford partisans. Moreover, the nomenclature of the corporation to manage the new creation was a stumbling block. Moomaw preferred the Stratford-Averett Foundation for Education, while Anderson liked the College of Averett-Stratford. In a humorous gesture, Averett history professor Charles P. Postelle moved in a faculty meeting that the Stratford preference be used on odd days and the Averett preference on even ones.[4]

Yet the major points of contention were financial. Anderson and Moomaw could never agree on a formula for cost and profit sharing. As early as autumn 1973, Anderson recognized that "the prospect of anything other than a further decline in dormitory enrollment next year [at Stratford] would appear to border on the miraculous." Therefore, he warned his board of trustees, "We must not make any agreement in which our financial resources are used to underwrite their possible insolvency."[5]

Since Stratford College was in a poorer financial situation than anyone realized, confederation soon became a dead issue. Historian Alvin Hall wrote:

> The beginning of the end came in February 1974, with the revelation that the college needed to raise $300,000 just to operate through the end of May. If the college did not make that total and recruit a minimum of 260 students for 1974–1975, Stratford would be unable to open in August.[6]

---

[4] Faculty Minutes, 20 March 1973, 1, 7 March 1974, 1–2; Conwell A. Anderson, Memorandum 19 February 1973, Coordination file; Anderson interview.

[5] Conwell A. Anderson to William H. Jefferson et al., October 1973, Conwell A. Anderson papers, Averett University Archives.

[6] Hall, *Stratford*, 68.

The students, faculty, and alumni of Stratford College launched a heroic effort to save the school. They were able to raise enough money to graduate the senior class in May 1974. Nevertheless, Stratford College was a victim of too few students and too much debt. Enrollment declined 43 percent between 1968 and 1974. Each decline in enrollment triggered an increase in tuition, which triggered another decline in enrollment. The national trend away from single-sex institutions made recruiting difficult. Stratford's ambitious building program saddled the college with a debt of $1.5 million; monthly debt service alone amounted to $14,000. Unable to raise the few hundred thousand dollars necessary for opening in August free of debts other than the mortgage, Stratford closed permanently on 28 June 1974. Almost immediately Memorial Hospital bought the property.[7]

The attempt at coordination and subsequent failure of Stratford had important repercussions for Averett. Anderson and his subordinates sincerely wanted coordination to succeed. Even though Stratford would have profited the most, Averett still stood to benefit. Several private foundations that funded innovative programs in higher education were considering grants to aid the Averett-Stratford coordination in order to provide a national model of educational efficiency and effectiveness. Thus, instead of gloating over Stratford's demise, President Anderson regretted the lost opportunities. Yet the regret was secondary to the difficulties, frustrations, and disagreements inherent in Anderson's protracted negotiations with Stratford, his long days of administering Averett, his long nights of planning for Averett-Stratford, and his feeling of helplessness as he watched the death of a concept that held so much promise. All of this took a heavy toll on President Anderson's health. Senior faculty members at Averett recall that the experience of coordination aged President Anderson as no other experience in his presidency. Gone were the heady success, halcyon days, and easy victories of his first six years.[8]

Certainly, Averett College benefited in the short term. Three days after Stratford announced it would close, President Anderson invited each Stratford student to transfer to Averett. He promised automatic

[7] *Greensboro [N.C.] Daily News*, 30 June 1974, A-11, Hall, *Stratford*, 68; Faculty Minutes, 12 February 1974, 2; Anderson interview.

[8] Anderson interview; Mary Joan Davis, interview, 13 April 1983; Ausband interview; Brachman interview.

admission, acceptance of all credits with grades of D or above, and
graduation from Averett under degree requirements in the Stratford
catalog. Ninety-six students accepted his offer. Most were seniors, but
for at least a year the Stratford contingent not only enhanced the flavor of
student life by participating in plays, concerts, art exhibits, and
intramural sports; they also added needed revenue to the college budget.[9]

Stratford's death also shocked Danville, and the saddened
community grew more aware of Averett's importance and more attentive
to Averett's needs. Averett College, as Danville's only remaining senior
college, became increasingly the de facto city college of Danville,
although without an official connection. Averett saw in Stratford's
demise a cautionary tale confirming its own policy of avoiding financial
gambles, aggressively recruiting potential students and financial support,
and focusing on a curriculum that emphasized quality and career
education. Inside Averett, the vice president for development and the
director of admissions quickly became members of the inner circle of
administrators. For Stratford's convenience in 1973, Averett adopted
Stratford's 4-1-4-1-1 academic calendar, which quickly proved to be so
flexible and popular that Averett was glad to retain it. This new Averett
Option encouraged such innovative educational experiences as study
abroad in the one-month January term when travel rates were cheapest.[10]

After Stratford's demise, Averett also picked up Stratford's interest
in horsemanship and developed a program in equestrian studies leading
to a baccalaureate degree. Offering both instruction and experience in
riding, training, teaching, and stable management, the program prepared
students for careers with breeding farms, training centers, show and hunt
stables, and private programs in horsemanship. The classroom and field
experience was rigorous. In addition to general education requirements in
the liberal arts and sciences, students mastered zoology, human anatomy,
physiology, kinesiology, small business management, and a host of
equestrian and related business courses. The program quickly achieved a
regional reputation for excellence. In 1978 the Averett team placed
second in annual competition of the National Riding Committee. Later
that year it won first place in the International Intercollegiate Riding

---

[9] Copy of unaddressed letter, 25 June 1974, Anderson papers.
[10] Faculty Minutes, 22 February 1973, 1–3, 28–29 August 1974, 2; Anderson interview.

Competition at Potsdam, New York. Riding against Averett were teams from Bermuda, Canada, the Netherlands, West Germany, Great Britain, and Switzerland, in addition to other American teams.[11]

The addition of horsemanship to the curriculum was indicative of Averett's receptivity to innovation within a framework of liberal arts and career education. So, too, were a new master's program in education, an evening college, and majors in social work, special education, and English/journalism. To emphasize the academic character of athletics, an intercollegiate athletic program was developed as a discipline within the Division of Natural Sciences. Effective 1 March 1976, Averett joined the Dixie Intercollegiate Athletic Conference of the National Collegiate Athletic Association. Competing in eight sports—men's golf, men's soccer, women's field hockey, co-educational riding, men's and women's basketball, and men's and women's tennis—the Averett Cougars quickly became a respected competitor, if not a dominant power. In 1978 the Averett men's basketball team finished second in the conference. In 1979 and 1980 the soccer teams won both conference and state championships.

However, not all curricular changes met with unanimous support of the faculty, which had to approve curricular additions. President Anderson described his approach to such matters with the word "boldness," meaning innovations to ensure that the college would serve needs in the decades ahead. "Boldness" found friends among the faculty when it meant new majors in mathematics/management, English/drama, English/journalism, and management/psychology, and when it meant establishment of a graduate program. "Boldness" found fewer friends when it meant changing the Department of Religion and Philosophy into the Department of Christian Studies. Faculty approval of this move came only after a lengthy discussion of whether this change involved any desertion of the liberal arts. "Boldness" found many critics when it meant an administrative decision to phase out the unprofitable foreign languages major. Some critics were displeased with what they perceived to be an abandonment of the liberal arts; others, that faculty approval had not been sought for discarding a major.[12]

---

[11] Catalogue supplement titled *Equestrian Studies* [1978]; News release, 6 September 1978, Development Office files.

[12] Faculty Minutes, 28–29 August 1974, 20 November 1975, 1; Anderson, President's Annual Report, 30 May 1975, 28 May 1976, 27 May 1977; Lee, President's

Nevertheless, Averett's evolving curriculum was a major factor in stabilizing enrollment in the last half of Anderson's presidency. In 1973–1979, enrollment fluctuated only slightly between 1,050 and 1,100 students. Since annual budgets were figured at fewer than 1,050 students, the college avoided the embarrassment of operating at a deficit.[13]

The smoothness with which the college was able to conduct its financial affairs carried over into denominational relations and campus religious life. In 1973 the Reverend Kirkland H. Lashley came to Danville as director of campus ministries for the Virginia Baptist General Board. His responsibilities included shepherding Baptist and other Christian students at all institutions of higher learning in the city. A youthful thirty-four years of age, Lashley possessed qualities of an ideal campus minister. Always available and a good listener, he was a good counselor with whom students felt comfortable discussing problems. He helped them reconcile fundamentalist backgrounds with historical and scientific scholarship. Under Lashley's encouragement the Baptist Student Union emerged as a dynamic campus organization. With participation as the only qualification for membership, the BSU claimed approximately a hundred supporters and sixty members every year during his six-year tenure. In addition to Thursday meetings at West Main Baptist Church, BSU activities included freshman orientation, weekly Bible study, folk teams, choral groups, big brother/big sister care for needy youngsters, visits to prison farms and detention homes, and a summer missions program that sent one member to Israel as a camp nurse and other members to beaches and tourist areas as evangelists.[14]

Lashley's arrival coincided with a change in relationship between Averett College and its parent denomination. In 1973 the General Assembly of Virginia created the Tuition Assistance Loan Program to help Virginia students in private colleges in the Old Dominion. To remain consistent with Virginia's tradition of separating church and state, the legislature decreed that only students who attended nonsectarian colleges were eligible. Three changes in Averett's charter were necessary to qualify. A provision giving the leadership of the Baptist General Association of Virginia the right to vote on matters affecting college real

---

Annual Report, 30 May 1980.

[13] See Anderson, President's Annual Reports, 1973–1979.

[14] Kirk Lashley, Annual Report to President Conwell Anderson, 29 April 1977, Averett University Archives.

estate had to be deleted. So did the requirement that 70 percent of the trustees be members of churches in the Baptist General Association. And finally, the number of trustees nominated by the association to Averett's self-perpetuating board of trustees could not be more than one-third. Other Baptist colleges in Virginia long since altered their charters in these respects; and in fact, if not on paper, the Baptist leadership had for some time simply nominated trustees recommended to them by President Anderson.[15]

Nevertheless, Anderson feared Baptists might view changes in the charter as an attempt to sever a precious historic relationship and alter a long-standing religious commitment. Though the threat was probably more imagined than real, the recent collapse of Stratford and the endemic risk of demagoguery in fundamentalist circles made President Anderson cautious. He had the board of trustees make the necessary charter changes and then mounted a gigantic educational effort to convince Baptists that only the words, and not the mission of the institution, were altered. The effort paid off. Averett secured state aid and also retained denominational support. The increasing importance of state aid bore out the wisdom of changes to the charter. In 1981, state aid to more than 550 Averett students totaled $402,176, a figure representing 20 percent of all student aid and almost 10 percent of the total institutional budget.[16]

In 1975–1976 President Anderson took stock of Averett's progress after a decade of his leadership. Enrollment had doubled; the proportion of professors with the Ph.D. degree had increased to 43 percent; and the school had awarded 1,300 baccalaureate degrees. Also, the valuation of campus properties had doubled, the operating budget had tripled, and grant and gift support had increased fourfold. The growth came largely from the driving leadership of the president. But these hard-won victories began to take their toll on his health. In autumn 1975, while en route to a presidential inauguration at Virginia Polytechnic Institute, President Anderson suffered what he believed to be a bout of influenza but turned out to be a heart attack. His condition required cardiac bypass surgery at

---

[15] Anderson interview.

[16] Conwell A. Anderson, "Observations Regarding the Charter Changes Made at Averett College, 9 October 1974," "Reports and Papers to the Virginia Baptist General Board, 1918–1979," Averett University Archives, hereinafter cited as Reports to Baptist Board; Anderson, President's Annual Report, 24 May 1974; 1975 Self-Study, 80; Lee, President's Annual Report, 5 June 1981.

Duke University in March 1976. Back at the helm by spring commencement, he was presented with a Lenox bicentennial bowl by the faculty as a gesture of support and appreciation for his ten years of leadership. Yet he never fully recovered from the effects of heart attack and surgery, which rendered his leadership less dynamic during his last four years.[17]

President Anderson's "second administration" began and ended in disappointment: it opened with the ill-fated plan to merge with Stratford and closed with the failure of Averett's new relocation plans to generate interest and enthusiasm among potential donors. After months of careful and detailed study by both the administration and executive committee of the board, on 14 October 1977, the board of trustees agreed that the existing seventeen-acre campus simply was not large enough to provide physical facilities commensurate with Averett's expanding academic and athletic programs. Educational consultant R. Orin Cornett, formerly connected with the Southern Baptist Convention and later with the US Department of Health, Education, and Welfare, recommended complete relocation over partial expansion into the surrounding residential areas, which would be piecemeal, expensive, and contentious. Board chairman William H. Jefferson, Jr., appointed committees to identify sites and select architects and campus planners. The committee in charge of site selection refused to rule out sites in other localities. In fact, a trustee from South Hill, Virginia, purportedly pledged $1 million if the college relocated there. An unauthorized newspaper account of this rumor so upset Danvillians that Anderson had to turn much of his time to allaying their fears. Speculation ended on 17 November 1978, when Dan River Mills offered 112 acres of land located on Route 29 two and one-half miles south of the present campus. Bordered by the Dan River on the north, Route 29 on the south, Country Club Parkway on the east, and River Oak Drive on the west, the site was a beautiful forest with rolling hills and hardwood timber.[18]

The college announced plans to relocate there in three phases. Phase One, with a completion date of 1982, involved four academic buildings,

---

[17] Faculty Minutes, 13 May 1976, 2; Anderson interview.

[18] News release, 14 October 1977, 17 November 1978, Development Office files; Anderson, President's Annual Report, 2 June 1978; R. Orin Cornett, "Report on the Advisability and Feasibility of a New Campus for Averett College," 29 July 1977, Averett University Archives.

the administrative building, and the student center. Projected costs were approximately $9 million. Phase Two, scheduled for completion in 1984, involved the physical education facilities. During the first two phases boarding students would use dormitories, dining facilities, and the library on the old campus and commute to classes and athletic events on the new one. Phase Three, with a completion date of 1988, entailed completion of dormitories and new library. In 1978 dollars, the entire cost of all three phases was $26 million. Unfortunately, inflation, business recession, and a conviction that colleges should spend money for programs instead of bricks and mortar, combined with fears that a projected nationwide decline in enrollment in the 1980s would disrupt higher education, kept potential donors at arm's length.[19]

Understandably, between 1976 and 1978, President Anderson spent most of his time on matters pertaining to campus relocation. Yet hours spent planning for relocation meant time not spent with faculty and its concerns about institutional life and direction. Some faculty feared that abolition of the French major implied a slackening emphasis on the liberal arts. Many were disturbed by recent changes in the tenure policy that might threaten academic freedom.[20] Others were concerned about long-range curricular planning, begun in 1977–1978. Although they realized how necessary and important such planning was, the faculty

---

[19] News release, 17 November 1978, Development Office files; *Chanticleer*, 13 December 1978. Despite the failure of relocation, the college did expand its physical facilities during the last half of Conwell Anderson's presidency. In 1977 retiring trustee W. Curtis English purchased for the college the two-story Jordan house at the corner of West Main and Robertson Streets adjacent to the Averett campus. The college used this majestic American foursquare with Doric portico as the admissions office. This purchase was further indication of the college's interest in preserving and using the historic houses on West Main Street. In 1969 the college purchased for the Department of Fine arts a three-story Queen Anne house adjacent to the future site of the Blount Library. The department painted the exterior of the structure in keeping with color schemes popular in 1890 when the house was built.

[20] In 1976 President Anderson asked for a redefinition of the college tenure policy in order to define the condition of financial exigency under which a tenured faculty member could be dismissed. Anderson and several trustees believed that Stratford's lack of flexibility in this regard had prevented that college from reducing the size of its faculty, thus hastening the school's demise. Accordingly, Anderson charged a faculty committee under Dean Godsey to prepare a statement defining financial exigency. The resulting definition was grudgingly accepted by the faculty, who did not want a groundswell among trustees for abolishing tenure—yet at least one division and two departments refused to sign the statement of acceptance.

objected strongly when President Anderson relegated it to a junior administrator with neither background nor experience in curricular affairs and to whom they were not accountable. Many faculty were concerned that they did not have a forum where issues and matters relating only to faculty could be discussed openly and frankly. All were hurt by the unexpected resignation of Dean Kirby Godsey in early 1977 and perhaps looked for someone to blame. Godsey, who left to become dean and later president of Mercer University, was a man of charm, charisma, political acumen, wisdom, and statesmanship. His departure was cushioned only by Anderson's appointment of Malcom W. Huckabee, the popular chairman of the Division of Social Science, as dean.[21]

Faculty activism, which spread across America in the 1960s but bypassed Averett due to its preoccupation with the move to senior-college status, emerged in 1977–1978. Faculty members began holding weekly meetings to draw up a constitution, affirming their hopes for the college. The document defined the term "teaching faculty," instituted separate teaching-faculty meetings, and created an elected six-member council whose responsibilities included appointment of faculty members to the college's standing committees and interpretation of faculty concerns to the administration. With President Anderson's acquiescence, the board of trustees approved this constitution. Anderson recognized there had been and would be honest disagreements over principles between president and faculty. He even expressed the belief that giving faculty a more prominent role in institutional life probably would relieve frustrations and contribute to smoother administration. Future harmony bore out the wisdom of his decision.[22]

Despite the rewards of a college presidency, Conwell Anderson concluded by spring 1978 that he should resign. Still a young man at fifty-two years of age, he enjoyed the challenges of office. He had spent most of his professional life in college administration and half of that at Averett College. Nevertheless, since the bypass surgery in 1976 had not brought complete recovery, his cardiologist recommended a less demanding and tension-filled profession. Anderson might have remained president if the college had not faced internal and external problems of

---

[21] See Anderson, President's Annual Report, 2 June 1978.

[22] Ibid; "Constitution of the Averett College Teaching Faculty," Averett University Archives.

greater magnitude than he had strength. Specifically, the decision to relocate the campus demanded a vigorous fundraiser as leader. On 13 December 1978, he submitted his resignation, declaring that to ignore his physical limitations "would be harmful for Averett and for me."[23] With great regret the board accepted his resignation, effective 30 June 1979, named as acting president his assistant, Howard W. Lee, and began a search for a permanent replacement.[24]

Conwell Anderson was certainly the most significant leader in Averett's history to 1979. If Averett had not become a senior college, the institution would not have survived in an era when many institutions that resisted change became defunct because of competition with public community colleges. Without a career-oriented curriculum grounded firmly on the liberal arts, Averett's appeal to prospective students would have diminished. Anderson aggressively and successfully courted the two elements to institutional survival: donors and Baptists. The college earned a reputation for academic strength and progressiveness as Anderson assembled a faculty dedicated to instructional excellence and curricular innovation. A final significant contribution was his campaign to relocate the institution. Although ultimately unsuccessful, the campaign illustrated Anderson's determination to provide excellence in facilities as well as in academics and student life.

Anderson left a college that would be the envy of many college presidents. Under his leadership Averett totally altered its nature and mission but without losing qualities of friendliness, concern for the individual, and attention to humane values. Under his leadership the college reemphasized community orientation and became the only senior college within a radius of fifty miles. During the Anderson presidency it built Fugate Hall and Mary B. Blount Library, opened a reading center, and acquired a fine arts building, an admissions building, and an apartment complex on Mountain View Avenue. The institution awarded 1,993 baccalaureate degrees, increased the library holdings from approximately 12,000 to 57,000 volumes, and placed more than 500 graduates in teaching positions in the Old Dominion. The college doubled its enrollment, quintupled its operating budget, and upgraded faculty

---

[23] *Pendulum*, 1979, 23.
[24] Averett Board Minutes, 13 December 1978, 23 May 1979; Anderson interview.

credentials so that 43 percent of the faculty held earned doctorates.[25]

During the Anderson presidency, the curriculum and the procedure for curricular change became the province of the faculty. Additions to the curriculum originated in the five divisions, followed by dean's council approval and consideration by the full faculty.[26] The five divisions also had responsibility for routine administration of the curriculum. In 1978 the Division of Business Administration, the largest in the college, administered seven areas of specialization with 252 student majors. However, all divisions had respectable numbers. The second largest, Education, had 184 students seeking teacher certification. Mathematics and Natural Sciences followed closely with 181 student majors; Social Sciences had 172; Humanities and Fine Arts, 120. Throughout the college the career-oriented programs were the most popular. In the three divisions of Mathematics and Natural Sciences, Social Sciences, and Humanities and Fine Arts, the most popular majors were, respectively, equestrian studies, social work, and English/journalism.[27]

President Anderson also left a college whose leisure-time and academic pursuits complemented one another to develop what holistic educators called "the whole person". Just as academic pursuits involved a search for truth in a milieu of freedom of inquiry, so student life involved a search for identity and wholeness in a milieu of freedom of action within mutually accepted and reasonably based guidelines. Leisure time at Averett College in 1979 promoted social growth through plentiful opportunities in recreation, athletics, theater, music, student government, and student publications. Jane or Joe College might spend Monday discharging duties as a class officer, serving as a member of the judicial board with jurisdiction over social code violations, and auditioning for the Averett Players, the student drama group. Tuesday might be spent reporting, writing, editing, or doing layout for *Chanticleer,* the *Pendulum,* or the *Ember,* playing intramural sports, and raising funds for a local charity under the auspices of the Averett

---

[25] See Anderson, President's Annual Reports, 1967–1979. The apartment building on Mountain View Avenue was a gift from Sue Leggett Miller, class of 1959.

[26] The Dean's Council was composed of the academic dean, the five division chairs, the librarian, and two at-large faculty members. Membership was fluid, since division chairs rotated within the divisions every four years.

[27] Catalogue supplement titled *Business Administration* [1978]; Peggy Aron, "Number of Students by Major, 1976–1983," typescript, Averett Registrar's Office.

chapters of Circle K or Jaycees. Wednesday was perfect for political activity as an Averett Young Republican, planning the next fraternity party, or joining friends at the "Snake Pit" on Piney Forest Road for an evening of refreshments. Thursday might bring the BSU luncheon meeting, cheerleader practice, and dinner at the president's house for members of the President's Council. Friday was suitable for a statewide business conference under the auspices of the Averett Chapter of the Society for the Advancement of Management, an Alpha Chi banquet, and a play by the drama department. Saturday might be spent at an Averett Singers' concert, an afternoon intercollegiate soccer game, or an evening dance. After morning worship and possibly an afternoon equestrian competition at Grenadier Farm, Sunday became a day of reflection and stocktaking, which offered Joe or Jane an opportunity to count up the number of classes missed during the week and plan for graduation in the distant future. Any free time on Sunday could be allotted to fourteen other clubs, courts, and councils on campus.[28]

Black student life blossomed during these years. After the trustees signed the Assurance of Compliance with the Civil Rights Act of 1964 and appealed to students of all races, black students eagerly applied for admission. By 1972–1973 black students staged an annual Black Studies Week in February, featuring guest speakers and performers such as the Harambee Dancers from Virginia State College. In October 1973, black students organized Black Leaders of Averett College (BLAC) to guide their affairs, promote interracial understanding, develop black student leadership, and stimulate black awareness. The following year a black student, Paula Simms, was selected as Averett's princess for Virginia's annual Apple Blossom Festival.[29]

The only incident in student life President Anderson preferred to forget came in March 1974 when streaking, or nude racing, became a national craze. Inspired by a "Lone Streaker" at the University of Northern Colorado who was attired only in Lone Ranger mask and cowboy hat as he raced through the student center shouting, "Off, off and away," Averett students decided to make their college the first in Virginia to field streakers. One evening in early March, the celebrants at a birthday party removed all clothing, donned black capes, and raced

---

[28] See *1979–1980 Catalogue*, 34–37.
[29] *Chanticleer*, 26 October 1973, 8 March 1974.

back and forth across campus. The next evening the Danville police were called to direct traffic when local residents turned out to view an anticipated repeat performance. Several commentators tried to explain this nationwide phenomenon. Some saw it as a campus rite akin to the panty raid, others as a reaction against rigorous demands of the reform movements in the 1960s. Whatever its explanation, streaking at Averett College was a statement by students that henceforth they must be counted in the mainstream of collegiate life in America.[30]

The 1970s was an easier decade for students than the 1960s. Gone were severe demands for reform. In their place was the Me Decade, encouraging self-centeredness, designer clothing, good manners, and career fulfillment. It seemed safe to trust students once again. Curfews, dating restrictions, overnight restrictions, and sign-in/sign-out requirements disappeared at Averett College. An Open House policy allowed male and female students to visit each other's rooms on certain days.[31] Students enjoyed television programs that glorified youth but usually avoided moral dilemmas or social comment: *Happy Days, Donny and Marie, The Love Boat, Fantasy Island, Mork and Mindy,* and reruns of *The Andy Griffith Show* and *Hogan's Heroes.* Also popular were *The Waltons* and *Little House on the Prairie,* purveyors of traditional American values.[32]

The music Averett students enjoyed in the 1970s was a continuation of music from the 1960s. Soul music, folk music, the Nashville Sound, and electric rock remained popular. Disco music, which emphasized melody and rhythm over lyrics, sprang from rock. Favorite rock artists at Averett included Bread, Three Dog Night, Jackson Browne, Styx, Fleetwood Mac, Rod Stewart with "Maggie May," Bruce Springsteen with "Born to Run," and Linda Ronstadt with "It's So Easy." Favorite disco artists included the Bee Gees with "More Than a Woman" and "Jive Talkin'" and Rick Dees with "Disco Duck." Favorite folk and Nashville Sound songs included "Take Me Home, Country Roads" and

---

[30] *Chanticleer,* 22 March 1974, Mary Joan Davis, interview, 13 April 1983.

[31] *Student Handbook* 1973–1974, 30; 1974–1975, 26; 1975–1976; 1976–1977; 1977–1978.

[32] Letter to author from: Carol Diane Blosser, October 1982; Martha Salley, October 1982; Sarah Ann Wood, October 1982; Johncie L. Flannagan, October 1982; Howard G. Todd, October 1982; Debra Sue Doolittle, October 1982; Marsha K. Flora, October 1982; Gerald D. Boone, Jr., October 1982; Randy James Richardson, October 1982; Mrs. Franklin Lee Tolbert, October 1982; Mrs. Kim Crawford Love, October 1982; Patricia Carol Boyd, October 1982

"Thank God I'm a Country Boy" by John Denver and "The South's Gonna Do It Again" by the Charlie Daniels Band. Interestingly, the South and country life, glorified by such songs of the 1970s, had been objects of vilification in the previous decade.[33]

Unlike the 1960s, songs of the 1970s avoided social comment. Instead, they often focused on romantic love and personal relationships. Averett students liked Billy Joel's "Just the Way You Are," Debbie Boone's "You Light Up My Life," James Taylor's "You've Got a Friend," and the Carpenters' "We've Only Just Begun." The piece by Billy Joel was a simple ballad in which a young man assures his lover she need not change to please him. The song by the Carpenters described a couple in a new relationship looking forward with confidence to the future. How different these songs were from songs of protest enjoyed by Averett students a decade earlier.[34]

Nevertheless, one Averett favorite—"I Am Woman," sung by Helen Reddy—overflowed with social comment. The artist spoke for women everywhere when she warned, "No one's ever gonna keep me down again."[35] Perhaps the song's popularity among both male and female students at Averett bespoke determination to succeed in spite of setbacks such as failure to relocate the campus or failing health of a president.

---

[33] Letter to author from: Kim Crawford Love, October 1982; Mrs. Franklin Lee Tolbert, October 1982; Brenda K. Lee, October 1982; Gerald D. Boone, Jr., October 1982; Mrs. Debra Sue Doolittle, October 1982; Johncie L. Flannagan, letter to author, October 1982; Carol Diane Blosser, October 1982; Milton Okun, introduction to *Great Songs of the 70s*, ed. Milton Okun (New York: New York Times, 1978) vi–x.

[34] *Great Songs of the 70's*, 130–33, 252–54; and Milton Okun, introduction to *Great Songs of the 70s*, vii, ix. Letter to author from: Margaret E. Tyree, October 1982; Marsha K. Flora, October 1982; Johncie L. Flannagan, October 1982.

[35] Helen Reddy (words) and Ray Burton (music), "I Am Woman," in *Great Songs of the 70s*, 103–4.

12

The Presidency of Howard W. Lee, 1980–1985

In April 1979, board chairman William H. Jefferson, Jr., appointed a presidential search committee to undertake the task of replacing Conwell Anderson. For the first time in the school's history, the committee was broadly representative: four trustees, two faculty members, two alumnae, and one administrator. After screening applications, identifying prospects, and interviewing applicants from early spring to late fall, the committee gradually realized the best available choice was acting president Howard W. Lee, who was persuaded to accept a permanent appointment on 1 January 1980.

Like Anderson and Bishop before him, Lee was an adopted Virginian. He was born in Toronto, Canada, on 30 January 1916. To the envy of young friends, his father, William Victor Lee, was superintendent of a candy company. His mother, Anna Spade Lee, was a homemaker with primary responsibility for raising five sons. Young Howard belonged to a large gang of neighborhood boys who spent afternoons after school playing stickball in the street; as catcher, Howard was responsible for watching for policemen patrolling the area on bicycles. He also enjoyed his family's Canadian Baptist Church, a large ecclesiastical gothic structure with a pastor whose demeanor and dress always bordered on the formal. Lee's fondness for dignity and formality in worship probably developed during these years. So did his insistence on elevating human needs above racial or cultural barriers, an attitude he learned from a mother and grandmother who were active in the church's literacy project for Asian immigrants.[1]

While Lee was in elementary school, his family moved to Windsor,

---

[1] Howard W. Lee, interview with author, Averett College, 25 March 1983, hereinafter cited as Lee interview.

Canada, and later to Detroit. There he finished school and developed a passion for sports and scouting. While in Boy Scouts, Lee earned more than thirty merit badges and worked at odd jobs to help his troop purchase an old truck for transportation to and from summer jamborees. Later, he transferred to Sea Scouts, developed skills as a sailor, and spent many weekends each year marking courses for boat races sponsored by local yacht clubs on the Detroit River. Ironically, his potential for seamanship was limited by seasickness.[2]

Although gregarious and competitive by nature, Lee also enjoyed solitude, which he often used as a background for his ingenuity and craftsmanship. He liked to take apart and then reassemble lamps and electrical appliances. A course in woodworking in high school made him a lifelong designer and builder of wooden furniture. As a young teenager he painted the family garage and his own room. He also made PLEASE KEEP OFF THE GRASS signs for homeowners in his neighborhood and repaired windows broken by errant fast balls. For extracurricular reading he preferred stories of adventurous youth, such as *Tom Sawyer*, magazines of the "fix-it" genre, such as *Popular Mechanics*, and biographies of biblical heroes given him by his parents and grandparents.[3]

Partly because of this interest in Bible figures, but more owing to his Christian upbringing, Lee decided as early as age eleven to make the pulpit ministry his vocation. He carried this decision with him to William Jewell College in Liberty, Missouri, although a healthy youthful rebellion led him to join a fraternity. Eventually, in fact, he became its president. During his sophomore year he met junior Margaret Davidson, whom he had admired since his freshman year when the two were in the same Greek class. Yet because she was a straight-A student and Lee was not, it took him a year to overcome his shyness and introduce himself. Margaret Davidson graduated in May 1936 and entered Southern Baptist Theological Seminary in Louisville for work towards a Master's in Religious Education. She and Lee were married on 26 May 1937, the day after his graduation from William Jewell. That autumn he entered Southern Baptist Theological Seminary, where he earned Th.M. and Th.D. degrees. During his seminary years in Kentucky he served as

---

[2] Ibid.
[3] Ibid.

associate pastor of Broadway Baptist Church and pastor of Okolona
Baptist Church in Louisville. Although he could have remained at
Okolona, his desire to cut ties with his seminary town led him to
Danville, Virginia, in 1944, to serve as pastor of the new West Main
Baptist Church a block south of Averett College. For seven years the
congregation met in a house before constructing a sanctuary. In the next
twenty years, under Lee's guidance, the congregation added two
educational buildings and several hundred members. By 1984 the
physical plant was valued at $1.2 million, and the active membership
totaled over seven hundred.[4]

Lee combined religious and civic leadership while serving as pastor
of the West Main church. He was active in denominational life as
president of the Danville Ministerial Association (1949) and Pittsylvania
Baptist Association (1956–1957). Shortly thereafter he was elected to the
Virginia Baptist General Board (1959–1965; 1966–1971) and executive
committee of the Southern Baptist Convention (1967–1971). He was also
active in the community as president of the Danville chapter of the
American Red Cross (1947) and the Danville Rotary Club (1950–1951).
He wrote a weekly column titled "Insight" for the *Bee*, Danville's
afternoon newspaper. In 1968 an appreciative community recognized his
contributions by awarding him the Kiwanis Club's Citizenship Award
for Outstanding Community Service, which had been bestowed on Curtis
Bishop seventeen years earlier.[5]

Lee's civic interests did not always elicit favorable comment,
especially when he joined the local movement for civil rights. In the
1950s he lobbied for black membership in the Danville Ministerial
Association. During racial unrest in the early 1960s, he joined with
clergy from churches on Main and West Main Streets in an appeal to city
council for fairer treatment of blacks. At least two of these ministers
were not allowed to return to their pulpits; within a year all but a handful
answered calls elsewhere. Lee remained in Danville and continued to
speak out for Christian brotherhood. During demonstrations in 1963, he
insisted that anyone seeking to worship at West Main Baptist Church be
seated without segregation. Later he marched in demonstrations and
publicly affirmed his friendship and respect for the Reverend Doyle

---

[4] Ibid.

[5] Biographical information sheet on Howard W. Lee, Averett University Archives.

Thomas, pastor of Loyal Baptist Church and president of the Danville chapter of the National Association for the Advancement of Colored People.[6]

Because of widespread recognition of Lee's integrity, his house was never vandalized, his pulpit never threatened, and his social acceptance never withdrawn. To many people Howard Lee was the social conscience of Danville, a benchmark by which to judge the rightness of individual actions. His brand of Christianity left no room for selective application of the teachings of Jesus. His winsome personality—particularly his ability to use humor deftly—often defused the anger of opponents. Always careful to present his views gently and nondogmatically, he was equally careful to tolerate views opposed to his own. A man of patience and tact, he worked hard to bring an opponent to recognition of error without recognition of defeat.

In 1970, when Lee was completing his twenty-sixth year at West Main Baptist Church, he and President Anderson frequently discussed Averett's denominational relations. Concerned about the strength of sentiment among many Baptists in favor of reducing support for educational institutions, Anderson knew Lee could be an effective spokesman for Averett College by virtue of his stature within the denomination and positions of leadership on Baptist boards and committees. Anderson also appreciated the great confidence and affection accorded to both Howard and Margaret Lee by an adoring community. All who knew Margaret Lee commented on her "love of life" and "genuine concern for those around her"; Howard Lee they praised for "his love of people, his integrity, his commitment to values, his understanding of people, his ability to counsel, and his experience over the years."[7] Although happy in his pastorate, Lee found his experience as an adjunct professor at Averett beginning in 1946 pleasant and rewarding, and he began to consider a change of career. In 1971, after months of deliberation, Lee became Anderson's assistant, the position he vacated in 1979 to become acting president.[8]

Shrouding the early years of Lee's presidency was a mood of national pessimism. Article after article in popular and professional

---

[6] Lee interview.

[7] *Chanticleer,* 19, November 1980.

[8] Lee interview.

publications predicted the demise of colleges like Averett in view of a declining pool of applicants, competition from less expensive public institutions, and a saturated private fundraising environment.[9] Domestic problems of inflation, recession, and unemployment defied solution, while America's influence in the world waned. News reports of real or imagined machinations by public servants continued to erode confidence in political leadership. The Iranian hostage crisis of 1979–1981 held America up to scorn in the arena of world opinion. Averett's mock US presidential election in May 1980 reflected this national disenchantment. The undecided category received more votes than any of the candidates; Averett's own history professor Charles Postelle tied for fourth place with Senator Edward Kennedy and George Bush. Whether intended seriously or facetiously, Postelle's inclusion pointed to disgust with politics-as-usual, dissatisfaction with shopworn symbols, and a plea for someone with answers.[10]

Lee, ever the optimist, chose to see this time of challenge as a time of opportunity. Without fully comprehending the details, he was aware that dramatic and beneficial changes were taking place in American higher education. Indeed, he governed Averett at the midpoint of a twenty-year period that saw the number of students enrolled in higher education across America increase 28 percent, the number of faculty grow 46 percent, the number of degrees conferred swell 35 percent, and current fund revenues mushroom 373 percent.[11] Lee also comprehended the immensity of his task. He thus set about to insure Averett's permanence by carefully managing day-to-day operations, maintaining enrollment and retention, improving facilities, vigorously pursuing donors, expanding the quality of student life, broadening curricular offerings, and upgrading faculty credentials.

Upgrading faculty was an ongoing process. Averett, a relatively new four-year institution, badly needed professors with Ph.D. degrees to demonstrate professional competence and gain academic respectability.

---

[9] John R. Thelin, "Institutional History in Our Own Time: Higher Education's Shift from Managerial Revolution to Enterprising Evolution," *CASE International Journal of Educational Advancement* 1/1 (June 2000): 9–10.

[10] News release, 27 February 1980, Development Office files; *Chanticleer,* 3 April 1980, 6 May 1980.

[11] Arthur M. Cohen, *The Shaping of American Higher Education: Emergence and Growth of the Contemporary System* (San Francisco: Jossey-Bass, 1998) 292.

President Lee increased the percentage of professors holding the doctorate from 43 percent to 50 percent, among this proportion every faculty member in the departments of biology, chemistry, history, foreign languages, and religion.[12] Unfortunately, faculty salaries did not keep pace and, when factored for inflation, remained largely unchanged from 1981 to 1985. In fact, by 1985 Averett ranked fourth from the bottom among Virginia's nineteen private colleges and universities. The average salary at Averett was also below that of the local two-year community college. The only concession to faculty was the addition of a sabbatical program funded initially by a federal grant.[13]

The curriculum improved, if faculty salaries did not. The college added an academic computer center, created a major in mathematics/computer science, and received accreditation from the Council of Social Work Education for the social work program. Approval for the master's program in education came from the Southern Association of Colleges and Schools. New majors in chemistry and music were added, coupled with a master's-level program in business administration. By autumn 1985, forty-six graduate students were enrolled in the business program. Realizing Averett could not, and probably should not, compete with community colleges for students seeking degrees in secretarial studies, the faculty voted to phase out that program in 1985. Equestrian Studies became a separate department and major, and the college added a Bachelor of Fine Arts degree for students who planned graduate work in studio art.[14]

Much more ambitious were programs in nursing and aviation. In 1981 a study of health care in southside Virginia revealed that hospitals within a thirty-mile radius of Danville would employ 600 nurses with the Bachelor of Science in Nursing (BSN) degree within the next five years. With encouragement from these hospitals, in 1982 Averett created a BSN program and hired Dr. Terry Pitts of Martinsville to head it. Enrollees would be registered nurses who had passed board examinations and wanted baccalaureate-level instruction. Memorial Hospital of Danville helped by offering tuition reimbursement at 50 percent of the

---

[12] Averett College, Institutional Self-Study, 1985–1987, 100, Averett University Archives.

[13] Ibid., 112; Averett College, Fact Book, 1985–86, Averett University Archives.

[14] Howard W. Lee, Annual Report to the Board, 30 May 1980–31 May 1985; 1985–87 Self-Study, 62–63.

cost. Averett graduated its first three BSNs in spring 1985; two were from the hospital in Danville.[15]

The program was not successful, however, and eventually it had to be abandoned. It lost $19,000 in 1983–84 and $50,000 in 1984–85. Part of the difficulty lay in the rigorous and unpopular schedule. One nursing graduate, Memorial's Sandra Mills, groused, "I would come home from work, cook supper, go to school, and return home in time to go to bed. Luckily, my family was very supportive."[16] Another problem was cost, which students felt they could not easily recoup given the small differential between the salaries of RNs and BSNs.[17]

The aviation program was more successful, growing quickly from fifteen students in 1981 to fifty students by 1985. Developed by George Falk, the college's director of financial aid who had been a B-17 pilot during World War II, it provided general education classes, business courses, and flight training that entitled the graduate to a Bachelor of Science in Business with a concentration in aviation management. Graduates also earned a pilot's license, a commercial license, instrument and multi-engine ratings, and instructor certification. Students took general education and business courses on the Averett campus and flight training through General Aviation, Inc., at Danville Municipal Airport. They progressed from a two-seater Piper Tomahawk to a four-seater Piper Warrior in the first two years, followed by a four-seater Piper Arrow to a twin-engine Piper Seneca in their last two years. In the process each student accumulated at least 228 hours in flight, although many gained as many as 400 hours. Graduates quickly found employment with airlines, air carriers, and large corporations.[18]

Unlike the program in aviation, a portion of whose instruction was on-campus, degree programs established in Northern Virginia and South Boston were held entirely off-campus. In 1980, academic dean Malcom Huckabee conferred with officials from Danville Community College and the Westinghouse plant in South Boston, thirty miles east of

[15] *Corridors* (newsletter published by Memorial Hospital of Danville VA), August 1985; Lee, Annual Report to the Board, 4 June 1982; *Chanticleer*, 16 December 1983.

[16] *Corridors*, August 1985.

[17] Minutes, Executive Committee of the Board, 9 March 1984 Averett University Archives; Lee, Annual Report to the Board, 31 May 1985.

[18] *Chanticleer*, 20 May 1980, 19 November 1980; undated clipping, *Danville Register*, Newspaper Clippings, 1977–1986, Averett University Archives.

Danville, to establish an on-site baccalaureate program in business for Westinghouse employees. Ten students enrolled and twenty eventually graduated before the program was discontinued in 1987. In autumn 1984, Averett opened a baccalaureate program in religion for the Korean community in Northern Virginia. Columbia Baptist Church in Falls Church housed the operation. Fifteen faculty members (eight with doctorates and seven with master's degrees) taught the courses in Korean or had the instruction translated into Korean. Students were subject to the same degree requirements as those on the Danville campus. As an incentive, the college charged only one-half of on-campus tuition. Eventually, 102 students received Averett diplomas. Most of them remained in Northern Virginia to take pastorates or positions in youth ministry or religious education in a number of Korean Baptist congregations in the area. Both the Korean program and the Westinghouse program symbolized Averett's desire to be bold in meeting the educational needs of regional and denominational constituents.[19]

However, this academic boldness did not involve tampering with Averett's curricular common core, which put Averett at odds with national trends. By the end of Lee's presidency, 80 percent of the nation's colleges and universities did not require a course in foreign languages, 42 percent did not require a course in history, 54 percent did not require a course in mathematics, and 48 percent did not require courses in either American or British literature. Fewer than 30 percent of the nation's graduates had even taken a course in Western civilization. The Averett faculty, embracing the Renaissance model that an educated person needs breadth before depth and requires a foundation on which to build an understanding of humankind, refused to entertain motions to alter prescribed courses in Western civilization, mathematics, natural science, British literature, foreign languages, fine and performing arts, and religion and philosophy.[20]

Modernized facilities went hand in hand with a modern if prescriptive curriculum. President Lee took office saddled with a trustee decision to relocate the campus in stages to the Dan River Mills property bounded by West Main Street, Country Club Drive, and River Oak

---

[19] 1985–87 Self-Study, 89–91.
[20] See Cohen, *Shaping*, 357–58.

Drive. From the beginning Lee doubted the wisdom of the decision. The existing campus was more space-efficient and could be made more energy-efficient than a new, sprawling one. Worse, in uncertain economic times, potential donors for such a mammoth undertaking were scarce. In September 1980, Lee confided his fears to friend and trustee George Shields, who served on both the site relocation committee and executive committee of the board. Lee bemoaned the fact that the project failed to generate "an enthusiastic core of constituents," and he was even more concerned that "a number of trustees" did "not accept the validity of the original study" to relocate. Lee concluded, "I think the Executive Committee should review the decision in the light of present economic circumstances and projections."[21] After securing commitments from potential donors of only $500,000, on 20 November 1981, the board heeded Lee's advice, scrapped plans for relocation, and voted to concentrate instead on improving the existing campus.[22]

Almost immediately, Lee recommended construction of an academic building with classrooms, laboratories, and faculty offices. Because Averett had added little classroom space since 1966, Lee reasoned correctly that the existing physical plant was appropriate only to a single-sex female institution with half the student body of 1981. Faculty offices, classrooms, and laboratories were scattered in seven different buildings and needed to be centralized. The new nursing program and chemistry major demanded additional, more modern laboratories. Averett needed dormitory space that could easily be provided by converting classrooms and faculty offices in Davenport Hall. Moreover, land was available adjacent to the proposed building site for construction of a parking lot, or parking garage, to serve 60 percent of the student body who commuted and constantly groused about scarcity of parking. Finally, land adjacent to the proposed building site could become an attractively landscaped commons tying together the new academic building, auditorium/gymnasium, Main-to-Bishop Hall complex, and Fugate Hall.[23]

After several months of study and gentle lobbying by the president,

---

[21] Howard W. Lee to George H. Shields, Jr., 25 September 1980, Howard W. Lee Papers, Averett University Archives, hereinafter cited as Lee Papers.

[22] Minutes, Board of Trustees, 20 November 1981; *Danville Register*, 22 November 1981, n.p. Averett University Archives

[23] Lee, Annual Report to the Board, 4 June 1982.

on 4 June 1982, the board voted to raise $3 million for constructing and furnishing a new academic building and renovating several older ones. Local architects Calvert, Lewis, and Smith executed the preliminary plans. Under the direction of new vice president for institutional advancement G. Rodney Beals, the new campaign took the theme "Averett Is Building." Trustees F. W. (Bill) Townes III and Julian Stinson agreed to serve as co-chairs. Beneath them were a host of subcommittees to solicit businesses, alumni, foundations, and friends. The trustees agreed not to make the campaign public until $1 million was raised. In the meantime, Beals made plans for the usual kickoff dinner, mass mailings, open houses, special donor solicitations, radiothons, and building dedication.[24]

Success came more rapidly than anyone expected. Within three months 125 donors pledged $1 million, thus ending the silent phase of the campaign. Over half of the $1 million came from twenty-two of the thirty trustees. By April 1983, pledges stood at $1.5 million, the figure previously set for drawing the final architectural plans. The following month the executive committee of the board established three qualifications for naming the new building: generosity towards its construction, substantial contributions to the life of southside Virginia, and significant impact on Averett College. Martinsville contractor and Averett trustee J. Burness Frith met all three. Not only did his family pledge $250,000, but he also secured several generous pledges from friends. The board subsequently voted to name the building Ada Nunn Frith Hall in honor of his mother, a former rural schoolteacher with a lifelong commitment to higher education. In August 1983, bids were advertised and opened after the $1.8 million necessary for construction, minus furnishings, was pledged. English Construction Company of Altavista was lowest of nine bidders and secured the contract.[25]

For the next eighteen months, fundraising and construction went hand in hand. In autumn 1983 the college formally broke ground for the new building. In May 1984, Mary B. Blount, for whom Blount Library was named, pledged $250,000 for the construction of a

[24] Ibid; Minutes, Executive Committee of the Board of Trustees, 25 March 1982; Minutes, Board of Trustees, 4 June 1982.

[25] Minutes, Executive Committee of the Board of Trustees, 22 September 1982, 1 April 1983, 9 May 1983, 8 August 1983; Lee, Annual Report to the Board, 3 June 1983; Minutes, Board of Trustees, 3 June 1983.

chapel/auditorium within Frith Hall. A Kresge Foundation grant of $150,000, which required a matching sum, came two months later and brought the total to $2.85 million. By November the match had been met, and the total figure exceeded $3 million. Averett trustees, friends, foundations, alumni, and businesses like Goodyear Tire and Rubber Company, Dan River Mills, Dibrell Brothers, Philip Morris, English Construction Company, and Bassett Furniture made Frith Hall a reality.[26] Lee was able to recognize these donors at the college's 125th anniversary celebration, held 2–8 December 1984. Lee commented proudly, "Modern buildings certainly symbolize the quality of education we are trying to provide."[27]

Partial occupancy (the first three floors) did not come until early March 1985; full occupancy followed six weeks later. When finally completed, the four-story masonry and steel structure of almost 34,000 square feet had seventeen classrooms, eight laboratories, and thirty-one faculty offices. The building could accommodate 650 students. Frith Hall was not only the first classroom building added since the college went four-year and co-educational; it was also the most ambitious fundraising effort in the school's history.[28]

However, Frith Hall represented only one part of the "Averett Is Building" Campaign. A second segment was construction of an attractively landscaped commons to tie together several buildings. This work was made possible by a generous donation from the family of Robert S. Jordan, Jr., in whose memory the commons was constructed and named. Behind Frith Hall the college converted three tennis courts into a resurfaced parking lot with eighty-three spaces—replacing spots lost to a 1981 enlargement of the athletic field, courtesy of a grant from Jacob M. (Jack) Kleinoder, which had created a campus parking crisis. Simultaneously, Dan River Mills swapped several acres of land on Memorial Drive for the city-owned public park bordered by Surry Lane and Rambler Drive adjacent to the Averett campus. At the urging of Dan River president and Averett board chairman Lester Hudson, Dan River

---

[26] Mary B. Blount to Howard W. Lee, 22 May 1984, Lee Papers; Averett College, news release, 27 July 1984; folder marked "Campaign for Funds: Academic Building," Lee Papers.

[27] *Danville Register*, 2 December 1984, n.p; *Chanticleer*, 5 December 1984.

[28] *Chanticleer*, 29 September 1983; *Danville Register*, 5 March 1985, n.p; 1985–87 Self-Study, 328.

Mills donated the park to Averett, which immediately constructed six tennis courts on the site. As soon as Frith Hall was completed, the former faculty offices in Davenport Hall became dormitory rooms ready for occupancy in the fall of 1985.[29]

Averett was successful in raising funds for other acquisitions of property. President Lee stepped up the effort, begun under President Anderson, to acquire houses in the block behind Blount Library bordered by Robertson Avenue, Woodland Drive, and Townes Street. By the end of Lee's administration, nine were in college hands, opening the way for future buildings and parking facilities. In January 1983, Mrs. A. B. Carrington, Jr., purchased and donated a residence at 500 Hawthorne Drive adjacent to campus for use as the president's house. Six months and $25,000 in renovations later, the Lees moved into the Carrington donation and converted the former President's House into headquarters for the Office of Institutional Advancement, housing the functions of development, alumni affairs, and news and information.[30]

The final acquisition of property involved the equestrian studies program. Local dentist Dr. Jesse Wall agreed to lease his fifty-five-acre Twelve Gates Farm nine miles south of Danville. The facility included an 80-by-200-foot indoor arena, an outdoor arena, a forty-stall, double-aisle barn with tack room, exercise paddocks, a cross-country course, a galloping track, and a dressage ring. Twelve Gates Farm provided better and more modern facilities for the sixty students taking classes in riding, training, teaching, equine care, stable management, and equine first aid.[31]

President Lee knew that careful management of finances was as important as modern facilities in keeping Averett competitive and viable. He paid attention to the prediction by the Carnegie Council that college enrollment nationwide would decline for at least the next decade. Because the Danville area itself was already losing population, he concentrated efforts on retaining a greater number of dormitory students,

---

[29] Minutes, Board of Trustees, 5 June 1981, 11 November 1982, 18 November 1983; Minutes, Executive Committee of the Board, 8 August 1983; Lee, Annual Report to the Board, 31 May 1985.

[30] Lee, Annual Report to the Board, 4 June 1982, 3 June 1983, 1 June 1984; Minutes, Board of Trustees, 16 November 1984; Howard W. Lee to the Board of Trustees, 28 January 1983, Lee Papers; Minutes, Executive Committee of the Board, 1 April 1983.

[31] *Chanticleer*, 20 February 1985; Lee, Annual Report to the Board, 31 May 1985; Averett College, Catalog Supplement, 1981–82.

whose additional fees for room and board made them more valuable from a budgetary standpoint. The college also advertised its expanded evening college, graduate offerings, noncredit continuing education courses, and nursing program to compensate for the anticipated deficit in traditional enrollment. In addition, by working to achieve and maintain an almost equal ratio of male to female students, Averett avoided a reputation as a single-sex or one-sex-dominant institution. As a result, Averett experienced only a modest decline in enrollment—from 1,028 students in 1980 to 952 students by 1985.[32]

Equally important, the institution used financial aid adroitly to halt the decline in enrollment. Certainly, by 1980 such assistance was crucial to the health of all institutions. Approximately half of Averett's revenue represented awards of federal, state, and private financial aid. In 1984–85, two-thirds of its students received some form of monetary assistance. To its disadvantage, Averett was what is commonly called a tuition-driven institution. Tuition and academic fees comprised 65 to 70 percent of revenue during the Lee years, which in the face of uncertain enrollments made long-range planning difficult. Because the trustees refused to operate at a deficit, fluctuations in enrollment caused maintenance to be deferred, departmental budgets slashed, and even faculty salaries frozen. To its advantage, Averett had more elasticity in the way it awarded financial aid than public institutions. Lee exploited this flexibility by substantially increasing the number and amount of institutional scholarships (in reality, tuition discounts). During President Anderson's last year, for example, institutional scholarships amounted to only $145,000; during President Lee's first year, they skyrocketed to $491,000—over $100,000 more than the Baptist General Association of Virginia contributed annually to the school. In light of such figures, Lee was able to assure Baptists statewide that every penny of denominational aid enabled needy Baptist students to attend college. Under President Lee, institutional scholarships accounted for 10 percent of the budget.[33]

---

[32] *Chanticleer*, 31 October 1984; Minutes, Executive Committee of the Board, 15 February 1983; Lee, Annual Report to the Board, 30 May 1980–31 May 1985.

[33] Averett College, Fact Book, 1983–84, Averett University Archives; Lee, Annual Report to the Board, 5 June 1981, 31 May 1985; 1985–87 Self-Study, 294, 307; Cohen, *Shaping*, 302–304. See also Philip G. Altbach, Robert O. Berdahl, and Patricia J. Gumport, eds., *American Higher Education in the Twenty-first Century* (Baltimore, MD: Johns Hopkins University Press, 1999) 64.

Still, revenues gained from tuition, fees, and charges for room and board represented only 80 percent of the cost of a student's education. The Office of Development, under former dean of students Mary Jo Davis, raised the remaining 20 percent each year in Current Fund drives. The college was fortunate to have experienced trustees like O. Lewis Roach of Danville to chair drives, and the institution met its current fund goal each year during the Lee presidency. In fact, from 1980 to 1985, alumni gifts increased 143 percent, those from businesses 112 percent, foundations 681 percent, friends 462 percent, and parents 1,180 percent. This burgeoning success in fundraising, particularly for capital spending, decreased the debt-to-equity ratio from 32 percent in 1979–80 to less than 18 percent in 1984–85.[34]

Lee's one area of financial shortsightedness was his decision not to focus on institutional endowment, which stood at $146,000 in 1980 and only $257,000 in 1985. Lee took the position that Averett had what he called a "living endowment" from Virginia Baptists. Their annual contributions of over $300,000, a hefty 8 percent of the annual budget, represented, he said, the annual earnings on a hypothetical endowment of $6 million, assuming a 5 percent return on investment. But his reasoning ignored the reality that denominational contributions were not guaranteed, given changing attitudes among Southern Baptists. Nor did he consider that many national rankings of colleges and universities were based partly on the size of endowments.[35]

Neither were students concerned with such matters as endowments. They wanted success and glory on the athletic field, and they were not disappointed. In 1980 the soccer team under Coach Vesa Hiltunen won the Dixie Conference championship for the second consecutive year. With a record for the season of 19-2-1, they also defeated Virginia Tech, Emory University, and Stetson University before advancing to the quarterfinals of the NCAA Division III playoffs. The following year the soccer squad was almost as successful, amassing a record of 14-2-1 before falling in sudden-death overtime to the nation's top-ranked Division III team, Glassboro State, in the first round of NCAA playoffs. In both years the soccer team received national exposure in the press. So

---

[34] Averett College, news release, 9 November 1983; Lee, Annual Report to the Board, 1 June 1984, 31 May 1985; 1985–87 Self-Study, 277.

[35] 1985–87 Self-Study, 280.

did soccer star Pekka Kaartinen, who earned All-American designation in 1980 and 1981. He was joined in 1985 by tennis star Tapio Martti, who won the Dixie Conference singles championship, advanced to the NCAA playoffs, and became Averett's first nationally ranked tennis player. Women's softball placed second in 1980 and third in 1981 in the state tournament of the Association of Intercollegiate Athletics for Women.[36]

Students also wanted plentiful leisure-time activities. College-sponsored events stretched throughout the year. The school year began with a freshman mixer in the ballroom of the King of the Sea Restaurant. Then came Rat Night, a tradition that began shortly after the college became co-educational under President Anderson. On the appointed evening upperclassmen took freshmen to the front lawn for anointing with lard, eggs, pancake syrup, and solid food, like flaky tuna, that adhered to the lard. The previous day each upperclassman had contributed a dollar to the anointment fund, which usually proved to be insufficient. The freshmen were then informed they must make up the deficit. "Freshmen will be freshmen, so they believe it and pay," one commentator observed.[37] The evening's activities "did force everyone to take a shower," he continued, "though I heard one guy mutter as he pulled the shower curtain closed, 'There's a first time for everything.'"[38] Despite Lee's early opposition to this affair—he called it "insensitive to the basics of human rights" and "degrading to persons of both sexes in a way that one would not expect to find on a college campus of mature individuals"—the student body was able to retain Rat Night until the last year of Lee's presidency.[39] By that time most institutions were discouraging such activity because of inherent legal liability.

There was less controversy surrounding other college-sponsored events. Homecoming in October continued to be popular. Its early afternoon parade of floats and homecoming princesses in convertibles stretching from campus to Bonner Field, followed by a soccer game and crowning of a queen at halftime, were well attended. A dance with music from a live band concluded the festivities. The traditional Halloween

---

' [36] *Chanticleer*, 6 May 1980, 4 November 1980, 11 March 1981, 20 November 1981; Lee; Annual Report to the Board, 30 May 1980, 31 May 1985.

[37] *Chanticleer*, 3 October 1984.

[38] Ibid.

[39] Undated notice titled "Students," Lee Papers.

Celebration three weeks later featured favorite horror movies such as *The Texas Chainsaw Massacre* and *American Werewolf in London* in the Bottom Inn. The evening concluded with breakfast at midnight served by faculty and administrators. Students gathered during the Christmas season to light luminaries and decorate the parlor. They also looked forward to a Valentine dance and a spring formal.[40]

Campus organizations remained strong. The Baptist Student Union remained the largest: in addition to attending weekly meetings at West Main Baptist Church on Thursdays at 11:15 A.M., members flocked to conventions and conferences at Eagle Eyrie, participated in missions and outreach programs in localities as diverse as the W. W. Moore Detention Center in Danville and the slums of New York City, and furnished a gospel choir, puppet ministry, and revival/creative worship team for area churches. At the other end of the spectrum, the AIH fraternity and Little Sisters social sorority sponsored frequent parties at suites in Fugate Hall and the AIH fraternity house in Eden, North Carolina, which mysteriously burned to the ground in October 1984. Destroyed in the blaze were all of the furnishings—four sofas, a bar, and a stove. Regardless of mission and function, all campus organizations showed their civic spirit by raising funds for such organizations as the Juvenile Diabetes Foundation, the March of Dimes, the American Cancer Society, and the Empty Stocking Fund.[41]

Politically, Averett students reflected national trends. In the college-sponsored mock presidential election of 1984, President Reagan swamped former vice president Walter Mondale with 73 percent of the vote. The only sizeable support for Mondale came from faculty and black students, the only two pockets of liberal sentiment on campus. Mondale secured 84 percent of the black vote and 74 percent of the faculty vote. Nevertheless, student John Phoenix, class of 1985, mirrored national opinion when he announced his support for Reagan, even though Phoenix sided with Mondale on issues such as abortion, school prayer, and nuclear disarmament. The lack of strong leadership recently displayed by President Jimmy Carter was too vivid a memory to allow students the luxury of voting for candidates whose stands on issues

---

[40] *Chanticleer*, 9 October 1980, 27 October 1982.

[41] *Chanticleer*, 31 October 1984, Lee, Annual Report to the Board, 5 June 1981, 3 June 1983, 31 May 1985.

simply mirrored their own.[42]

Students during the Lee years enjoyed the inventions and innovations that made college life pleasurable. Music Television (MTV) and boom boxes suddenly were everywhere. In dorms and at home, students carried boom boxes that blared recordings by the Rolling Stones, David Bowie, Billy Idol, and Elton John. Video jockeys on MTV joined artists like Donna Summer, Michael Jackson, Prince, Culture Club, and Men At Work as teenage idols. In dormitory rooms, bedrooms at home, and cars with radios, students sang along with any of the five top-ten singles from Michael Jackson's album *Thriller:* "Billie Jean," "Beat It," "The Girl Is Mine," "Human Nature," and "Wanna Be Starting Something."

In addition, in 1980 Averett seniors, allowed to live off campus for the first time, quickly discovered the pros and cons. "You have to learn to take care of yourself, pay bills, and cook and clean because nobody else will do it for you anymore," groused Cheryl Wilson, who moved to the nearby Canterbury Apartments. Ximena Criswell focused on benefits. "You can have friends over anytime you want; you can have parties. You don't have to put up with loud stereos and loud televisions." Everyone nodded with approval as Betsy Martin added, "You can party without worrying about school rules."[43]

Also new to Averett during the Lee years was the Kissing Bandit. At lunch one midday in September 1981, an unknown male dressed in black cape, mask, and hood swept into the dining hall, passionately kissed several unsuspecting female students, and quickly disappeared into the adjacent corridors. He repeated the prank for several days. The reviews were mixed. One woman complained the kiss "was too hard and it hurt." Another was more charitable. "Damn, it was good!" she exclaimed. Several upperclassmen finally seized and unmasked the hapless rogue, who, it turned out, was freshman John Thomasson of Collinsville. The next day as Thomasson strode into the dining hall dressed in street clothes, another Kissing Bandit appeared, giving notice that the phenomenon had not run its course. Not long thereafter a Kissing Bandette showed up to return the favor to male diners. These kinds of campus high jinks relieved the stress of academic life and created

---

[42] *Danville Register*, 26 October 1984, n.p; *Chanticleer*, 31 October 1984.
[43] *Chanticleer*, 19 November 1980; *Pendulum*, 1984.

memories to pass on to children.[44]

The residence life staff that dealt with most of these pranks were the Resident Assistants (RAs), undergraduates with at least sophomore standing and a 2.25 grade point average who oversaw halls in the dormitories in return for a meager stipend and the opportunity to preregister for classes. They had to know and enforce rules, attend to administrative duties such as room inventories, communicate college information to students, and advise and counsel. The job, probably the most difficult on campus, demanded patience, self-control, compassion, tolerance, wisdom, and skills in communication. Although she found the job "a great way to get to know people," Sherry Harper complained that the position was ill paid. "It's a twenty-four hour job," she said. "Divide twenty-four hours a day into $150 and you get just over two cents an hour. This is not minimum wage for a ten-dollar-an-hour job." Ann Crittendon took the assignment, she admitted, primarily to "bring out leadership qualities in me." She also agreed with Harper that the toughest part was having to turn in friends for rule violations.[45]

Another fad of the Lee years was what students called "biscuitmania." Studying in dormitories late at night often brought on a condition called "midnight munchies," uncontrollable hunger pangs that could only be satisfied by a biscuit from the nearby Hardee's restaurant that stayed open twenty-four hours a day. Frequently, at midnight on weekdays, students would descend in droves on Hardee's for what they called "the best thing since the Big Mac," a reference to the hamburger made famous worldwide by the McDonald's chain.[46]

Not all weeknights were spent studying in dormitory or library, sometimes to students' regret. Because in 1981 the drinking age was eighteen (later nineteen) years, several local nightspots enticed Averett students with contests, giveaways, and low beer prices. The King's Lounge at 1010 Piney Forest Road, open daily for dancing from 7:00 P.M. to 1:00 A.M. and popularly known as "the Pit," was a particular favorite. The establishment had a dress code of sorts: shirttails had to be tucked into pants. Some students went on Monday nights when there was no cover charge. More went on Ladies' Night (Tuesdays and Thursdays).

[44] *Chanticleer*, 9 October 1981.

[45] *Chanticleer*, 3 April 1985.

[46] *Chanticleer*, 19 November 1982.

History faculty remember giving tests on Friday mornings to bleary-eyed, half-awake students who had spent the previous evening at the Pit instead of the library. By 1985 the weeknight for partying shifted from Thursday to Wednesday and from the Pit, which closed, to the Stallion's Cantina on Riverside Drive. Test scores on Friday immediately improved; those on Thursday plummeted.[47]

Of course, students would not be students unless they had complaints. The college was able to address some, but not others. Gripes about hot dogs, ham, and fish at almost every meal prompted Lee to change the food-service vendor. Ongoing criticism about the lack of available parking was one reason for construction of the eighty-three-space parking lot behind Frith Hall. Incidents of slashed tires in parking lots, and intoxicated "townies" roaming the halls and asking women for permission to search their rooms for suspected prowlers, led the college to hire a professional security service. Complaints of an inadequate student center prompted President Lee to create a student committee to recommend renovations for the Bottom Inn. Their suggestions led to new paint, carpeting, furniture, and fixtures, a snack bar, and a large-screen television with Home Box Office for sporting events and movies.[48]

Misleading recruiting information was a problem Lee soon solved. "This isn't the college they told me about," was a frequent complaint from freshmen. In truth, the Admissions Office's slide show, viewed by high school seniors and numerous guidance counselors, was obsolete. It showed one student seated in a broadcast studio, another by an indoor swimming pool, and a third beside a large athletic field. New freshmen were surprised to discover the broadcast studio was at WDVA radio station where the student was working part-time, the swimming pool had been drained for use as an art studio, and the college's only athletic field was used for all intramurals, intercollegiate competition, team practices, and free recreation. Lee quickly erased such erroneous impressions, and protests subsided.[49]

Another common complaint dealt with visitation between the sexes in dormitories. During the week the college had "closed days" on

---

[47] *Chanticleer*, 20 May 1981, 10 May 1985.

[48] *Chanticleer*, 9 October 1980, 25 March 1981, 27 October 1982, 29 September 1983, 10 May 1985.

[49] *Chanticleer*, 9 October 1980, 25 March 1981, 27 October 1982, 29 September 1983, 10 May 1985.

Monday, Tuesday, and Thursday, when members of the opposite sex were not allowed to visit in students' rooms. Some students objected, claiming that the limits on quiet and private study with their peers were unfair. Moreover, on "closed days," wrote *Chanticleer* editor Matt Pethybridge, "any date has to begin and end in a public place.... The idea of trying to share an intimate moment in the main parlor with eight other couples who are trying to do the same thing strikes us as particularly unromantic."[50] Faculty who attended college when dating was permitted only on weekends and then only in public areas were not very sympathetic. Nevertheless, gradually and incrementally, the college moved to "open hours" and "closed hours" on all seven days.

Other complaints were not so easily addressed. By 1980, student vandalism of college property was a $50,000-a-year problem. Since students were reluctant to turn in guilty parties, President Lee decreed that all residents of a hall would be assessed equally to repair deliberate damage to their living quarters. Students protested immediately, but President Lee stood his ground. Not surprisingly, the cost of repairing vandalized property declined to $1,000 a year by 1985.[51]

Aging and undependable heating and plumbing also generated complaints. One student remarked wryly that "nothing gets the old adrenalin flowing" in the morning quite like "icy water coming from the cold *and* hot faucets" of the shower. All the hot water, he was certain, was diverted to the heating system. Problem was, he claimed with little exaggeration, "some rooms are heatless," while others would "stay a toasty 96 degrees all winter, whether you want it or not." Try as they might, college maintenance personnel were never able to correct this deficiency.[52]

Nor could the college solve the perennial problem of friction between roommates. Students of any era will recognize the ten most common complaints during the Lee years, as recited in a *Chanticleer* column:

---

[50] *Chanticleer*, 27 October 1982.

[51] *Chanticleer*, 3 April 1980; 9 October 1980; Lee, Annual Report to the Board, 30 May 1980, 31 May 1985.

[52] *Chanticleer*, 11 March 1981.

1. Early in the morning Roommate B could not sleep because Roommate A arose, loudly brushed her teeth, turned on all the lights, exercised, and hummed her favorite tune as she dressed.
2. Roommate A dressed in Roommate B's clothes without her permission.
3. Roommate A put an album on the stereo while Roommate B was listening to the radio.
4. Roommate A locked the door as she left for class even though Roommate B, who was visiting next door, had left her key in the room.
5. Roommate A let her dirty laundry accumulate in front of Roommate B's bed.
6. Roommate A used the spare change on Roommate B's dresser to buy sodas.
7. Roommate A pinched food from Roommate B's care package from home.
8. Roommate A read Roommate B's mail.
9. Roommate A had parties in the room without inviting Roommate B.
10. Roommate A talked *ad nauseam* about her new boyfriend.[53]

Rules against drinking alcohol continued to confound everyone. During the Lee years the federal government successfully pressured states to raise their legal drinking age to twenty-one years. Aware that drinking was a rite of passage that could not be stamped out, the college was equally concerned that failure to enforce rules against underage drinking might lead to injury or death that would leave the institution liable for damages. Therefore, the college began to enforce more rigorously its policy against drinking on campus. Students were incensed. While condemning drunkenness, freshman Lisa Cannon observed in 1983, "We come to college in order to learn how to become responsible and educated adults. The choice of whether or not we indulge in social drinking should be our privilege." Sophomore Terri Martin added, "Because of the policy, Averett students are forced to drink socially off campus. Not only will drinking off campus lead to an

---

[53] *Chanticleer*, 25 March 1981.

increase in the number of deaths on the highway, but it will also contribute to a sharp increase in the number of alcohol related accidents."[54] The dean of students was willing to compromise by sentencing first-time offenders to a campus alcohol awareness program.[55]

By 1985, when Howard Lee retired, Averett College certainly bore his imprint. He carried the college safely through years of national pessimism and economic uncertainty. Under his leadership the college upgraded faculty, expanded the curriculum, and established a satellite campus for Korean students in Northern Virginia. More important, the institution added facilities—Frith Hall, a new president's house, and Twelve Gates Farm. These accomplishments were possible because Lee had extricated the college from the ill-advised decision to relocate the campus while skillfully managing the inevitable decline in enrollment and successfully courting Baptists, community leaders, and potential donors. Two other facts attest to Lee's success. First, unlike most presidents, he ended his career at least as popular with students and faculty as when he began. Second, because an organization often assumes the personality and character of its chief executive officer, Averett College from 1980 to 1985 was a blend of classical, Renaissance, and Christian virtues that characterized Howard Lee. Perhaps this was his greatest legacy.

---

[54] *Chanticleer*, 29 September 1983.

[55] *Chanticleer*, 20 March 1985.

13

The Presidency of Frank R. Campbell

In the 1890s, when Ohio State University was searching for a new president, one of its trustees, Rutherford B. Hayes, described the perfect candidate. "We are looking for a man," said Hayes, "of fine appearance, of commanding presence, one who will impress the public; he must be a fine speaker at public assemblies; he must be a great scholar and a great teacher; he must be a preacher, also, as some think; he must be a man of winning manners; he must have tact so that he can get along with and govern the faculty; he must be popular with the students; he must also be a man of business training, a man of affairs; he must be a great administrator." Hayes paused, smiled, and then added: "Gentlemen, there is no such man."[1]

For Averett College in 1985, there was such a man—Frank R. Campbell. Born in Roanoke, Virginia, on 4 January 1936, Campbell was the first son and eldest child of Clarence Robert Campbell and Frances Slayton Campbell. His father was a lifelong employee in the treasury department of Norfolk and Western Railroad; his mother was a homemaker. The family lived in southeast Roanoke on Kenwood Boulevard until young Campbell's tenth year, when they relocated seven blocks away to a home on Tazewell Avenue. From there he attended Jamison Elementary School, Stonewall Jackson Junior High School, and Jefferson Senior High School before entering Carson-Newman College in 1954.[2]

Frank Campbell was a typical lad of the 1940s and 1950s. While still in elementary school, he worked a paper route to earn spending

---

[1] Quoted in Rudolph, *American College,* 419.

[2] Frank R. Campbell, interview with author, Averett College, 24 June 2002, hereinafter cited as Campbell interview.

money. In high school he gave up his paper route and began to work for the *Roanoke Times* from 11:00 P.M. until 4:00 A.M. on weekends and during summer months, stuffing circulars into newspapers and preparing bundles for delivery. This left him with free time to date young ladies and indulge in his passion—-sports. He idolized sports figures, beginning as a youth with older boys who played baseball at nearby Fallon Park and ending in adolescence with the famous power-hitting outfielder of the Boston Red Sox, Ted Williams. The Red Sox had a farm team in Roanoke that hired young Campbell to be batboy for opposing teams. On one occasion when the Boston club played an exhibition game against the Roanoke team, Ted Williams called to Campbell, "Hey, kid. Throw me my glove." Campbell still remembers with excitement: "I actually touched Ted Williams' glove!" His fascination also led him to collect baseball cards and sports magazines and listen by radio to the baseball games of the day.[3]

Naturally, his interest in sports took him into interscholastic competition. Campbell gained citywide recognition as an All-City center in the sandlot football program during junior high school. At Jefferson Senior High School, he gave up football to concentrate on baseball and basketball. In basketball he was a starting forward and team captain his senior year. In baseball, his favorite sport, he played second and later third base and was invited by the New York Giants to try out for a spot on one of their farm teams. Interestingly, fierce competitiveness in interscholastic athletics is one of two traits shared by presidents Anderson, Lee, and Campbell.[4]

The other trait is active involvement in church. As a youth Campbell began attending and later joined the Waverley Place Baptist Church. He participated in a male youth group called RAs, or Royal Ambassadors, and worked his way to Ambassador Plenipotentiary, the highest distinction. He was also active in Cub Scout and Boy Scout programs. At Waverley Place he met the Reverend Charles Jolly, who believed that a Christian lifestyle is best encouraged by a vibrant youth program. Jolly not only urged Campbell to participate in the many and varied youth activities, but he also introduced him to the family babysitter, Janet Hale, who was two years Campbell's junior. The pair

---

[3] Ibid; *Chanticleer*, 14 December 1992.
[4] Campbell interview.

dated for five years until their marriage in 1957.[5]

In an unusual way Pastor Jolly also directed Campbell's future. When Campbell was eighteen years of age, a revival at the Waverley Place church led several teenagers to refocus their lives. Campbell dreamed of becoming a professional baseball player and, after that, a coach, but the revival convinced him to devote at least a part of his life to Christian service. This call, however, was not specific; he was unsure whether he should pursue a religious avocation such as lay leadership and Sunday school teaching, or a religious vocation such as missionary work or the pulpit ministry. On the last evening of the revival, he came forward to commit his life to Christian service. Pastor Jolly, sensing the young man's gifts, turned to the congregation and announced young Campbell had decided to become a pulpit minister. The announcement caught Campbell by surprise. He had not committed to anything of the sort. But the more he pondered, the more it appealed to him, and the idea's appeal was substantially enhanced by handsome preministerial scholarships at Carson-Newman College in Jefferson City, Tennessee, which he planned to attend.[6]

Fortunately, Carson-Newman had three professors who helped Campbell confirm his decision. Although a history/political science major with minors in sociology, Greek, and religion, Campbell developed his closest relationships with religion professors Dan Taylor, Douglas Harris, and Russell Bradley Jones. Taylor taught Greek to Campbell for three years and made him appreciate the New Testament in its original language. Harris encouraged Campbell to think historically and critically about the text, dispelling in the process the notion that Christian ministry was simply memorization of Bible passages. Jones, as author of the textbook used in Campbell's introductory class in religion, impressed on the new student the importance of basing biblical knowledge upon sound scholarship.[7]

Meanwhile Frank Campbell and Janet Hale, who was still in high school, continued a long-distance romance. The pair corresponded by mail, talked by telephone occasionally, and dated in the summers and on sporadic weekends when he came home. Her freshman year at Blue

---

[5] Ibid.
[6] Ibid.
[7] Ibid.

Mountain College in Blue Mountain, Mississippi, which separated the pair for long periods, only proved the adage that absence makes the heart grow fonder. As a result they were married on 5 July 1957, at the end of his third collegiate year and her first. He was able to support himself and his new wife with a part-time pastorate at English Creek Baptist Church in Newport, Tennessee, near Carson-Newman College. The congregation was so pleased with his ministry that they obtained an offer of a teaching position in the local public schools to supplement his church salary, should he agree to remain permanently.[8]

Although Campbell graduated cum laude from Carson-Newman in 1958, he had been an indifferent student in high school. Doubtless, he now suspected a career behind a schoolteacher's desk in high school might be no more rewarding than his previous experience in front of one. In addition, daughter Cathy was born in the summer of 1958, followed almost three years later by daughter Donna. Four mouths to feed required a larger pastorate than the seventy-six-member English Creek church. Thus, Campbell turned down the offer and enrolled at Southeastern Baptist Theological Seminary in Wake Forest, North Carolina. In 1961 he graduated with the degree of Master of Divinity. During his stay at Southeastern, Campbell supported his family and paid for his education by serving as pastor of two small churches in Oxford, North Carolina. He spent the next twenty-four years in pastorates at Baptist churches in Raleigh and Statesville. Along the way he earned the degrees of Master of Theology (1965) and Doctor of Ministry (1975) from alma mater Southeastern. He wrote two books—*God's Message in Troubled Times* and *Equipping Deacons in Church Growth Skills*—and scores of articles. In Statesville, where he chaired the Mayor's Citizen Advisory Committee and served on the boards of numerous local charities, a grateful community named him Citizen of the Year in 1983.[9]

Friends and casual acquaintances alike found Campbell to be a comfortable blend of personal traits. At six feet tall and 180 pounds, he was handsome and athletically proportioned. Both in and out of the pulpit, he was eloquent. He was also kind and compassionate, traits that undergirded his role in pastoral care. He visited shut-ins in his congregations several times each year and willingly cut short a vacation

---

[8] Ibid.

[9] Biographical data sheet on Frank Campbell, Averett University Archives.

so he could attend to emergencies in his congregation. Campbell was industrious; he frequently worked seventy-five-hour weeks and seven days each week. Outside of his role as clergyman, he was friendly, witty, and gracious. He could quickly put people at ease. A voracious reader of biographies and autobiographies, he was conversant on many topics. Campbell's close friends knew him as family-oriented. He devoted several hours each week to time with his daughters. Moreover, his wife was always his best friend and confidante. In competitive sports such as golf and tennis, Campbell competed against himself but not against his opponents; he always wanted them to play their best.[10]

His approachability and skills in conciliation, organization, and preaching early marked him for positions of influence in the Baptist hierarchy. In the one-million-member Baptist State Convention of North Carolina, he served as a member of the board of trustees of Wake Forest University, which in 1980 awarded him a Doctor of Divinity degree. He also served as a member of the executive committee of the board of trustees of North Carolina Baptist Hospital, vice chairman and member of the executive committee of the board of trustees of the *Biblical Recorder*, chairman of the board of trustees of the Medical Center of North Carolina Baptist Hospital and Bowman-Gray School of Medicine, and president of the Council on Christian Higher Education. To no one's surprise, the Baptist State Convention of North Carolina elected Campbell its president for 1981–1983. Meanwhile, in the fifteen-million-member Southern Baptist Convention, Campbell became a member of the powerful Committee on Boards and vice chairman of the board of trustees of Southeastern Baptist Theological Seminary.[11]

Despite involvement in higher education as a former student, alumnus, trustee, adjunct professor at both Gardner-Webb College and Southeastern Baptist Theological Seminary, and overseer of denominational colleges and universities in North Carolina, Campbell assumed the Averett mantle knowing only what is called the "external" presidency—fundraising, public relations, and denominational relations. He did not know the "internal" presidency of budgeting, overseeing the physical plant, managing collegiate personnel, and supervising academic matters.

---

[10] Campbell interview; Janet Campbell, telephone interview with author, 26 June 2002; Richard Stoakley, telephone interview with author, 26 June 2002.

[11] Biographical data sheet on Frank Campbell, Averett University Archives.

Nevertheless, because of his skills in administration, he had little trouble mastering these responsibilities. Perhaps more critically, he arrived without a strategic vision—a notion of what the college should be in five years and ten years. In this area, he was keen to learn, quick to grow, and willing to take conservative risks.[12]

His quest for vision was evident in his convocation address in September 1985, two months after assuming the presidency. Although eloquently delivered and entirely appropriate to a collegiate community anxious about the unknown quantity who now was its leader, the address was replete with inspiring phrases that could have been delivered by any president at any of several hundred institutions. To the gathering of faculty, staff, students, and sprinkling of trustees, Campbell pledged to "release the creative talents of a great faculty." He asked that his presidency be judged by his "ability to pull individual talents together to make a smooth team." He promised "democratic administration with strong executive leadership," affirmed the importance of "academic freedom," and applauded Averett for remaining true to its "emphasis on the liberal arts done with excellence," coupled with a "genuine concern for the student." Campbell also warned that "times are hard for higher education today" but "opportunity is always implicit in adversity."[13]

Nonetheless, near the end of his speech, Campbell looked to the future. Averett, he said, must concentrate on building an endowment large enough to assure financial independence. No doubt he arrived at this conclusion through experience. As president of the Council on Christian Higher Education in the Baptist State Convention of North Carolina, he visited and studied the state's seven Baptist colleges and universities to determine what factors made them successful or unsuccessful. He also befriended their presidents. Of these he most admired James Ralph Scales of Wake Forest University, who became Campbell's mentor in collegiate administration. Scales brought academic excellence and respectability to his institution by building a sizeable endowment that could be used for salaries and scholarships to attract and retain outstanding faculty and students. Moreover, a strong endowment lessened Wake Forest's dependence on its parent denomination and

---

[12] Campbell interview.

[13] Frank R. Campbell, "Convocation Address, September 17, 1985," Frank R. Campbell Papers, Averett Library.

made the university immune from denominational meddling. Campbell was coming to realize he must do the same for Averett.[14]

By the time of Campbell's formal inauguration ceremony seven months later, his vision for Averett had crystallized. Once again he stressed the indispensability of endowment. To this he added a second necessity—adult education. He carefully outlined with demographic data both the burgeoning aging population and increasing number of adults not currently served by the traditional, four-year baccalaureate experience. Averett, he said, must develop a new educational delivery system to offer both undergraduate and graduate programs to nontraditional adult students. These two focuses—endowment and adult education—would be Campbell's agenda in his early presidency.[15] Indeed, they would form the two cornerstones of his legacy.

He began with the endowment, which was sorely needed. Owing to the battle between fundamentalists and moderates over use of Baptist resources, Averett could not depend forever on a large annual contribution from the Baptist General Association of Virginia (BGAV). Income from a hefty endowment would be needed to make up for the inevitable decline in Baptist money. In addition, Averett would need quick access to a large sum of cash, should the opportunity arise to acquire the aging Forest Hills Elementary School adjacent to campus. For such a purchase, funds could come only from the unrestricted portion of an endowment. Moreover, faculty salaries remained completely dependent on a tuition-driven budget. Endowed professorships could relieve pressure on the budget and even remove the necessity of raising tuition every year to pay for salary increases. In addition, in 1985, Averett's student scholarships amounted to simply discounts of tuition. Endowed scholarships would serve the dual purpose of removing the need to discount tuition and allowing Averett to compete for brighter students.[16]

In May 1986, Campbell secured board approval for a $10 million endowment campaign. At his request the board also created the Averett Future Fund for the eventual purchase of neighborhood property such as the Forest Hills school. Both funds grew rapidly, despite the eventual

[14] Ibid.

[15] Frank R. Campbell, "Inauguration Address, 22 April 1986," Frank R. Campbell Papers, Averett Library.

[16] Frank R. Campbell, Report to the Board of Trustees, 5 May 1995; Minutes, Board of Trustees, 29 May 1987.

decision by the school board to retain and refurbish the elementary school. Within six months the endowment mushroomed from $240,000 to $1.33 million. Another $1 million came the following year. In 1988 the board approved another $5 million endowment goal when it also approved a $50 million Caring for the Future Campaign, to be completed by the year 2000. Total Current Fund contributions were expected to top $20 million; total endowment, $15 million; and total capital gifts, $15 million. To everyone's surprise the endowment had reached a healthy $24 million by July 2001, when Averett ceased to be a college and became Averett University.[17]

Development of a unique delivery system for nontraditional adult learners came on the heels of initial plans to raise endowment. In fact, the most ambitious, innovative, and successful new program in the Commonwealth of Virginia during the late 1980s and early 1990s was Averett's Graduate and Professional Studies (GPS), known before 1998 as the Averett Adult Curriculum for Excellence (AACE). A year into his presidency, Campbell laid the groundwork for moving into adult education. He began by highlighting changing demographics, pointing out that by 1992 half of the nation's college students would be above twenty-four years of age. Part-time students would equal full-timers, and resident population would, on average, account for only one-sixth of the total student population. Obviously, he concluded, Averett had a unique opportunity to serve a host of currently underserved adults.

In addition, Campbell realized that a college's attractiveness depended on its history, location, curriculum, quality, and religious affiliation, and the usual marketing advantages of small class size, emphasis on teaching, and caring faculty and staff. On many of these measures, Averett suffered by comparison. Its history as a four-year institution was brief. To many Virginians, the name Averett was synonymous with a junior college for girls. The college was located near North Carolina's Research Triangle and abundant shopping and recreation in Greensboro, Winston-Salem, and Raleigh/Durham. But several key competitors were in, and not just near, these areas. Averett could appeal to Virginia Baptists, but not as much as Bluefield College to conservatives or the University of Richmond to moderates. Averett could tout benefits such as

---

[17] Campbell, Report the Board, 30 May 1986, 21 November 1986, 29 May 1987, 1 November 1988, 12 May 2000.

small class size, but so could competitors. In quality its students were at the average in SAT scores, again like many competitors. In short, for Averett to flourish it would have to emphasize higher education with a vocational emphasis delivered innovatively to the nontraditional student.[18]

That emphasis began in spring 1988, when Averett's AACE program opened evening classes for adult learners at various locations in southside Virginia. Classes at Tyson's Corner near Washington, DC, followed in September. AACE quickly proved to be popular. Three-credit-hour classes, called modules, met for four hours once a week for up to seven weeks. Students were required to meet in study groups an equal number of times for an equal number of hours. They could take nine courses a year and complete a baccalaureate degree in five years. The MBA degree required an additional two years of study using the same format. The college designed modules, selected faculty, and provided instruction. It contracted with the Institute for Professional Development (IPD) in Phoenix, Arizona, to handle recruitment.[19]

Despite AACE requirements that students be at least twenty-three years of age, IPD had no trouble meeting its first-year goal of two hundred students. In fact, within a year more than twice that number were enrolled in thirty-two classes at several sites in Northern Virginia (NOVA) and Southern Virginia (SOVA). The average age of the student body was a mature thirty-four years.[20] By April 1991, SOVA added sites in Lynchburg, Roanoke, Martinsville, South Boston, Bluefield, and Wytheville to serve 176 undergraduates and 126 graduate students. NOVA expanded onto military posts near Washington and enrolled 362 individuals divided almost equally between undergraduates and graduate students. AACE was already planning to open sites in Richmond and Tidewater. After only three years of operation, AACE was generating almost 18 percent of Averett's revenue and a half-million dollars annually in sheer profit.[21]

Growth and expansion continued throughout most of the 1990s. The regional campus in Richmond opened in 1993. Its 316 students swelled the AACE student body to more than 1,400 students, twice as many as

---

[18] Campbell, Report to the Board, 21 November 1988; Cohen, Shaping, 304.
[19] Campbell, Report to the Board, 6 May 1988.
[20] Campbell, Report to the Board, 5 May 1989.
[21] Campbell, Report to the Board, 3 May 1991.

matriculated at Danville's residential campus. Averett not only became the recognized leader in adult education in the Commonwealth of Virginia, but AACE's annual profits topped $1 million—the equivalent of earnings on an endowment of $20 million. These earnings helped the college retire debt, improve facilities in Danville, and offer scholarships to deserving students in both the traditional and AACE program. In fact, by May 1994, total annual revenues from AACE amounted to approximately one-third of the college budget. The following year AACE's regional campus serving Hampton Roads opened in Virginia Beach. That same year AACE enrollment reached its peak of 1,638 students.[22]

AACE entered a new era in February 1995, when it unveiled a distance-learning network for use eventually on US Marine bases around the world. Employing voice-activated video cameras and monitors, Marines as far away as Japan and as close as Camp Lejeune, North Carolina, could participate in simultaneous discussions in AACE classes leading to the MBA degree at Averett. The Marine Corps was especially supportive. Because the US military was downsizing, Marines could no longer count on a twenty-year career and a lifelong pension. They now wanted opportunities to earn advanced degrees that would prepare them for civilian life. At the same time, because the Marine Corps often transferred its personnel several times during an average career, Marines could not depend on a fixed-classroom, residential-campus setting. Distance learning best met their needs. The Corps helped out by offering to pay 75 percent of the cost of tuition. Within three years, twenty-one Marines earned master's degrees through Averett's Distance Learning Network.[23]

Other changes in Averett's academic program during the Campbell years were also profound. The best description would be evolution without revolution. Across America in the 1990s, traditionalists usually lost the debate with multiculturalists and deconstructionists over the relative importance of reason and rational discourse in the curriculum. Also in contention was whether courses of study emphasizing ethnic identity were more relevant than a core curriculum highlighting the

---

[22] Campbell, Report to the Board, 1 May 1992, 13 May 1994, 5 May 1995; Board Minutes Averett College Board of Trustees, 5 May 1995. Averett University Archives

[23] *Richmond Times Dispatch*, 1 February 1995, 1B, 3B.

Western experience and based on the works and ideas of what multiculturalists called DWMs (dead white males). Another issue was whether the arts and sciences can unveil universal truth, or whether truth simply depends upon the intellectual environment and personal motives of artists, writers, scientists, and historians. The Averett faculty, which controlled the curriculum and was dominated by traditionalists, insisted on the validity of the Western experience. They championed the role of logic, reason, and rational discourse in the educational process. The faculty also insisted on the existence of universal truth, and they decried the dangers of triviality when supposedly educated citizens discard the classics.[24]

As a result, the faculty merely adjusted the curriculum to accommodate evolving technology and vocational opportunities. In the process the college dropped the cost-ineffective majors of nursing and social work. It added but later dropped a program in air traffic control, closed the Northern Virginia International Program (Korean Program), and downgraded Church Ministries from a major to a minor. Averett then added majors, anchored in a comprehensive liberal arts foundation, in airway science management, aviation/criminal justice, environmental science, journalism, mathematical decision science, golf management, sports medicine, athletic training, and political science. New minors came in coaching, computer information systems, and Spanish. A new interdisciplinary program for students majoring in art, computer science/mathematics, or psychology was added in human-computer interaction. New degrees at all levels included the associate degree in air traffic control, the baccalaureate degree in business administration (e-commerce), and the master's degree in teaching and special education.[25]

Four new programs—honors, interdisciplinary studies, leadership studies, and study abroad—placed Averett in the mainstream of academic life in America. Although new to this institution, these programs were not new to American higher education. The honors program, for example, with its emphasis on a seminar format and senior thesis, began in 1922 at Swarthmore College. It spread across America in the next two decades but did not reach Averett until 1993. With rigid

---

[24] Cohen, *Shaping*, 444–45.

[25] Campbell, Report to the Board, 6 May 1988, 3 May 1991, 1 May 1992, 9 May 1997, 8 May 1998; Board Minutes Averett University Board of Trustees, 20 November 1992, 5 May 1995, 10 November 2000; *Chanticleer*, 19 October 1992, 7 May 1999.

admissions requirements that restricted enrollment to the best and brightest, Averett's new Honors Program combined out-of-classroom experiences, such as field trips, with four colloquia and at least three electives. These courses emphasized a strong oral and written component, student-generated information, and student-led discussion. A required senior honors project demonstrated the capacity to undertake substantial creative work or original research. Students completing approximately 20 percent of their coursework as honors courses earned an honors designation at graduation. An average of twenty students participated in this program yearly.[26]

Slightly fewer students—fifteen—were involved in the eighteen-hour minor in leadership studies. This interdisciplinary program combined required courses in psychology, political science, business administration, and leadership with mentoring and experiential learning designed to produce a leader who could think critically, articulate professionally, appreciate diverse points of view, work in concert, interact successfully, act decisively, and judge soundly.[27]

The most controversial innovation, at least among freshmen, was interdisciplinary studies. Commonly called IDS at Averett and Freshmen Topics or the Freshman Experience elsewhere, the required three-credit-hour course dealt with a different theme each year. The logic behind the program was undeniable. It would enable students to understand the interrelatedness of disciplines by examining a topic from an interdisciplinary point of view. Students in IDS would improve skills in oral and written communication through formal debates, less formal small-group discussions, and short papers. The class would encourage teamwork, improve skills in individual research, and lead students to base opinions on fact, not intuition. Finally, the heavy study-skills component would encourage wise time management and skillful note taking, test taking, listening, summarizing, memorizing, and reading for understanding. Students approached IDS 101 with apprehension. The heavy reading and writing requirements struck many as excessive. Others regarded the emphasis on study skills and time management as trivial and demeaning. On the other hand they enjoyed debates and guest lecturers. After a symbolic boycott of IDS classes in the program's first

---

[26] *Catalog* 2000–2002, 133–35.
[27] Ibid., 141–42; *Danville Register and Bee*, 4 September 1996, n.p.

year (1988), freshmen gradually came to regard the class as inevitable and made the best of it.[28]

The final new program—study abroad—had its roots in the Anderson and Lee years when professors Stephen Ausband in English, Elizabeth Compton in education, Jack Hayes in history, John Laughlin in religion, and Elizabeth Smith in theater began to take students to the British Isles and Israel for short stints in connection with regularly offered classes. During the Campbell years the practice became routine and systematic. Each summer Professor Laughlin went with students to Israel for three weeks of work on an archaeological dig at Banias. Every odd year students accompanied Professor Hayes to the British Isles for study during spring break. In even years Professor William Trakas in the Department of History led students to central and eastern Europe during the May term. Later, the Department of Education arranged a student-teacher exchange with the University of Derby in the United Kingdom for three weeks each spring. Biology participated with annual two-week trips to study the ecology of sites as diverse as Costa Rica and Finland. Students in the Department of Foreign Languages studied in Costa Rica and at the University of Quebec. Finally, Averett offered both semester-abroad and year-abroad programs through cooperative arrangements with universities in China and Russia and an exchange program with Hong Kong Baptist University.[29]

Not only did the equestrian studies department send students to a summer-long course in England to qualify for a British Horse Society Assistant Instructor's Certificate, but also, in autumn 1997, five Averett riders represented the United States of America in international eques-trian competition at the Techniques de Randonnée Equestre en Compe-tition (TREC) World Championship in St. Pierre D'Albigny near Lyon, France. They competed with national teams from Canada, Tunisia, and eight Western European nations. The competition, combining cross-country events and obstacle courses, required riders to navigate a twenty-five-mile course over rough terrain with nothing but a map and compass. The Averett riders, entered as Team U.S.A., won first place among the five national teams who had not competed previously, a triumph that gave Averett international exposure and plentiful local and statewide

---

[28] Campbell, Report to the Board, 6 May 1988, 4 May 1990.
[29] *Chanticleer*, 2 March 1994, 26 September 1997; *Catalog* 2000–2002, 31.

publicity.[30]

Other changes at Averett continued to place the institution in the mainstream of American higher education. Discarding the once-popular January Term brought a corresponding reduction in faculty workload from nine courses per year to eight. Part-time faculty increased. Nationally, the percentage of part-time faculty doubled from 22 percent in 1970 to 41 percent in 1995. The increase at Averett was more dramatic--from less than 10 percent in 1970 to 61 percent by 2001. Averett also reflected the national trend of professors "staying and graying." In 1987 the average age at Averett for assistant, associate, and full professors were 39, 47, and 48 years, respectively. By 2000 the average ages had increased to 45, 47, and 55 years. The effort nationally to update campuses with modern technology was reflected at Averett in the purchase of computers for each faculty member, requirement that students demonstrate computer literacy as a precondition for graduation, general use of programs such as PowerPoint and Blackboard, installation of several computer labs, converting the campus network to the Internet, increasing the number of servers for administrative use from one in 1985 to ten by 2001 and those for students from none in 1985 to three by 2001, installation of digital video equipment, laying of fiber optic cables over the entire campus, and installation in several classrooms of video projectors harnessed to computers with access to the Internet.[31]

Capital improvements kept pace with advances in technology. In fact, Frank Campbell's impact on physical facilities was greater than that of any president, despite his modest start. The lean and inflationary years of the late 1970s and early 1980s had forced the college to defer building maintenance in order to balance the annual operating budget. Campbell's arrival on campus in summer 1985 coincided with vocal student discontent over dilapidated dormitories. He immediately set out to refurbish every dormitory, starting with Danville Hall and ending with Fugate Hall. Finally, in 1991 he was able to scrap the deferred-maintenance model in favor of a continuous-care one.[32]

---

[30] *Richmond Times Dispatch*, 13 September 1997; *Chanticleer*, 26 September 1997, 20 October 1997. See also Kelly Stock , letter to author , January 2002.

[31] Campbell, Report to the Board, 29 May 1987, 3 May 1991, 5 May 1995, Cohen, *Shaping*, 352; Averett College, Fact Book, 1987–88, 15.

[32] Campbell, Report to the Board, 30 May 1986, 6 May 1988, 4 May 1990, 11 October 1991.

Meanwhile, more houses were acquired in the block directly behind Blount Library for future campus expansion. Two were purchased in 1987, three in 1988, and seven more in the next eight years. The college used several of them to house administrative departments such as financial aid, AACE, and student center. Others were demolished to expand open space on campus.[33]

The most important acquisition in Campbell's first five years came in 1989 when trustee Carrington Bidgood persuaded his aunt, Ruth Carrington, to donate her home on Hawthorne Drive. The school sold the home at auction for over $500,000, the largest gift in college history to that point. After designating $100,000 of the proceeds for refurbishing the president's home, the trustees placed the remainder in the endowment for scholarships.[34]

Nineteen ninety-one was a banner year. Since 1981 music courses had been taught in classrooms at West Main Baptist Church adjacent to campus, a stopgap arrangement that was ultimately not satisfactory because of a dearth of good instruments, practice rooms, studios, and offices. In 1988 President Campbell began efforts to acquire Sacred Heart Catholic Church, fifty yards east of campus on West Main Street. In April 1990, he signed a contract to purchase the property for $250,000, only to have the bishop of Richmond withhold approval of the sale because the parish's plans for relocation were judged not to be "fiscally viable."[35]

Meanwhile, President Campbell and director of development Mary Jo Davis were courting a potential donor introduced by board member Lewis Roach. She was Emily Swain Grousbeck, a Danville native and music major at Randolph-Macon Institute (later Stratford College) who sang in choral productions with the New York Symphony Orchestra. In summer 1990, she graciously agreed to contribute $1 million towards the construction of a 6,800-square-foot music building on campus. Completed in summer 1991, the Emily Swain Grousbeck Music Building

---

[33] Campbell, Report to the Board, 18 November 1988, 7 May 1993; Minutes of the Board Averett University Board of Trustees, 29 May 1987; Averett College, Fact Book, 1990–1991, 43.

[34] Campbell, Report to the Board, 5 May 1989; Board Minutes Averett University Board of Trustees, 1 May 1992.

[35] Walter F. Sullivan to Frank R. Campbell, 5 April 1990, Campbell Papers, Averett University Archives.

contained two large classrooms, four office/studios, five practice rooms, a seminar room, and a library. Music classes began there in the fall semester. With the Art Building on West Main Street, the dramatic arts program located in Pritchett Auditorium, and the music program in Grousbeck, the fine and performing arts were finally housed in permanent facilities.[36]

The banner year of 1991 also brought both an unusual acquisition and the end of a chronic parking shortage. The former came when Mrs. A. C. Conway, Jr., donated her Cape Cod house at 161 Mountain View Avenue across the street from Frith Hall. She reserved her right to lifetime occupancy of the dwelling. In addition, the college improved parking by adding a paved sixty-four-space lot at Townes Street on property recently leveled after the demolition of houses the college had purchased. For the first time in its history, Averett had a surplus of parking spaces. Never again would neighbors complain. It seemed as though an era was ending.[37]

The equestrian program finally got permanent facilities in spring 1990, when trustee George Shields and his business partner, Marshall Kendall, donated eighty acres of land eight miles from campus off Shady Grove Road in Caswell County, North Carolina. The college immediately cleared the land, created three large pastures, and constructed a state-of-the-art equestrian center. The complex, located on hilly and rolling land, featured a twenty-stall barn with three tack rooms, a 30-by-60-meter indoor arena with additional space for stalls, outside dressage and jumping arenas, a round pen, six paddocks, three additional large pastures, cross-country jumps, and access to nearby trails. The college occupied the facility in September 1993.[38] In the next seven years, Shields added thirty-five additional acres, bringing the total acreage to 115.

Three years later, on 19 October 1996, Averett dedicated the David S. Blount Chapel in Frith Hall. With 172 seats and attractive, modern furnishings, the hall finally provided the college with a medium-sized

---

[36] *Danville Register and Bee,* 6 October 1990, n.p; *Chanticleer,* 25 October 1990; Campbell, Report to the Board, 3 May 1991.

[37] Campbell, Report to the Board, 3 May 1991; Frank R. Campbell, "Remarks to the Faculty, 1991," Campbell Papers.

[38] Board Minutes Averett University Board of Trustees, 4 May 1990, 1 May 1992, 7 May 1993, 13 May 1994.

space for cultural and religious events that would have overflowed the largest classroom but would have been dwarfed in the six-hundred-seat Pritchett Auditorium. The college funded the facility after Mary Blount's death in 1994 with the portion of her $2.8 million bequest that she had earmarked eleven years earlier for a chapel.[39]

The end of the decade brought badly needed apartment-style dormitories. Despite much-needed renovations, the other dormitories remained uninviting. In many instances they were drab and plagued with problems such as uneven climate control. Making matters worse was the interconnection of all dormitories, except Fugate, which continued to exude an aura of a 1950s-vintage girl's junior college. In addition, many Averett students of the 1990s, who grew up in homes with a private bedroom and bath for each child, found living in hall-style dormitories confining. As a result dormitory enrollment dropped from 438 students in the fall of 1982 to 305 students in 1997, after free falling to only 257 students in 1992.[40]

President Campbell began to take notice in 1998. A year later, on 18 November 1999, he and board chairman Robert Ashby broke ground for the Averett Commons. Built by the Capstone Development Corporation of Birmingham, Alabama, at a cost of $5.3 million, the complex consisted of three apartment-style dormitories to house 144 students. Each apartment had four single-occupancy bedrooms, two bathrooms, a living/dining combination, a fully furnished kitchen, a laundry room with washer and dryer, ample closets, and a spacious balcony. Students occupied these quarters in fall semester 2000. So popular was the notion of apartment-style living that during the signup period five months earlier, all of the rooms were spoken for on the first day. The wisdom of constructing the new dormitories was borne out by a 94 percent retention rate for Commons residents from fall to spring of 2000–2001.[41]

The capstone of Campbell's capital improvements campaign was North Campus. Since attaining senior status in 1969, Averett had suffered from inadequate athletic facilities. The narrow gymnasium, seating only three hundred spectators, was not suited for postseason tournaments

---

[39] *Danville Register and Bee,* 18 October 1996, n.p.

[40] Campbell, Report to the Board, 8 May 1998.

[41] Campbell, Report to the Board, 29 May 1987, 4 May 1990; 4 May 2001; Board Minutes Averett University Board of Trustees, 29 May 1987, 17 November 1989, 3 May 1991.

in volleyball and basketball, and its climate control was limited to heating. Even local high schools had better indoor facilities. Outside, the softball, baseball, and soccer programs lacked practice fields. Only soccer had a playing field on campus. Softball games were played at Ballou Park, baseball at Dan Daniel Park. In addition, the college had no center where the entire Averett community could gather. Commencement exercises, for example, were held at the City Auditorium in December or under a large tent on Kleinoder Field in the spring.

As soon as he arrived at Averett in 1985, Campbell recognized the need for a field house that could double as a convocation center. On 29 May 1987, after two years of lobbying, he persuaded the board to commit to the concept of such a facility. Concept could not become reality, however, until the college obtained a suitable site. Two years later, in November 1989, Danville developer John W. Daniel donated almost seventy acres of land in a tract known as the Carter Springs property on Mount Cross Road. Located four miles north of the West Main Street campus, the tract was valued at $610,000. Combined with the new Equestrian Center, the Averett campus suddenly swelled from 19 to 169 acres. In May 1991, the Board formally committed to a $10 million campaign to construct North Campus, complete with modern athletic facilities and convocation center. This Averett Tomorrow Campaign would remain in its silent phase until $4 million was pledged.[42]

Steady progress ensued through 1993. Two board chairs, Claude B. Owen and Elizabeth Walker, personally or through their businesses each donated $500,000. By May 1993, an additional thirty-eight contributors brought the total to $3.3 million. By November, the estate of Danville newspaper publisher Elizabeth Stuart James Grant added another $1 million. On 14 September 1993, at fall convocation, board chairman Richard Wright announced the inauguration of the public phase of Averett Tomorrow. The following May, English Construction Company began site development.[43]

Then came the bad news. Through much of 1994–1995, the

---

[42] Campbell, Report to the Board, 29 May 1987, 4 May 1990; Board Minutes Averett University Board of Trustees, 29 May 1987, 17 November 1989, 3 May 1991.

[43] Board Minutes Averett University Board of Trustees, 20 November 1992, 7 May 1993, 10 November 1993; *Danville Register and Bee,* 15 September 1993, n.p; Campbell, Report to the Board, 3 May 1991, 1 May 1992, 13 May 1993.

campaign was unable to progress beyond a plateau of $5 million. Worse yet, the projected cost of the project escalated from $10 million to $12.5 million. Consequently, beginning in spring 1995, the college inaugurated a massive public relations drive to complete the Averett Tomorrow Campaign quickly. On May 5, amidst much fanfare, Campbell presided over an official groundbreaking ceremony at North Campus to coincide with construction of the athletic fields. He also announced formation of a Committee of Thirteen, made up of former and current trustees, to raise the additional $7.5 million. Within two years, pledges rose to $7.8 million, and the college began erecting the field house/convocation center. Use of the athletic fields in fall 1997 generated more interest and publicity, which, in turn, brought in additional contributions. By May 1998, the Averett Tomorrow Campaign passed the $10 million mark with contributions from sixty-seven businesses and 447 individuals. Over one-fourth of the total came from the generous Elizabeth Stuart James Grant Trust.[44]

When finally completed in late summer 1998 at a cost of $4.5 million, the E. Stuart James Grant Convocation/Athletic Center was modern in design, appearance, and appointments. Externally, it sported a silver metallic roof and two tones of masonry. Surrounding it were ample parking facilities, two soccer fields, a softball field, and baseball field. Inside, the 33,000-square-foot arena contained three basketball courts, fixed seating for 1,000 spectators, and temporary seating for 2,000 more. The structure also contained thirteen faculty offices, three classrooms, a fitness center, a training room, locker rooms, restrooms, laundry, and maintenance areas.[45]

The college officially dedicated this facility at Homecoming on Saturday morning, 18 October 1998, in a "Run with the Scissors" ceremony. After formally retiring the old gymnasium on Mountain View Avenue, college officials drove four miles to North Campus. Meanwhile, forty former Averett athletes from as far away as Finland participated in a relay carrying scissors that would cut the ribbon officially to open the Grant Center. The forty-first runner was former vice president for development G. Rodney Beals, who handed the scissors to President

---

[44] Campbell, Report to the Board, 5 May 1995, 9 May 1997, 8 May 1998; *Danville Register and Bee,* 16 April 1997, , n.p., 22 October 1998, n.p; Averett News Release, 13 April 1995, 5 May 1995.

[45] *Chanticleer,* 9 November 1998.

Campbell. After speeches by city authorities, members of the Grant family, and college officials, Campbell cut the ribbon to open the new facility.[46]

Two years later, in 2000, the college completed development of North Campus with construction of a football complex to house the new football program. Included were a playing field, a practice field, and a 7,800-square-foot field house with team rooms, coaches' offices, classrooms, and an equipment room. Planning and some construction also began on a stadium of 3,000 seats, press box, and concession area. The facility, minus permanent seating, was ready for the Cougars' opening home game on 9 September 2000, against Gallaudet University.[47]

Like his predecessor, Campbell had to adjust Averett to a changing educational environment in the United States. In the process Averett evolved into an institution markedly different from the one Campbell inherited in 1985. Shortly after becoming president he reduced the number of cost centers by contracting with private firms to operate internal housekeeping, maintenance, and bookstore. He then quickly moved to improve Averett's regional image. In the early 1990s, based on such factors as financial resources, faculty credentials, student/faculty ratio, and graduation rates, *U.S. News and World Report* produced a guide entitled *America's Best Colleges*, which listed Averett in the fourth quartile of Southern liberal arts colleges. By improving such factors as endowment and percentage of alumni giving, Campbell was able to move Averett into the second quartile. However, a reclassification by the Carnegie System shifted Averett from the designation of liberal arts college to comprehensive regional university because of the large number of advanced degrees the institution awarded each year. Averett subsequently fell from the second quartile of the former category into the fourth quartile of the latter. There Averett remained until the late 1990s, when it advanced into the third quartile of comprehensive regional universities. Yet because its competitor group now included reputable and well-established schools such as the University of Richmond and Stetson University, Campbell was able to boast that "this ranking serves, once again, as an acknowledgement that Averett College remains

---

[46] Campbell, Report to the Board, 7 May 1999.

[47] Averett news release, 27 April 2000, Averett University Archives.

competitive with some of the finest colleges and universities in the
nation." The result was regional recognition as an institution rising in
quality and reputation.[48]

Perhaps more important for the future was creation in 2000 of the
Institute for Advanced Learning and Research through a partnership with
Danville Community College (DCC) and Virginia Polytechnic Institute
(VPI). In the mid-1990s several public officials, led by state senator
Charles Hawkins of Chatham, began looking for ways to revitalize the
Southside economy. Hawkins identified three possible solutions: an
Interstate highway, a major airport, or a major university. For various
reasons, the first two were not attainable. Hawkins therefore persuaded
the state legislature to appropriate money to study the feasibility of
creating a state-supported university in Danville. Several Averett
partisans, including former mayor Linwood Wright and board members
Charles Majors, Ben Davenport, Whittington Clement, and Robert
Ashby, lobbied to have Averett included in any state-supported scheme.
These men also formed the nucleus of the Future of the Piedmont
Foundation that was planning for the area's economic revitalization. Like
the political cadre led by Senator Hawkins, leaders in this group saw
availability of higher education locally as a key component in attracting
new industry, improving technology, and developing a workforce based
on human intelligence rather than brawn. A lean state budget kept the
concept of a state-supported university in Danville from becoming a
reality. However, as a result of initial overtures by VPI alumnus and
Averett board member Ben Davenport, Virginia Polytechnic Institute
indicated an interest in creating a partnership with Averett and DCC.
Prodded by local delegate Whittington Clement, the state legislature
bowed to the wisdom of combining state money with private money and
approved the scheme with little opposition.[49]

The New Institute held great promise. Danville and Pittsylvania
County promised to provide funding for initial facilities in a proposed
cyberpark at the junction of US 29 and US 58. The money was slated to
come from a portion of each jurisdiction's share of the Virginia Tobacco
Indemnification Settlement. At the Institute students would be able to

---

[48] News release, 13 October 1995, 18 October 1993; Campbell, Report to the Board,
30 May 1986, 5 May 1989; *Chanticleer*, 15 October 1993; *Danville Register and Bee*, 19
October 1994, n.p.

[49] Campbell interview.

complete an associate degree through DCC, a baccalaureate degree from Averett, and advanced degrees, including a doctorate, through VPI.[50]

Simultaneous with creation of the Institute was a change in nomenclature of Averett from college to university. Although the board first discussed this transition in 1995, a decision was delayed because of accreditation issues raised by the Southern Association of Colleges and Schools (SACS) in 1997. That hurdle cleared, the Averett community under board chairman Robert Ashby began to talk seriously about the wisdom of such a step. The advantages were obvious. State Senator Hawkins wanted a university in the Southside to stimulate regional development. Averett partisans feared that failure to act might invite extension of another institution into the area (in fact, Old Dominion University was already offering baccalaureate degrees through distance learning on the premises of Danville Community College). In addition, Averett might have more success in recruiting international students who, when they finished secondary school, were accustomed to attending university, not college. Sister institutions such as Shenandoah, Hollins, and Eastern Mennonite had already adopted the moniker of university. The Carnegie System and *U.S. News and World Report* had for several years classified Averett as a university because of its high percentage of master's degrees. Moreover, the switch from college to university would not involve additional expenses of upgrading its academic program, as Averett's faculty, facilities, and opportunities for research were at least as impressive and extensive as those of many other private universities. Finally, by having undergraduate study in the arts and sciences, graduate study in education and business, advanced teaching facilities, research capabilities, and vocational and professional programs, Averett already satisfied current criteria for a university. With all arguments favoring the name change, the board voted in November 2000 to become Averett University, effective 1 July 2001.[51]

Interspersed with hours preparing the transition to university status and creating the Institute was energy devoted to expanding the athletic program. Campbell realized not only the importance of developing each student athletically as well as academically, but also the fact that

---

[50] Board Minutes Averett University Board of Trustees, 10 November 2000, 4 May 2001.

[51] Board Minutes Averett University Board of Trustees, 10 November 2000; Frank R. Campbell, Remarks to the Faculty, August 1999, Campbell Papers.

retention of students at Averett was tied to extracurricular involvement. As a result he emphasized intercollegiate athletics. During his administration, the Averett Cougars became the team to beat in the Dixie Conference in women's volleyball, women's tennis, and men's tennis. The women's volleyball team won the conference championship each year from 1991 through 2000. The women's tennis team did likewise in every year from 1994 through 2000 except 1998. The men's tennis teams were conference champions in six of the fourteen years from 1987 through 2000 and received NCAA postseason bids each year from 1996 through 2000. In addition, individual athletes achieved national recognition. In 1987 Tapio Martti of the men's tennis team finished in the final four of the NCAA Division III Tournament. In 1996 and 1997, Elina Tolppa of the women's tennis team won the National Rolex Championship in Memphis, Tennessee.[52]

In the other thirteen intercollegiate sports, Averett was usually competitive if not dominant. The women's cross country team won a Dixie Conference Championship in 1997 but failed to place thereafter. The women's softball team was conference co-champion in 1995. Men's basketball won the conference title in 1990 and even reached the "sweet sixteen" of the NCAA Division III postseason tournament. Unfortunately, that autumn the Dixie Conference put the men's basketball program on probation for two years because of recruiting violations. Thereafter, the men's team was able to eke out only a second-place conference finish in the regular season of 1998, a second-place finish at the conference tournament in 2000, and a second-place finish in both regular-season and conference play in 2001. The baseball program began in 1995 with a twenty-two game junior college schedule. Dixie Conference competition began the following year, when the team won twelve games and lost nineteen. Averett's best record of 28-12 came in 2000. Between 1985 and 2001, fifteen athletes were selected as All-Americans: ten were in tennis, two in golf, and one each in volleyball, basketball, and baseball.[53]

---

[52] Board Minutes Averett University Board of Trustees, 29 May 1987; *Chanticleer*, 25 April 1997, 17 November 1997.

[53] Board Minutes Averett University Board of Trustees, 4 May 1990; Campbell, Report to the Board, 4 May 1990, 5 May 1995; *Pendulum*, 1990, 108; *Chanticleer*, 15 November 1990, 31 January 1991, 21 April 1995; *Danville Register and Bee*, 18 February 1996, n.p.

Averett's boldest move in intercollegiate athletics came in 2000 with a football program. Although beginning in New Jersey in 1869 with a contest between Princeton and Rutgers, football evolved into a Southern sport after World War II. Football offered great appeal to Americans and particularly Southerners. It was a social leveler; it recognized individual achievement while at the same time stressing teamwork; it put a premium on ingenuity, encouraged competition, and bred esprit de corps. With detailed rules and regulations, it encouraged fair play and honor, both of which were historically glorified in the chivalrous South. More importantly for Averett, football was the sport most often calculated to reverse female dominance in a student body. In fact, Averett's male-female ratio on the Danville campus had slipped from 42:58 in fall 1993 to 39:61 in 1997. The 106 players who dressed for football in late summer 2000 brought the ratio to a respectable 48:52. On the other hand, a win-loss record that year of one and nine gave promise of better days to come.[54]

Regionally, Averett dominated intercollegiate competition in one sport not recognized by the NCAA: flying. From 1991 through 1995, the aviation program won four consecutive titles in regional competition sponsored by the National Intercollegiate Flying Association (NIFA). Averett flyers placed either first or second in the next five years. These meets combined ground events in navigation, aircraft recognition, simulation, and rules and regulations, with flight events in message drop, short field, power off, and navigation.[55]

Despite a successful intercollegiate athletic program, Campbell had to cope with trials and occasional failures in other areas. Problems with enrollment bedeviled him throughout his presidency. Traditional enrollment (the Danville campus and Korean program in Northern Virginia) averaged about 970 students in his first five years before dropping to 808 students in 1992–1993. Residence hall enrollment plunged even more dramatically, from 403 students in autumn 1985 to 257 in 1992. These figures partially reflected national demographic trends. The number of high school graduates peaked at 2.77 million in 1988 before declining steadily to 2.44 million in 1992. Not until 1995

---

[54] Rudolph, *American College,* 373, 381–82; Averett College, Fact Book, 1997; Campbell, Report to the Board, 4 May 2001.

[55] *Chanticleer,* 25 November 1996.

would the annual total begin to increase, and not until 1998 would the 1988 figure be reached again.[56]

Campbell, not waiting for the increase in 1995, quickly devised a strategy to combat the ten-year trough from 1988 to 1998. In 1988, he inaugurated the AACE program to add in off-campus adult learners what the college was losing in traditional eighteen- to-twenty-four-year-olds. AACE enrollment grew from 542 in June 1990 to 1,638 in May 1995. As a result, in 1990 Averett experienced the largest increase in total enrollment of any college in Virginia. The following year its increase was third largest of fifty-six schools in the Southern Baptist Convention. Only new-student enrollment at Baylor University and Wake Forest University exceeded that of Averett.[57]

The second piece of his enrollment strategy was reorganization of the administration. In 1992 Campbell created an Office of Enrollment Management under a dean with direct responsibility for the four functions of recruiting, admissions, financial aid, and retention. These four offices previously worked cooperatively but without coordination. The new dean quickly placed a renewed emphasis on retention through refurbishing dormitories and improving new-student orientation. He also budgeted more money for telemarketing and less for travel. Dividends were apparent immediately. Residence hall enrollment shot up from 257 in fall 1992 to 317 in 1993 and stabilized for the next five years.[58]

Demographics were not the only culprit. In the early 1980s private institutions nationwide adopted a "high tuition/high aid" strategy. They raised tuition and allowed wealthy students to pay the sticker price. Less affluent students received "scholarships" (in reality, tuition discounts) that reduced their costs while at the same time flattering their ego. The average tuition discount nationwide rose from 29 percent in 1990 to 39 percent in 1999. As a result, students expected to receive at least one scholarship. At the same time, they quickly caught on to the ploy of tuition discounts and began choosing a college based on total cost rather than size of scholarship. This pattern cut both ways at Averett. The college did not raise tuition as much as many sister institutions.

---

[56] Campbell, Report to the Board, 5 May 1989, 13 May 1994; Board Minutes Averett University Board of Trustees, 6 May 1988.

[57] Campbell, Report to the Board, 29 May 1987, 4 May 1990; folder titled "AACE enrollment," Campbell Papers.

[58] Campbell, Report to the Board, 4 May 2001.

Consequently, it was able to keep discounts a full 12 percentage points below the national average in 1999 and still attract students. On the other hand, Averett suffered in a bidding war with more affluent colleges whose endowments allowed them to discount tuition less but at the same time offer more in real scholarships. Campbell's solution to this quandary was a determined effort to raise the portion of Averett's endowment earmarked for scholarships. The amount of money distributed from the endowment each year for scholarships rose from zero in 1985 to $240,000 in 2000–2001.[59]

The last two pieces of his enrollment strategy were an innovative pilot program, coupled with fiscal retrenchment. As early as 1991, chief academic officer Malcom Huckabee suggested to the State Council of Higher Education for Virginia (SCHEV) that the Commonwealth subsidize the baccalaureate education of community-college transfers into private senior colleges like Averett. The subsidy, equal to Virginia's portion of the cost of educating the student at a public senior college, would be available to what were called "place-bound" students who could not leave their locality to attend a public senior college because of commitments such as job or family. In 1995 Whittington W. Clement, Danville's delegate in the General Assembly and an Averett trustee, guided a Community College Transfer Program through the legislature. As a pilot program lasting only two years and applicable only to community-college transfers at three colleges (Averett, St. Paul's College in Lawrenceville, and Bluefield College in Bluefield), this innovative scheme earmarked one hundred scholarships of $3,500, divided almost equally among the three schools. Eventually, because of unclaimed scholarships at St. Paul's and Bluefield, forty-seven transfers from Danville Community College were able to earn their baccalaureate degrees at Averett.[60]

The most painful segment of the enrollment strategy was fiscal retrenchment in areas not involved in recruitment, admission, retention, and financial aid. In 1990–1991, because of the adverse demographic trough, 45 percent of colleges and universities nationwide reported midyear budget cuts. Other institutions reduced costs by increasing class

---

[59] Campbell, Report to the Board, 12 May 2000.

[60] Board Minutes Averett University Board of Trustees, 18 November 1995; *Danville Register and Bee,* 10 September 1995, n.p.

size and reducing the number of multiple sections of classes. Because of the infusion of AACE revenue, Averett was able to avoid retrenchment until fall 1992, when salaries were frozen. A 4 percent salary increase in February partially made up for the cuts. Salaries were frozen again in 1998–1999, although a 5 percent increase in 1999–2000 removed some of the sting. In addition, departmental budgets were frozen occasionally.[61]

The success of the four-part strategy became even more apparent in the late 1990s. Between autumn 1998 and 2001, traditional enrollment increased 43 percent. In 1999–2000, that of residential students was the best in a decade, and the residence-hall headcount of 478 in the fall of 2001 was the best in almost three decades.[62]

Enrollment was not the only factor exerting pressure on the budget. Almost equal was the need to increase faculty salaries. When Campbell took office, Averett's faculty salaries were among the lowest of twenty-one private colleges in the Commonwealth. Quickly realizing a pay raise was essential, not only to recruit and retain competent faculty but also to gain membership in the prestigious Virginia Foundation for Independent Colleges, Campbell increased compensation for some faculty by 25 percent over a three-year period. However, much of the emphasis was put on improving salaries for assistant and associate professors, tending to narrow the differential between the lower ranks and full professor and resulting in grumbling in the top rank. In the late 1980s rival institutions also increased faculty compensation significantly, leaving Averett professors in nearly their same comparable position. Campbell then worked hard to create endowed professorships to relieve pressure on the annual operating budget. Yet despite the fact that donors endowed professorships in history and chemistry (coupled with an average annual increase in faculty pay at or above the consumer price index), Averett professors still finished the decade of the 1990s ahead of only two private Virginia colleges out of twenty-one in full-professor and associate-professor pay, and ahead of only seven in assistant-professor pay. More embarrassing, the only college behind Averett in full-

---

[61] Campbell, "Remarks to Faculty and Staff, August 1991," Campbell Papers; Campbell, Report to the Board, 7 May 1993, 7 May 1999.

[62] Frank R. Campbell, President's Annual Report, 4 May 2001; Campbell, Report to the Board, 12 May 2000; "Residence Halls Headcount," typescript, Admissions Office, Averett University.

professor pay in 1987 was ahead in 2000. Two of the three colleges behind Averett in associate-professor pay in 1987 were ahead in 2000. Clearly, Campbell's efforts in this area accomplished little.[63]

At the same time enrollment was declining and salary pressures were increasing, denominational aid was in jeopardy. Internecine warfare between fundamentalists and moderates in the Southern Baptist Convention in general, and the Baptist General Association of Virginia (BGAV) in particular, led to a decline in giving to the cooperative programs that funded such outreaches as higher education. Nevertheless, Campbell bemoaned the fact that BGAV gave only 14 percent of its dollars to higher education while similar programs in neighboring states contributed 22 to 28 percent. The pressure of his complaints did seem to help, and so did Campbell's constant lobbying. In 1992 Averett received more BGAV aid than any other Baptist institution in Virginia, despite the fact the dollars amounted to only about 5 percent of the total college budget. At the same time, the 5 percent was equivalent to the earnings on an endowment of $4 million. By 1990–2001, however, BGAV contributions dwindled to slightly over $300,000, or just over 1 percent of the annual college budget.[64]

Added to budgetary pressures were those from the local community. An integral part of Averett's mission was community outreach, which it fulfilled through a host of cultural events. The community was unanimous in appreciation of the monthly concert/lecture series, three dramatic productions each year, weekly "Fit For Life" programs for cardiac patients, and an array of camps and conferences. Less appreciated was a controversy that reverberated throughout the Southern Baptist Convention and eventually cost a seminary professor her job.

On 28 January 1992, as part of Averett's annual Staley Lecture Series, Professor Molly Marshall of Southern Baptist Theological Seminary in Louisville spoke on the topic "Gender Identity and Language about God." She decried as erroneous, even idolatrous, the common tendency to make God, who is a spiritual being, male by use of

---

[63] Averett College, Fact Book, 1988–1989; *Chronicle of Higher Education,* 20 April 2001, A20–A22; Campbell, Report to the Board, 29 May 1987, 6 May 1988; Board Minutes Averett University Board of Trustees, 6 May 1988.

[64] Campbell, Report to the Board, 6 May 1988, 5 May 1989, 1 May 1992; Board Minutes Averett University Board of Trustees, 20 November 1992, 18 November 1994, 3 May 1996, 8 May 1998.

gender pronoun labeling. Furthermore, she pointed to many nonpersonal and female metaphors for God in scriptures. She ended by pleading for inclusive language in discussions about God.[65]

Trouble started the next day when the local daily newspaper printed portions of her remarks out of context and with key words missing. The conservative Danville-area Concerned Baptist Laymen (CBL) immediately swung into action. Publicly assailing Marshall as a heretic, the group fired off a letter to several trustees of Southern Baptist Theological Seminary "urgently requesting" her dismissal. "Her radical feminist views," they explained, constituted "an open affront to the very foundations of our Christian Faith."[66] Two weeks later, CBL members and supporters paid to have the letter printed in the local daily newspaper. They agreed with the CBL chairman who proclaimed, "Jesus referred to Him as God the Father. How much more evidence do you need?"[67]

Worse was to come. Critical letters poured into President Campbell's office from throughout the South. The Richmond-area Concerned Baptist Laymen publicly expressed "shock and outrage" at her remarks and dubbed them "spiritually X-rated."[68] Even the executive committee of the local Pittsylvania Baptist Association, representing 48 churches and 15,000 members, expressed to Campbell "displeasure and disapproval for your allowing Professor Molly Marshall—or any other professor whether as a guest speaker or as a member of the faculty—to express and expound such views as God having no gender."[69]

Attempts to defend Marshall fell on deaf ears, especially among local conservatives. Campbell tried to defuse the controversy by stating publicly that the audience at Marshall's lecture heard "nothing faintly resembling the article in the paper."[70] In a letter to a Virginia Baptist clergyman, Campbell took exception to the common tendency to

---

[65] Malcom W. Huckabee to Trustees of the Southern Baptist Theological Seminary, 17 February 1992, Malcom Huckabee Papers, Averett University; *Danville Register and Bee,* 29 January 1992, 1, 5A; 29 February 1992, 5A; *Religious Herald* 165 (20 February 1992): 5.

[66] *Danville Register and Bee,* 14 February 1992, 1A.

[67] *Danville Register and Bee,* 29 February 1992, 5A.

[68] Richmond Area for Concerned Baptist Laymen to Malcom W. Huckabee, 3 March 1992, Campbell Papers.

[69] Alden L. Hicks to Frank R. Campbell, 21 February 1992, Campbell Papers.

[70] *Baptist Messenger,* 20 February 1992.

anthropomorphize the Almighty: "I think for us to demand that God be like us," he wrote, "is to diminish the nature and character of God."[71] Chief academic officer Malcom Huckabee wrote seminary trustees to deny that Marshall made the statements imputed to her by the local chairman of the Concerned Baptist Laymen. He added for emphasis, "As [he] was not present at either lecture we can only assume that he was misinformed." Labeling the quotations by the local CBL chairman as "a caricature of what was presented," Huckabee concluded that "we find his actions deplorable." [72] The Reverend Bruce Wilson, a local moderate, pleaded that Marshall be judged "on the basis of what she actually said and did, and not on superficially-rendered newspaper articles and second-hand evaluations from a man [the local CBL chairman] with a widely reputed doctrinal agenda."[73] Unfortunately for Marshall and for freedom of inquiry, her moderate-to-liberal views on this and other issues eventually led to her dismissal from the faculty of the Louisville school.

Spillover from the Molly Marshall affair affected decisions on campus for some time to come. Thereafter, the Staley Lecture Committee took pains not to bring in controversial female speakers. More immediately, the Campbell administration felt compelled to cancel a film that, under less turbulent circumstances, might have been shown with little comment: *Henry and June*, which contained nudity, strong language, and graphic homosexual encounters. When the Averett College Activities Board (ACAB), which scheduled films for student entertainment, billed the film as "an erotic masterpiece," several students complained the film was inconsistent with the institution's Baptist heritage and statement of mission.[74]

Campbell was in a bind and he knew it. Although religiously moderate, he and Averett had not seen fit to take sides publicly in the controversy between fundamentalists and moderates in the SBC and the BGAV. To show the film would pose double jeopardy: even many moderates would be offended by the frank subject matter, and all fundamentalists would claim Averett had taken sides against them. In

---

[71] Frank R. Campbell to Dr. Paul L. Brown, 19 March 1992, Campbell Papers.

[72] Malcom Huckabee to Trustees of Southern Baptist Theological Seminary, 17 February 1992, Huckabee Papers.

[73] Bruce Wilson to Dr. Julian Pentecost, 13 February 1992, Campbell Papers.

[74] Campbell, Remarks to the Faculty, 18 February 1992, Campbell Papers.

addition, Averett was in the midst of a demographic slump in high school graduates and thus potential freshmen. To show the film in the winter of 1992 might be just enough to persuade young conservative Baptists to enroll elsewhere. On the other hand, Campbell considered censorship inherently undemocratic and hostile to intellectual growth and maturation. He agonized for several days before finally deciding to cancel the film. He concluded that academic freedom was not involved because the film would be shown for entertainment and not as a vehicle for teaching. He further noted that none of Averett's external constituencies would have condoned such use of Baptist money. Campbell defended his action by saying simply that showing such a movie would be "inconsistent with the mission of the college."[75]

Reactions ran the gamut. Physical Education instructor Stephanie D. O'Brien labeled the cancellation "a wise decision based on the mission of our institution."[76] History professor William Trakas took the opposite view. Asserting publicly that the cancellation smacked of Nazi Germany and Stalinist Russia, he was certain Campbell's actions made Averett "look like a Mickey Mouse institution."[77] Trustee James R. Rowles was mystified that "any faculty member who is at all knowledgeable concerning the fundamentalist takeover [of state Baptist associations across the South] would want to add fuel to their fire."[78] One student bemoaned the hypocrisy evident in ACAB's being forced to cancel *Henry and June* but being allowed to show *Lethal Weapon*—in the latter movie, the writer noted, "Mel Gibson puts a hole through someone with an elephant gun" and "has meaningless sex" with "numerous blonde bimbos."[79] One hundred eighty-four other students signed a petition to protest the cancellation. On the other side, several students questioned whether freedom of speech and press are "advantageous for a society if the people within that society use that liberation to foster their own immorality."[80] Coverage by the Associated Press and *Chronicle of Higher Education* focused on censorship to the exclusion of other issues,

---

[75] Ibid; *Chanticleer*, 6 February 1992; See also Frank R. Campbell to Tim Thornton, 19 March 1992, Campbell Papers.

[76] O'Brien to Campbell, 24 February 1992, Campbell Papers.

[77] *Chanticleer*, 6 February 1992.

[78] James R. Rowles to Frank R. Campbell, 11 February 1992, Campbell Papers.

[79] *Chanticleer*, 24 February 1992.

[80] Ibid.

and nationwide, Averett was made to look repressive.[81]

Yet the flaps over Molly Marshall and *Henry and June* were minor distractions when compared to a deteriorating relationship with the Southern Association of Colleges and Schools (SACS), the regional accrediting body without whose endorsement no college or university can exist. Federal guidelines simply prohibit federal aid to students at any institution not regionally accredited. A year into Campbell's presidency, he led the college successfully through its third ten-year accreditation review with SACS. Seven years later, in fall 1993, a SACS committee making a site visit to Averett's new AACE operations in Bluefield and Richmond determined Averett was out of compliance with SACS guidelines on faculty credentials. At issue were such matters as what constituted an appropriate terminal degree for teaching graduate courses. Averett, for example, argued for the Doctor of Business Administration; SACS insisted on the Ph.D. in Business Administration. Rather than discharge the less qualified D.B.A.'s and hire instructors with the Ph.D. degree, which Campbell admitted later should have been done "on the spot," the college chose to protest. In 1994 SACS requested a progress report relating to upgrading faculty at Bluefield and Richmond. In January 1995, the Committee judged Averett's response inadequate and requested another progress report, which the college submitted in October 1995. A SACS follow-up committee on the Bluefield/Richmond situation visited campus and issued an unfavorable report that included twenty-eight recommendations for change. SACS's recommendations (which are obligatory, not discretionary) dealt not only with faculty credentials but also with effectiveness, comparability of outcomes in the traditional and AACE programs, admission criteria, part-time faculty, and faculty workload. SACS gave the college two years in which to bring the Bluefield and Richmond programs into compliance. As Campbell later admitted, "This is when the clock started ticking."[82]

In June 1996, Averett administrators appeared before SACS. Campbell later confessed the tone of the meeting was "adversarial," owing partly to Averett's chief academic officer Malcom Huckabee, who challenged the right of certain SACS committee members to prescribe a workload for AACE faculty. SACS's subsequent report found Averett

---

[81] Ibid.

[82] Campbell, "Remarks to the Faculty, August 21, 1997," Campbell Papers.

out of compliance in several areas. Worse, SACS placed the college on notice (a private but nonetheless undesirable sanction) for one year. Campbell later admitted, "It should have been a wake-up call—more of a wake-up call than it was." Although normal procedure called for SACS to send a special committee to campus in fall 1996 to monitor progress towards compliance, instead SACS decided to allow the committee making the ten-year reaffirmation visit for the entire institution in January 1997 to see that the problems at the two AACE sites had been resolved.[83]

The ten-year visit by the reaffirmation committee in late January 1997 went badly. The group examined approximately 170 faculty folders and determined that at least eighty-four faculty did not hold degrees appropriate for their areas of teaching responsibility. Almost all were in the AACE program and most were at Bluefield and Richmond. This determination, coupled with institutional deficiencies in administrative structure, comparability of outcomes between traditional and nontraditional programs, access to library materials for nontraditional students, allocation of resources, and strategic planning and assessment, resulted in ninety-one recommendations (in reality, demands for change) that had to be corrected for accreditation to be reaffirmed.[84]

Worse was to come. The college immediately had to decertify eighty-four unqualified part-time faculty who were teaching 215 courses, replacing them with five qualified full-time and several qualified part-time faculty. Although the college quickly corrected deficiencies in comparability, planning and assessment, library access, and administrative structure, it simply did not have enough time to respond to the report of the reaffirmation committee in March 1997 and the concerns raised by SACS in 1995 about the sites at Bluefield and Richmond. The two-year time limit imposed by SACS in 1995 expired in December 1997 without all of the issues at Bluefield/Richmond addressed. SACS, therefore, put Averett on probation, a public sanction and the last step before denial of reaccreditation.[85]

This action got Campbell's attention. He accepted the resignation of his chief academic officer and replaced him with Elizabeth Compton,

---

[83] Ibid.
[84] Ibid.
[85] Ibid.

dean of Arts and Sciences. Within two months she and the new dean of Arts and Sciences, Richard Vinson, who had directed the campus self-study, quickly corrected the remaining deficiencies. In summer 1998, SACS removed Averett from probation and reaffirmed the institution's accreditation for another ten years. By June 2002, relations between Averett and SACS had improved to the point that SACS waived the customary site visit and accepted Averett's written report as satisfactory completion of its fifth-year review. SACS even commented that the fifth-year report, prepared by academic vice president Susan Dunton, was so expertly crafted as to be a model for other institutions.

Probation had other repercussions. Campbell was forced to take a more aggressive roll in recruiting students and defending the institution with the news media. Recruiters for traditional competitors were warning high school seniors to avoid Averett because the college was certain to lose its accreditation and go out of business. Recruiters for nontraditional rivals, meanwhile, were casting aspersions on the integrity of the AACE program. As a result, in 1998–1999, Averett experienced shortfalls of sixty traditional students and 200 AACE students before finally stabilizing enrollment in 1999–2000. In addition, because of the tarnish on AACE, the trustees changed its name to Graduate and Professional Studies (GPS). Perhaps worst of all, many Averett faculty members lost faith in their president.[86]

Postmortems can be invidious, especially so close in time to an event. Nevertheless, many persons appear to share responsibility for the SACS debacle. The president's cabinet erred in not correcting deficiencies in the Bluefield and Richmond operations, and in institutional planning and assessment, in timely fashion. In addition, the president would have been better served if he had followed the Russian maxim of "trust but verify" in relations with his cabinet. Moreover, one cabinet-level administrator was responsible for planning, while another was responsible for assessment, but there was no mechanism to insure proper communication between the two. As a result, not until summer 1996, only six months before the crucial visit by the reaffirmation committee, did Averett discover that its process of strategic planning and

---

[86] Campbell, Report to the Board, 9 May 1997, 7 May 1999; Board Minutes Averett University Board of Trustees, 21 November 1997, 20 November 1998; Minutes of the Executive Committee of the Board, 18 September 1997, 6 October 1998; Frank R. Campbell, Report to the Faculty, 21 August 1997.

assessment was flawed. This determination came just as SACS was placing the college on notice because of faculty credentials at Bluefield and Richmond. Concluding incorrectly, as future events would show, that deficiencies in planning and assessment were more serious than notice, the administration erred by concentrating on the former problem almost to the exclusion of the latter. In effect, it simply continued to debate with SACS over what constituted appropriate faculty credentials. Believing Averett was being held to a higher standard on the matter of faculty credentials than other institutions, one cabinet-level administrator displayed a confrontational tone towards SACS when a cooperative one might have won the day. Finally, owing to administrative secrecy, faculty were never informed of the private sanction of notice or the running feud over Bluefield and Richmond. Had they known, faculty would have applied pressure on appropriate administrators to correct the deficiencies in faculty credentials that a faculty self-study committee uncovered six months before the visit by the reaffirmation committee in January 1997. Perhaps the best that can be said for the reaccredidation disaster is that faculty, administration, and trustees were determined never to repeat the experience of notice and probation.

† † †

Even though worries over re-accreditation plagued the Campbell administration for several years, student life was largely unaffected by these concerns. Nevertheless, student life was altered by demographic, technological, and cultural changes. During the Campbell years, the Averett student body became slightly more Virginian, male, and minority. Eighty-two percent of students in 1983 hailed from Virginia; in 2001, the proportion stood at 88 percent. The ratio of male to female at 37:63 on all campuses in 1983 fluctuated during the Campbell years but stood at 42:58 in 2001. In 1983, 82 percent of students were Caucasian; in 2001, the figure had decreased to 74 percent. This decline in Caucasian enrollment and growth in minority students reflects the disappearance of Generation X and the appearance of the Millennials, a more ethnically diverse generation. Nevertheless, some patterns remained. Students under both presidents read *Sports Illustrated*, *Time*, *Newsweek*, and *Cosmopolitan*, drank beer, and worked part-time or full-time to help pay college expenses. In the latter regard Averett was no different from most other institutions. Sixty percent of students nationwide in the year 2000 worked at jobs; at Averett the proportion was 63 percent. Finally, students under both Lee and Campbell faced and answered the age-old questions of how to set goals for life and career, establish harmonious relationships with peers, and adjust to adulthood.[87]

In terms of personal habits, however, there was a world of difference between Lee students and Campbell students. The latter carried cell phones, drank wine, used the Internet, surfed the Web, enjoyed Napster, and downloaded music. They sported tattoos, indulged in body piercing, worked out assiduously at the YMCA or the student fitness center, and adjusted to constant and rapid change brought on by sophisticated technology. They expected to have instant information through the Internet, easy and anonymous communication via chat rooms, and instant recreation through video games. In fact, hours spent each week in front of computer screens often surpassed those in front of television sets. Although not touched personally by violence, in the 1990s Averett students had to cope with the national phenomenon of multiple deaths from disgruntled workers "going postal," dissatisfied students assassinating fellow students in high schools, and terrorists detonating bombs in skyscrapers and federal buildings. As a result, they yearned for stability and consistency in interpersonal relations but within an environment of flux and innovation in technology.[88]

Lee students and Campbell students also differed in their preferences for television entertainment. The most popular show at Averett during the Lee years was *M.A.S.H.*, a preachy situation comedy about the Korean War but in reality a metaphor about Vietnam and, by extension, American imperialism. Averett alumnus Richard Breen remembers dormitory students in the early 1980s would "pack the lounge" on Fourth Bishop whenever *M.A.S.H.* was shown. "If you got up to get a drink of water," he recalls, "you immediately lost your seat."[89] No doubt the show's gentle cynicism appealed to students disillusioned by contemporary developments such as the Iran hostage crisis and economic recession. Also, the setting was the 1950s, a period for which

---

[87] Julie Stockenberg, "Student Satisfaction Inventory, February 2001," Dean of Students Office, Averett University.

[88] Julie Stockenberg, conference materials, Virginia Association of Student Personnel Administrators Conference, 15 November 2001, Wintergreen, VA.

[89] Richard Breen, interview with author, Averett College 28 January 2002.

Reagan-era Americans were beginning to feel nostalgia. Moreover, college students liked the humorous way *M.A.S.H.* dealt with issues like racism, which was seldom mentioned on television.[90]

By contrast, Averett students during the Campbell years of the mid-1990s fixed on *Friends* and *Seinfeld*. They could identify with both shows' cast of college-educated young adults who were unattached and bent on enjoying life but who continually experienced problems in their relationships. *Friends* had clever scripts and attractive and appealing characters that all young viewers wanted as friends and mates. The show also featured interesting plots, sexual humor, and identifiable situations. What made each episode so tantalizing was the possibility of the guys and girls pairing up romantically. Both shows were so popular that Thursday evening in the mid-1990s became "must-see TV night" on NBC. *Friends* aired at 8:00 P.M. and *Seinfeld* at 9:00 P.M. Students would delay studying or partying until at least 9:30 each Thursday.[91]

Seinfeld, the other popular situation-comedy, featured four flawed, eccentric, dysfunctional, and less appealing thirty-somethings in Upper Manhattan who seemed to be afraid of the demands and responsibilities of adulthood. The show appealed to those who hoped to relocate after graduation to a major metropolitan area where they could live like yuppies while acting socially like adolescents. The inability of the main characters to form lasting romantic relationships was emblematic of the college student's fear of commitment and desire to delay making the lasting commitment of marriage for more years than his parents or grandparents had. *Seinfeld* titillated Averett students by dealing with issues not commonly talked about in polite society, such as male and female masturbation, which would have been taboo on primetime television in the Lee years when *M.A.S.H.* was popular.[92]

By the year 2000, as a campus survey revealed, an interesting but inexplicable discrepancy existed at Averett between the academic motivation of males and females that probably did not exist in 1985. Female students were 11 percent more willing than their counterparts nationwide to make necessary sacrifices in order to be successful. By

---

[90] Steven D. Stark, *Glued to the Set: The 60 Television Shows and Events That Made Us Who We Are Today* (New York: Dell, 1997) 278–85.

[91] Rene Lambert, interview with author, Averett College, 29 January 2002; Kara Cocke, telephone interview with author, 31 January 2002.

[92] Stark, *Glued to the Set,* 378–84; Cocke, interview; Lambert, interview.

contrast, Averett males were 7 percent less willing than the national average. Females were 6 percent above the national average in enjoyment of reading and discussing concepts; males were 20 percent below. Females were 10 percent above average in determination to complete their baccalaureate education; males were 13 percent less determined. Apparently, men regarded Averett as a party school or a venue for playing athletics, while women regarded it as an excellent place to earn a baccalaureate education.[93]

Yet in what are called social coping skills, Averett students of both sexes were well adjusted and relatively mature. Judged against their peers nationwide, they were above the norm in ability to make decisions, act independently of social pressures, join in social activities, feel comfortable in positions of leadership, and feel secure in the campus social scene.[94] The background of Averett students tells why. In high school over three-fourths of them participated in athletics, almost one-third performed in dramatic productions, over one-half held positions of leadership, almost one-half belonged to a club or service organization, and one in four worked on a publication. Participation in such activities bred social skills and maturity. On the other hand, the average SAT score at Averett was 5 percent below the national average, which partly explained why Averett students ranked 5 to 9 percent below the national average in academic self-confidence.[95]

Because of above-average social skills and maturity, Averett students adjusted more quickly to college life. The greatest challenge for freshmen was having to make their own decisions for the first time. "It was frightening," remembered freshman Melissa Jennings in a yearbook feature. Matthew Sloan added, "I found it difficult, at first, to decide on going to class, or studying, and on what to do with all of my free time." Most students quickly took cues from seniors who seemed "able to take six classes, work, party, and run campus organizations without a problem." Another adjustment for freshmen, according to Neil Griffin, was "meeting people who had different outlooks on life and who had experienced things I hadn't." Most freshmen quickly learned simply to

---

[93] Julie Stockenberg, "Retention Management Survey at Averett College, September, 2000," Dean of Students Office, Averett University.

[94] Ibid.

[95] Ibid.

appreciate the diversity of the Averett student body.[96]

Problems of adjustment for upperclassmen were different. Sophomores, who felt generally well adjusted and were three years from graduation and responsibilities of adulthood, seemed to forget how to budget time and money. The proverbial sophomore slump was common. So were empty pockets. "I have big bills and small checks," groused sophomore Nathalie Williams. Junior year brought comfort, confidence, and a feeling of well-being. For the typical male junior, the yearbook noted, "social patterns are concrete, priorities are set, and he has a reasonable idea of where he is going in the next few decades." Having fun without guilt was now permissible. Seniors, who by now were only taking courses in their major or related fields, were certain of graduation but uncertain of the immediate future beyond it. Their anxieties sprang from the process of planning weddings or applying for jobs or graduate schools. Many were also anxious over student loans that soon would have to be repaid.[97]

The educational level of Averett parents posed a daunting challenge for counselors in the offices of student affairs and academic affairs when dealing with students at all levels. Approximately 10 percent of parents did not finish high school, and an additional one-third had only a high school education. Thus, four in ten had no experience in a collegiate setting. Students from these homes were subject to a variety of attitudes and expectations about higher education that ranged from strong encouragement ("I want you to have opportunities in life that I never had") to apathy ("I was able to succeed in life without a college education and you can, too") to hostility ("Don't try to rise above your 'raising'"). When these students found themselves in academic crisis, counselors often had to deal with varying parental attitudes before devising strategies to overcome the academic difficulty. Similarly, these four in ten students had no system of support at home to give advice on age-old adjustment problems such as obnoxious roommates, school rules that appeared unfair or restrictive, and the relative importance of clubs and organizations. Conversely, children of the 11 percent of fathers and 7 percent of mothers with master's and doctoral degrees felt a keen appreciation for the value of higher education and usually had to meet

---

[96] *Pendulum,* 1990, 72–73.
[97] Ibid., 55–56.

high parental expectations. Academic failure on their part was unacceptable, unless the failure was a conscious or unconscious attempt to punish overbearing parents. Again, counselors were forced to serve in loco parentis.[98]

For most students, regardless of background, life in the dormitories during the Campbell years was pleasant. As soon as he became president, Campbell initiated a program of renovating every building on campus, beginning with the dormitories. Then in 1995, telephone jacks and cable television connections were installed in all rooms, making individual access to the Internet possible. Students appreciated this attention to improving their physical environment. In fact, the only physical alteration generating opposition came in 1990 when a section of the student dining hall was partitioned to create a separate Trustees Dining Room. In the process the main entrance to the student dining hall was walled over and a new one created off the alley running along the east side of Bishop and Danville Halls. The administration quickly learned that students will always have the last word. The day after the project was completed, a door was painted on the wall where the previous entrance to the student dining hall had been. Authorities painted out the door, only to find it painted back the next day. After several more paint-outs and paint-ins, the administration gave up the battle and left the outline of the door on the wall. Several months passed, students grew accustomed to the new entrance, and the false door finally vanished.[99]

Students in the dormitories were practically unanimous in likes and dislikes. "The [hall] phone [that] rings for the nineteenth time and still no one answers it," was a constant complaint.[100] So was "doing your own laundry." As one individual described it, the setting was particularly obnoxious: a "hot, moist room filled with irritated people fighting each other for the next available dryer," which would "suck away those precious quarters that students would rather feed into a soda machine." The best advice to newcomers was "trust mom." Otherwise, one risked having "pink skivvies" that had not been segregated from "red sweatpants," or a favorite sweater "shrinking three sizes" because of

---

[98] Stockenberg, "Retention Management Survey."

[99] Board Minutes Averett University Board of Trustees, 17 November 1995; Campbell, Report to the Board, 5 May 1995; *Chanticleer*, 30 September 1995, 25 October 1990.

[100] *Pendulum*, 1989, 84.

water too warm for the fabric.[101]

Other unwelcome distractions included "the ringing and buzzing of alarm clocks" each morning "anywhere from 6:30 A.M. to 11:00 A.M." because students retired the night before as early as 11:00 P.M. and as late as 5:00 A.M. Late alarms inevitably led to the midmorning spectacle of "a small brigade of sweat-pant-clad, bed-headed students wander[ing] into the dining hall rubbing the sleep out of their eyes."[102] Often, late alarms were the product of "cramming" for a test into the wee hours of the early morning. "Cramming has become an accepted routine in college life," one student observed. "Studying for a test in stages, days in advance, has definitely gone out of vogue."[103]

On the other hand, late alarms were not possible for students with 8:00 A.M. classes, which everyone despised. "They are quite literally the worst thing about college life," said junior Frank Shannaberger in 1989. Sophomore David Lea agreed: "Getting a semester without 8:00 A.M. classes is like winning the college equivalent of the lottery." Sophomore Jim Washington, who watched such classes be "the death of many a good weeknight party," wanted the surgeon general to ban them as "hazardous to your health."[104]

Averett's small size was seen as both a blessing and a curse. "It's hard to keep things private on [such a small] campus," said senior Stacy Sparks. "The 'Averett Grapevine' can really swing an innocent date way out of proportion...you know, like those casual dates that people make into serious relationships."[105] On the other hand, Averett's small size gave a familial tone to the student body. "Someone is always there for you," said senior Carolyn Sellers. Small, hall-style dormitories bred even more intimacy. "It's like having 30 sisters," she added.[106]

Other pleasures were "shaving cream fights" that would leave the hall "smell[ing] like menthol for days," and late-night "Hardee's runs" for snacks, "which invariably turned into bull sessions."[107] But most of all, students enjoyed snow and lots of it. In February 1993, a storm

---

[101] *Pendulum*, 1989, 23; see also Tara R. Huff, letter to author , February 2002.

[102] *Pendulum*, 1989, 102.

[103] *Pendulum*, 1989, 29.

[104] *Pendulum*, 1989, 26.

[105] *Pendulum*, 1989, 37.

[106] *Pendulum*, 1989, 84.

[107] Ibid.

blanketed campus and brought out the ingenuity in students. They created "slopes" on hills beside the Bottom Inn and nearby Frith Hall. On both the "Bottom Inn Double Diamond Slope" and the "Frith Downhill," students competed on trays from the dining hall that doubled as sleds. Teams were formed, and self-appointed judges on the upper floors of Bishop Hall and Jordan Commons awarded points for style, distance, and speed. The "Frith Downhill" was especially hazardous because sledders had to clear four brick steps before landing hard on the Commons patio. Students solved this problem by hauling mattresses from the dormitories to cushion the landing. The event continued well past midnight because everyone assumed classes would be cancelled the next day. They were not, and several students flunked tests. But these late-night sledders "could never look at those hills the same way" again.[108]

Although undergraduates typically complained about "nothing to do in Danville," by senior year they liked the city and its college too much to leave. For whatever reason, some remained for a fifth year, prompting *Chanticleer* to wonder whether many students simply had overstayed their welcome. Borrowing a line from David Letterman, the popular late-night television personality, the newspaper opined that a student had stayed too long if:

1. he could "tell you the story behind all the graffiti on the bathroom walls."
2. he heard other students complaining about the *old* computers in the computer laboratories which were *new* computers when he arrived.
3. a "security [officer] asks *him* for directions."
4. he has "a favorite toilet."[109]

Clubs remained popular during the Campbell years. BSU continued to be the largest. Over a hundred students participated with varying degrees of frequency and about half of them attended the weekly luncheon program on Thursdays at West Main Baptist Church. Other activities included fall and midwinter retreats, spring leadership training conferences, ministry teams to lead worship services and weekend

---

[108] *Chanticleer*, 28 March 1993.
[109] *Chanticleer*, 18 April, 1996.

revivals in area churches, community outreach programs with local charities, weekly Bible study groups in dormitories, weeklong mission trips during spring break, and a full-time summer mission program.[110]

Fraternities and sororities metamorphosed. In May 1988, the board of trustees decreed local fraternities would have to affiliate with national Greek-letter organizations with programs discouraging hazing and alcohol abuse. AIH fraternity, which was established in 1976 and stood enigmatically for Alphata Isota Hegmonius, changed in 1985 to the local Alpha Kappa Pi and affiliated in 1988 with national Sigma Pi. The group was never strong, and it died in the early 1990s. On 1 April 1989, a group of thirty-four male students chartered the Zeta Xi chapter of national Pi Kappa Phi. Almost simultaneously, another group was chartered by national Sigma Tau Gamma, which remained a weak chapter until 1995, when it folded. Among females, meanwhile, on 15 March 1992, the local Sigma Pi Omega sorority became a chapter of national Phi Sigma Sigma. A colony of national Alpha Sigma Alpha (ASA) was established in November 1993 and chartered on 9 April 1994. ASA would disappear in 1999, leaving one national sorority (the "Phi Sigs") and one national fraternity (the "Pi Kapps").[111]

In addition to enjoying the usual benefits of Greek life such as recreation, friendship, leadership, and access to national networks, the Pi Kapps and Phi Sigs devoted much of their free time to community service. Each year the sisters staged twenty-four-hour rock-a-thons to raise money for their national charity, the National Kidney Foundation. They also sang Christmas carols at nursing homes, conducted food drives for the Salvation Army, mentored several handicapped Girl Scouts, and hosted an Easter Egg Hunt for YMCA youth. The Pi Kapps, in addition to trick-or-treating for UNICEF and mentoring handicapped Cub Scouts, supported their national charity, PUSH (People Understanding the Severely Handicapped). In 1999–2000, through fundraising activities such as car washes, the Averett fraternity was fourth in the nation among chapters in fundraising for PUSH and first in amount raised per member. Averett brothers also participated in the summer Journey of Hope for

---

[110] David Blevins to Nancy Werst, 2 May 1986, in Campbell, Report to the Board, 30 May 1986. See also Maria Roulidis, letter to author , February 2002.

[111] *Chanticleer*, 7 November 1991, 3 November 1993; *Pendulum*, 1990, 120; Minutes, Board of Trustees, 6 May 1988; Campbell, Report to the Board, 5 May 1989, 13 May 1994.

PUSH, a two-month-long, three-thousand-mile bike ride from San Francisco to Washington, DC. In groups of twenty-five brothers from chapters all over the nation, they rode seventy-five miles a day, serving as goodwill ambassadors for the handicapped along the way and raising about $350,000 through donations from sponsors.[112]

On campus the Pi Kapps were known more for school spirit than community service. Like the fabled Cameron Crazies of Duke University, the Averett fraternity made life miserable for visiting basketball teams at home games. The brothers came en masse, sat behind the opposing team's bench, and led the cheers for Averett. What made them such a distraction were their outfits. The brothers dressed alike by theme—one night in togas, another night as women, yet another night in boxer shorts with blazers and ties.[113]

Off-campus hangouts waxed and waned in popularity. In the early years of Campbell's presidency, students flocked to the Busy Bee Café (which quaintly advertised "booths for ladies") for burgers and a frosty mug before going to the Tobacco Exchange for nightlife. Both closed in the early 1990s, forcing students to the nightclub Miami's, where the Pi Kapps sponsored the ever-popular college night on Thursday evenings. By the mid-1990s Sir Richard's Restaurant and Lounge, complete with a beach-volleyball court, became popular, joined by Phatty Bobalatti's and Ham's in the late 1990s. In addition to college nights, these establishments featured Karaoke Night, Live Stand-up Comedy Night, and Ladies Night, all of which had great appeal to Averett students.[114]

Students also looked forward to traditions associated with collegiate life. With the exception of Homecoming, the major ones were established in the Campbell years. In early September the college staged the Senior Pinning Ceremony, where seniors attended a reception to be recognized with an Averett pin by professors from their major department. Two weeks later came Averett on the Lawn, a midday barbecue with live entertainment following the late-morning fall convocation. The Christmas Celebration on an evening shortly before the end of fall semester featured a concert by the Averett Singers under the

---

[112] *Chanticleer*, 18 April 1996, 6 March 1998; Averett College, news release, 28 February 2000; Campbell, Report to the Board, 5 May 1989, 13 May 1994; *Danville Register and Bee*, 28 March 1996, n.p.

[113] *Chanticleer*, 9 February 1989.

[114] *Chanticleer*, 27 September 1999.

direction of Professor Gail Allen, a feast in the dining hall, reading the nativity story, singing Christmas carols on the Jordan Commons, and lighting a Christmas Tree on the hill between Jordan Commons and Mountain View Avenue. Occasionally, Santa and his elves even made an appearance to give out candy.

Throughout the year upperclassmen passed on to freshmen what was called the "haunted history of Averett." By the time of graduation, everyone knew someone who claimed to have seen the ghost of a despondent and romantically scorned female who reportedly "hurled herself from the window beneath the Main Hall portico" in a shocking suicide, or an Indian who regularly tormented the residents of Davenport Hall because the building was allegedly constructed on a sacred burial site, or the drama major who, being denied the leading role, supposedly hanged himself on stage just before the curtain went up for dress rehearsal. Despite the fact that all of these stories were fanciful, student testimonials to the presence of apparitions added credence to the legends. Crystal Giles, a resident of Third Main, was certain a ghost awakened her for cheerleading practice one Saturday morning by loudly opening her door "exactly at the time I needed to wake up." "I knew it was a ghost," she explained, "because my door was locked and shut."[115]

Despite the gruesome stories of ghosts and suicides, memories of the Campbell years were positive. Patricia Adkins, class of 1998, recalled the "crazy, spontaneous road trips," the delightful annual Pi Kappa Phi Rose Ball, and the residence halls where "life was like having all of your friends around all the time for one big slumber party."[116] Latarsha Kyler, class of 1997, remembered with fondness spring breaks at Myrtle Beach, movie nights sponsored by Residence Life, ordering pizza late at night, and sleeping late on weekends.[117] Jeff Davis, class of 1992, looked back on the fierce competitiveness of intramural sports, where the only trophy was a coveted maroon T-shirt the champions wore with pride. Suite Four of Fugate, where he lived, hosted the "Crypt Club" on Wednesday evenings at 10:00 P.M., when friends would gather to watch movies such as *Tales from the Crypt* and *Dream On*. During each night of final examinations the cafeteria opened from 9:00 P.M. to 10:00

---

[115] *Chanticleer*, 20 October 1997, 20 April 1994, 2 December 1999.

[116] Patricia Adkins, letter to author , February 2002.

[117] Latarsha Kyler, letter to author , January 2002.

P.M. for snacks. Food fights inevitably erupted to relieve the tension. Also, in plays put on by the theater department, stage crews often tried to make actors on stage break character. In *Exit the Body,* Davis said, the crew even resorted to "mooning" those on stage.[118] Sherry Harper-McCombs, class of 1986, remembered the fun of playing Trivial Pursuit in the Main Lobby and taking "library adventure trips," which usually coincided with concerts by rock artists, to libraries at nearby universities to gather material for term papers.[119] She also recalled with glee the panty-raids-in-reverse, when she and several female companions raided the dormitory rooms of male basketball players to steal underwear for display on a clothesline erected in front of the dining hall. Barb Russo, class of 1988, remembered the thrill of intercollegiate softball. She and many former teammates "still play summer softball together in Danville," she related, "even though I drive a couple of hours to do so."[120]

Meals in the dining hall stood out in everyone's memory. Stromboli and chicken patties were particular favorites. Students would smuggle chicken patties back to their rooms for snacks later. "Steak night was like the floor of the New York Stock Exchange," Jeff Davis remembered. No one skipped dinner on those nights, and the few vegetarians were able to barter or sell their steak tickets at premium prices. Regardless of the menu, "going to the dining hall was usually one of the best parts of the day," recalled Laura Leigh Daniel, class of 1999. "You could socialize with all your friends at once."[121]

Averett was certainly a watershed for students. Parent-child relations changed. "My parents began to see me as an adult who was capable of making her own decisions," Laura Leigh Daniel wrote. "In turn, I began to see them more as friends and not 'rule-enforcers.' I began to understand they only wanted what was best for me, and our relationship became stronger."[122] Jeff Davis remembered entering Averett as an uncertain teenager but leaving as a confident and mature adult. "I learned at Averett how to deal with people, both individually and in groups," he wrote. "The first time away from home offers a lot of

---

[118] Jeff Davis, letter to author , January 2002.

[119] Sherry Harper-McCombs, letter to author , 15 October 2001.

[120] Barb Russo, letter to author , October 2001.

[121] Laura Leigh Daniel, letter to author , October 2001; Jeff Davis, letter author.

[122] Daniel, letter to author.

independence and responsibility, and I was forced to grow up fast, think for myself on all issues, and take a stand on several things that I believed in instead of caving in to peer pressure. Standing up for myself built my self confidence."[123]

Commuting students often had a different experience. Many of them worked at jobs to support families and therefore left campus as soon as classes ended. To them the Averett experience was purely academic. Their memories are limited to favorite professors, favorite classes, and red tape here or there during registration. Other commuters would relax in the Bottom Inn between classes to munch popcorn or socialize with other commuters. Still others visited friends in the dormitories, played on athletic teams, or were active in Student Government Association, BSU, fraternities, or theatrical productions. Some who began as commuters later became dormitory residents in order to enjoy the best of both worlds.[124]

† † †

Owing to his accomplishments, Frank R. Campbell shares with Conwell Anderson the distinction of being the most important presidents in Averett's history. No president—even Bishop—could equal Campbell's impact on the physical facilities. Campbell converted the sleepy suburban campus of nineteen acres on West Main Street into fifty-eight sites across Virginia in the Graduate and Professional Studies Program, coupled with a sprawling four-campus network in the Danville area of some 204 acres. In addition to the West Main campus, the network in 2001 included the North Campus complex with its athletic fields, Grant Center, and field house; classroom facilities at Danville Airport; and the Equestrian Center in North Carolina. In the process Campbell also built the Emily Swain Grousbeck Music Center and three apartment-style dormitories. Moreover, he renovated every existing building on campus at least once and acquired for the college more than twenty nearby residences for future expansion on the West Main campus. By any measure, the endowment is really the Frank R. Campbell endowment. Its

---

[123] Jeff Davis , letter to author.
[124] Donna R. Mahalko, letter to author , October 2001; John Thorhauer, letter to author , January 2002; Linda Dalton, letter to author , December 2001,.

growth from $240,000 to $24 million was an increase of 9,900 percent, or about 700 percent a year. Put another way, the endowment he left was a hundred times larger than what he inherited. In addition, the AACE, or GPS, program not only made Averett the recognized leader in nontraditional adult education in the Commonwealth, but its revenues also cushioned the operating budget during lean times in the late 1980s and early 1990s. Perhaps most important, his emphasis on making Averett "the best private, church-related college in Virginia" changed the focus of the collegiate community from one of survival to one of excellence.

Other accomplishments also stand out. Campbell increased the annual budget from $5 million to $25 million. In his sixteen years as president of the college, he raised almost $50 million for capital improvements, endowment, and current funds. When the institution metamorphosed from college to university in 2001, it boasted a student body whose makeup more nearly reflected the population demographics of Virginia than any other private college: 74 percent white, 19 percent black, 1.7 percent Hispanic, 2.7 percent Asian, 1.6 percent nonresident, and 0.4 percent native American. Under his leadership Averett expanded its athletic program by building an athletic complex that remained the envy of schools in Division III of the NCAA. He also added the sports of football and baseball for men, soccer and lacrosse for women. During Campbell's tenure, Averett became competitive in the Dixie Conference in every sport and dominant in women's tennis and volleyball and men's tennis. Campbell insured that funds were available for technology, and he led in the formation of the innovative partnership with Danville Community College and Virginia Polytechnic Institute known as the Institute for Advanced Learning and Research. Certainly, these contributions towered over his failures: the accumulation of more than $7 million in debt after initially making the institution debt-free; a self-study process that put the college on probation for six months before full accreditation was granted; and faculty salaries near the bottom among sister schools in the Commonwealth and no better comparatively in 2001 than in 1985.

By the date of Averett's conversion to the status of university, supporters pointed with pride to its 142-year history. Through lean years and fat years, the institution managed to provide an education that encouraged social mobility, sparked civic participation, increased tolerance, raised the cultural bar of communities in which alumni settled, stimulated personal creativity, broadened outlooks, increased both the capacity to earn and the capacity to serve, instilled an appreciation for the Western heritage, and enriched the local economy.[125] By 2001, basic curricular changes had ended, and the college had grown comfortable with opportunities for career education on a foundation of the liberal arts and sciences. Institutional self-confidence blossomed with the passage of time as Averett graduates became successful in business and the professions, and as a profusion of appreciative and complimentary comments came from older Danvillians who returned to Averett to finish an interrupted baccalaureate program. Permanent senior-college traditions emerged. So did permanent and active senior-college organizations. The institution had come to represent all races, all major religions, all political persuasions, and all areas of the United States. It had also acquired a permanent and stable faculty, 72 percent of whom held earned doctorates. Averett—comfortable at last with its identity, secure in its mission, and shored up by loyal alumni, Baptists, and community leaders—began its first year as a university with pride in the accomplishments of the past and optimism for the future.

---

[125] See Cohen, *Shaping,* 424, 456–57.

A Note on Sources

Informative and revealing primary source material in the Averett archives made possible the writing of *The Lamp and the Cross: A History of Averett College, 1859-2001.* The annual reports of several presidents to the Virginia Baptist General Board (1918–present) and to the trustees of the college (1918–present), the minutes of faculty meetings (1951–present) and the board of trustees (1922–present), college catalogues (1868–present), student handbooks (1926–present), news releases, and scrapbooks furnished an official record of proceedings at the college. Regrettably, these reports and minutes have disappeared for the years before 1918. The personal and administrative papers of former provost Malcom Huckabee and former presidents Curtis Bishop, Conwell Anderson, Howard Lee, and Frank Campbell offered rare glimpses behind the scenes of public occurrences.

So did interviews with former presidents Anderson, Lee, and Campbell, former acting president Mary Fugate, present and former faculty members Stephen C. Ausband, Russell C. Brachman, Pauline Coll, Mary Elizabeth Compton, John P. Dever, David W. Gray, Richard M. Inlow, Carol S. Kushner, Margaret Lanham, Robert C. Marsh, Charles P. Postelle, and Charlotte Read, former dean of students and director of development Mary Jo Davis, and alumni Richard Breen, Kara Cocke, and Rene Lambert. *The Religious Herald*—the official publication of Virginia Baptists—and minutes of the Roanoke and Dan River Baptist Associations in the Virginia Baptist Historical Society at the University of Richmond were helpful with information on antebellum attitudes and efforts to establish the college. Topical collections in the Averett archives, such as the Averett Family file, the Delius file, the Carson Davenport file, the Graveyard Episode file, and the Averett-Stratford Coordination file, furnished information on later events. So did articles from the *Danville Commercial Appeal*, the *Danville Bee*, the *Danville Register*, and the *Richmond Times Dispatch*.

Most valuable for anecdotes and stories of human interest were

Chanticleer (the student newspaper, 1924–present), *Echoes* and *Pendulum* (the college yearbooks, 1904–present), and written reminiscences from the following alumni extending from the class of 1905 to the class of 1998: Patricia Adkins, Mrs. E. Wesley Appel, Mrs. Robert H. Auerbach, Mrs. Edith A. Barbour, Mrs. Jack M. Barts, Christine Riley Bettencourt, Mrs. Lord Beveridge, Carol Diane Blosser, Mrs. Gerald D. Boone, Jr., Mrs. E. Lacy Bowen, Noland Hubbard Bowling, Patricia Carol Boyd, Mrs. Cecil Buckner, Mrs. Annice W. Carneal, Elly S. Caro, Mrs. Ralph Chamberlain, Mrs. Tilmon Chamlee, Mrs. R. Thomas Clark, Jr., Lottie Hundley Coleman, Mrs. Ronald W. Collins, Mary Creath Colston, Mrs. O. E. Corder, Dr. Betty S. Cox, Shirley Marie Whittington Crute, Linda Dalton, Laura Leigh Daniel, Jeff Davis, Mrs. William Charles Davison, Frances DeDan, Rosemary Dempsey, Debra Sue Doolittle, Mrs. Robert F. Dove, Mrs. Robert F. Drewes, Mrs. Harvey Edmund Dunn, Ruth T. Dunn, Mrs. Charles G. Eastwood, Mrs. Coleman B. Edmunds, Mrs. John P. Elliott, Jr., Mrs. Edward Evans, Mrs. Herbert V. Ewell, Jr., Mrs. Bernard F. Fetter, Johncie L. Flannagan, Marsha K. Flora, Mrs. Ralph L. Forest, Mrs. George E. Fulford, Jr., Mildred Frances Hale Gardy, Lillian Smith George, Mrs. David Gladstone, Dorothy E. Goodman, Mrs. James C. Green, Mrs. Bruce Griffith, Louise Williams Griffith, Mrs. R. Stuart Grizzard, Mrs. Vigen Gurdian, Sherry Harper-McCombs, Mrs. Walter Irvin Henson, Mrs. Rene L. Herbst, Mrs. Richard A. Hevenor, Mrs. Kurt L. Hirchmann, Mrs. Walter R. Holloway, Mrs. Hylah Morton, Mrs. Ira H. Hurt, Jr., Elizabeth Coward Hutton, Kathryn R. Jacques, Mrs. Clifton W. Jenkins, Mrs. Burnell Jones, Mary Mustain Kirk, Mrs. Robert N. Kullman, Latarsha Kyler, Miss Roy Land, Mrs. Henry T. Law, Mrs. George E. Lawrence, Mrs. Lawrence L. Layman, Jr., Brenda K. Lee, Miss Martha H. Lester, Edna Henderson Lipscomb, Mrs. James R. Lockerman, Jr., Kim Crawford Love, Mrs. Frederick M. Lyon, Donna R. Mahalko, Mrs. George Mahler, Mrs. William L. Major, Mrs. Jack A. Mayes, Jr., Dot Sturdivant McAdams, Mrs. Robert McAlister, Nancy Adnia McDowell, Mrs. Charles D. McManus, Mrs. James S. Moore, Mrs. L. J. Morgan, Mrs. W. B. Moseley, Mrs. Leo A. Napoleon, Mrs. Paul F. Neal, Mrs. Warren E. Neubert, Sara Wells Nixon, Carolyn E. Odenheimer, Mrs. Z. B. Ogden, Jane L. Owen, Mrs. F. L. Owens, Mrs. Robert J. Owens, Mrs. Joseph Frederick Parker, Mrs. Peter W. Payne, Marion Beared Proehl, Mrs. Allen T. Pugh, Dorothy M. Putney, Polly

Milliner Ransome, Mrs. Stanley H. Rayner III, Mrs. Richard H. Reed, Mrs. Robert W. Rice, Randy James Richardson, Mrs. Raymond Ridgeway, Alger Robbins, Mrs. Jacob N. Rohme, Maria Roulidis, Barbara Russo, Martha Salley, Michelle Scott, Mrs. Howard H. Simms, Mrs. Jerome H. Simonds, Mrs. Gerald Sims, Mrs. Grady L. Sumner, Mrs. Francis S. Swienckowski, Mrs. Samuel R. Theal, Mrs. Kathryn B. Thompson, John Thorhauer, Mrs. Joan S. Thorp, Howard G. Todd, Mrs. Franklin Lee Tolbert, Mrs. R. Kenneth Tonning, Mrs. Eduardo J. Trinidad, Margaret E. Tyree, Mrs. Alfonso Vasquez, Mrs. Winfred I. Viele, Bridus G. Voss, Mrs. Carl T. Walker, Linda Hawks Walker, Mrs. Milford Weaver, D. Fred Willis, Gertrude Hodnett Wilson, Sara Ann Wood, and Bessie Moses Wooding.

Numerous other sources—primary and secondary, published and unpublished—were helpful. The two most important secondary sources were David W. Gray, "A History of Averett College," unpublished master's thesis, University of Richmond, 1960; and James A. Davis, "Dr. Curtis V. Bishop: Focus on a Junior College Career, 1930–1966," unpublished Ph.D. dissertation, University of Florida, 1973. These two works provided essential background, interpretation, biographical material, and chronological outline. Also helpful but much less detailed was Margaret Lanham's typescript titled "The Fugate Years: 1924–1969," in the Averett archives. Owing to a fire in the early 1900s, which destroyed the archives of the Danville *Register and Bee*, no good history of Danville, Virginia, exists. Jane Gray Hagan's *The Story of Danville* (New York: Stratford House, 1950) and Beatrice W. Hairston's *A Brief History of Danville, Virginia* (Richmond, VA: Dietz Press, 1955) are popular and topical rather than scholarly and chronological. For information on nineteenth-century Danville, the following works are useful as supplements to Hagan and Hairston: John H. Brubaker III, *The Last Capitol* (Danville, VA: Danville Museum of Fine Arts and History, 1979); Chesapeake and Ohio Railroad, *Historical, Industrial, and Statistical Review* (New York: Historical Publishing Company, 1887); the Commercial Association, *The City of Danville* (Danville VA: Waddill Printing Co., 1913); George W. Dame, *Historical Sketch of Roman Eagle Lodge, No. 122, A.F. and A.M.* (Richmond VA: I. N. Jones, 1895); George W. Dame, typescript titled "Facts Concerning the Early History of Danville," Danville vertical file, Danville Public Library; unknown author, typescript titled "Early Days in Danville,"

Piedmont Genealogical Collection, Danville Public Library; Frances Hallam Hurt, "Centennial of Averett College," *The Commonwealth: The Magazine of Virginia* 26 (December 1959); Robert Enoch Withers, typescript titled "Excerpts from Autobiography of an Octogenarian," Danville vertical file, Danville Public Library; unknown author, typescript titled "Reconstruction Days in Danville," Piedmont Genealogical Society Collection, Danville Public Library; James I. Robertson, Jr.,"Houses of Horror: Danville's Civil War Prisons," *Virginia Magazine of History and Biography* 69 (July 1961); unknown author, typescript titled "Story of the Danville Riot," Danville Genealogical Society Collection, Danville Public Library; R. A. Schoolfield, typescript titled "Reminiscences of R. A. Schoolfield," Danville vertical file, Danville Public Library; and Edward Pollock, *1885 Sketch Book of Danville, Virginia* (Danville VA: Womack Press, 1976 [1885]).

Several sources furnished biographical information on Averett presidents. The best is Clara G. Fountain, "The Presidents of Averett College," unpublished manuscript, Averett University Archives. Others include William Cathcart, ed., *The Baptist Encyclopedia: A Dictionary* (Philadelphia: Everts, 1881); John Lipscomb Johnson, *Autobiographical Notes* (privately printed, 1958); Louis H. Manarin, ed., *North Carolina Troops, 1861–1865: A Roster,* 13 vols. (Raleigh: North Carolina Department of Archives and History, 1966–1968); Benjamin Simpson, *Men, Places, and Things* (n.p.: Dance Brothers & Co., 1891); Rosemary Sprague, *Longwood College: A History* (Farmville, VA: Longwood College, 1989); and George Braxton Taylor, *Virginia Baptist Ministers* (Lynchburg VA: J. P. Bell Co., 1913).

An understanding of Baptists in Virginia is crucial to understanding the development of Averett College. The most useful work is Reuben E. Alley, *A History of Baptists in Virginia* (Richmond: Virginia Baptist General Board, 1974). Also helpful are Garnet Ryland, *The Baptists of Virginia: 1699–1926* (Richmond: Virginia Baptist Board of Missions and Education, 1955), and, despite its obvious biases, Charles F. Leek, *The History of Pittsylvania Baptist Association* (Danville VA: Pittsylvania Baptist Association, 1963).

No less essential is an appreciation of the college's state and regional background. The best work on Virginia is Virginius Dabney, *Virginia: The New Dominion* (Garden City NY: Doubleday, 1971). The best works for background on the eras of presidents such as Curtis Bishop are C. Vann Woodward, *Origins of the New South: 1877–1913* (Baton Rouge: Louisiana State University Press, 1967 [1951]; George B. Tindall, *The Emergence of the New South, 1913–1945* (Baton Rouge: Louisiana State University Press, 1967); the section on South Carolina in V. O. Key, Jr.,*Southern Politics in State and Nation* (New York: Knopf, 1949); Francis Butler Simkins, *Pitchfork Ben Tillman* (Baton Rouge: Louisiana State University Press, 1944); and Ben Robertson, *Red Mills and Cotton* (New York: Grosset and Dunlap, 1942).

Frederick Rudolph, *The American College and University: A History* (New York: Knopf, 1968, and Athens: University of Georgia Press, 1990) is the classic beginning for any study of higher education in the United States. Also valuable are Philip G. Altbach, Robert O. Berdahl, and Patricia J. Gimport, eds., *American Higher Education in the Twenty-first Century* (Baltimore MD.: Johns Hopkins University Press, 1999); Arthur M. Cohen, *The Shaping of American Higher Education: Emergence and Growth of the Contemporary System* (San Francisco CA: Jossey-Bass Publishers, 1998); and John R. Thelin, "Institutional History in Our Own Time: Higher Education's Shift from Managerial Revolution to Enterprising Evolution," *CASE International Journal of Educational Advancement* 1:1 (June 2000).

Barbara Miller Solomon, *In the Company of Educated Women: A History of Women and Higher Education in America* (New Haven CT: Yale University Press, 1985) is necessary for understanding the development of female institutions. Robert Russell Neely, "A History of Private Secondary Schools in Danville, Virginia," (master's thesis, University of Virginia, 1938), is informative but dated. The junior college movement is treated perceptively in four works: Walter Crosby Eells, *Present Status of Junior College Terminal Education* (Washington, DC: American Association of Junior Colleges, 1941); Win Kelley and Leslie Wilbur, *Teaching in the Community-Junior College* (New York: Appleton-Century-Crofts, 1970); Leland L. Medsker, *The Junior College: Progress and Prospect* (New York; McGraw-Hill,1960); and Carl E. Seashore, *The Junior College Movement* (New York: Henry Holt and Co., 1940).

William Randel's "Frederick Delius in America," *Virginia Magazine of History and Biography* 71 (1971) and Gerald Tetley's "Delius in Danville," *Virginia Cavalcade* 9 (summer 1959) illuminate

Delius's activities at Roanoke Female College. Likewise, Alvin L. Hall's *The History of Stratford College* (Danville VA: Womack Press, 1974) is prerequisite to understanding the Averett-Stratford coordination.

Index

CPSIA information can be obtained
at www.ICGtesting.com
Printed in the USA
LVHW111804110123
736941LV00002B/37